T0419539

BUSINESS ISSUES, COMPETITION AND ENTREPRENEURSHIP

THE U.S. AUTO INDUSTRY AND THE ROLE OF FEDERAL ASSISTANCE

BUSINESS ISSUES, COMPETITION AND ENTREPRENEURSHIP

Additional books in this series can be found on Nova's website under the Series tab.

Additional E-books in this series can be found on Nova's website under the E-books tab.

BUSINESS ISSUES, COMPETITION AND ENTREPRENEURSHIP

THE U.S. AUTO INDUSTRY AND THE ROLE OF FEDERAL ASSISTANCE

JAMES R. ELLIOT
EDITOR

Nova Science Publishers, Inc.
New York

For permission to use material from this book please contact us:
Telephone 631-231-7269; Fax 631-231-8175
Web Site: http://www.novapublishers.com

NOTICE TO THE READER

The Publisher has taken reasonable care in the preparation of this book, but makes no expressed or implied warranty of any kind and assumes no responsibility for any errors or omissions. No liability is assumed for incidental or consequential damages in connection with or arising out of information contained in this book. The Publisher shall not be liable for any special, consequential, or exemplary damages resulting, in whole or in part, from the readers' use of, or reliance upon, this material. Any parts of this book based on government reports are so indicated and copyright is claimed for those parts to the extent applicable to compilations of such works.

Independent verification should be sought for any data, advice or recommendations contained in this book. In addition, no responsibility is assumed by the publisher for any injury and/or damage to persons or property arising from any methods, products, instructions, ideas or otherwise contained in this publication.

This publication is designed to provide accurate and authoritative information with regard to the subject matter covered herein. It is sold with the clear understanding that the Publisher is not engaged in rendering legal or any other professional services. If legal or any other expert assistance is required, the services of a competent person should be sought. FROM A DECLARATION OF PARTICIPANTS JOINTLY ADOPTED BY A COMMITTEE OF THE AMERICAN BAR ASSOCIATION AND A COMMITTEE OF PUBLISHERS.

Additional color graphics may be available in the e-book version of this book.

LIBRARY OF CONGRESS CATALOGING-IN-PUBLICATION DATA
The U.S. auto industry and the role of federal assistance / editor James R.
Elliot.
p. cm.
Includes index.
ISBN 978-1-60741-322-6 (hardcover)
1. Automobile industry and trade--United States. 2. Automobile industry
and trade--Economic aspects--United States. 3. Economic assistance,
Domestic--United States. 4. Government lending--United States. 5. Economic
stabilization--United States. I. Elliot, James R.
HD9710.U52U177 2010
338.4'76292220973--dc22
2010012881

Published by Nova Science Publishers, Inc. ✤ *New York*

CONTENTS

PREFACE

The three domestically owned U.S. manufacturers of cars and light trucks are requesting federal financial assistance in the form of "bridge loans" to assure their ability to continue in business. The companies have been affected by a long-term decline in U.S. market share, the impact of a general decline in U.S. motor vehicle sales that has impacted all producers and the effects of a severe constriction of credit, resulting from problems in U.S. and global financial markets. This book reviews stipulations that Congress might impose on auto manufacturers as conditions of providing assistance.

Chapter 1 - On December 19, 2008, President George W. Bush provided financial assistance to General Motors (GM) and Chrysler. These two automakers had testified before Congress that if they did not receive federal financial assistance before the end of the year, they could be forced into bankruptcy. After Congress did not provide the assistance requested, the Treasury Department agreed to provide a total of $13.4 billion to GM and $4 billion to Chrysler from the Troubled Assets Relief Program (TARP), established by the Emergency Economic Stabilization and Recovery Act (EESA, P.L. 110-343). Ford, the third member of the "Detroit 3," testified that it did not need such assistance immediately, though it has said that it could potentially require a line of credit in 2009. The Bush Administration also loaned a further $6 billion under the TARP for General Motors Acceptance Corporation (GMAC), and $1.5 billion for Chrysler Financial, the two manufacturers' respective credit affiliates.

The Detroit 3 have been affected by a long-term decline in their U.S. motor vehicle sales market share, plus the impact of a general decline in U.S. motor vehicle sales in 2008 resulting from a severe constriction of credit related to problems in U.S. and global financial markets. The rise in gasoline prices in mid-2008 caused a sales decline and a structural shift in motor vehicle consumption patterns. Motor vehicle purchases fell substantially in late 2008 despite the subsequent decline in gasoline prices.

A bill to provide up to $25 billion in direct loans from the TARP to auto companies (S. 3688) was introduced in November 2008 by Senate Majority Leader Harry Reid. The Bush Administration instead proposed to make general-purpose loans from a program for advanced technology vehicle production set up under Section 136 of the Energy Independence and Security Act (EISA, P.L. 110-140). This bill had become law in December 2007, and was funded under P.L. 110-329. In December 2008, Representative Barney Frank introduced H.R. 7321, which would have allowed most of the EISA loan funding to be used to support "bridge loans." This bill was supported by the Democratic leadership of both houses, and the Bush

Administration. It passed the House on December 10 by 237-170. The bill was opposed by the Republican leadership in both bodies. Efforts to invoke cloture in the Senate in an attempt to pass the bill failed.

President Bush then provided loans for GM and Chrysler from the TARP, subject to a number of oversight conditions. Eligible companies are to establish an approved restructuring plan by March 31, 2009. They are to target debt reduction through conversion of bonded indebtedness and debt owed for retiree health care to corporate equity. This chapter analyzes the financial solution provisions, including bankruptcies as an alternative, and the impact of the loan provisions on pensions, voluntary employees' beneficiary associations (VEBAs), protection of taxpayers' investment, labor contracts, and executive compensation. Hourly workers are required under the plan to accept contract changes designed to make the companies' workforces more competitive with those of Japanese-owned auto manufacturers in the United States. The United Auto Workers union (UAW) and some Members of Congress have criticized the workforce contract targets as unfair, and may seek to change them under the new Obama Administration.

Completion of the loan package under TARP was allowed in the 111th Congress when S.J.Res. 5, a restrictive measure, was defeated 5 2-42 in the Senate on January 15, 2009. Auto loan provisions would be modified by a House measure (H.R. 384) approved on January 21, 2009, but this measure will have no effect without Senate action.

Chapter 2 - U.S. automakers are facing a myriad of unfavorable conditions, including a worsening economy and credit crunch that have dampened consumers' demand for new vehicles, high legacy costs, increased competition from foreign automakers, and stricter Corporate Average Fuel Economy (CAFE) standards. The last concern — the regulatory cost of higher fuel economy standards — led Congress to consider various federal programs, including grants and loans, to help automakers with the increased cost to comply with the new standards.

In December 2007, the Energy Independence and Security Act of 2007 (P.L. 110-140) authorized a program to provide loans to automakers and parts suppliers for the production of fuel-efficient cars and light trucks. The law authorized up to $25 billion in total loans. However, funds were not appropriated for the loan program until September 30, 2008, when the Consolidated Security, Disaster Assistance, and Continuing Appropriations Act (P.L. 110-329) was enacted. This act appropriated $7.5 billion to cover the subsidy cost of up to $25 billion total in loans, as well as $10 million for program implementation. The act further directed the Department of Energy (DOE) to implement an interim final rule within 60 days of enactment — this deadline would be November 29, 2008.

On November 5, 2008, DOE announced an interim final rule for the program. The rule will be effective the date it is published in the *Federal Register* (when this will happen is unclear). Once published, DOE will have a 30-day public comment period on the interim rule before issuing the final rule for the program. Loan funds will be separated into tranches, with applications for each tranche due every 90 days, until all loan authority has been expended. The application deadline for the first tranche is either the effective date of the program (the day it is published in the *Federal Register*), or December 31, 2008 — the rulemaking documents are contradictory on this point.

To qualify for a loan, an automaker must have an average fleet fuel economy no lower than that in Model Year 2005. Also, eligible facilities (either vehicle assembly or part making) must be located in the United States. Specific projects must result in the production of vehicles that achieve at least 25% higher fuel economy than Model Year 2005 models with similar size and performance. Further, applicants must be able to demonstrate their financial viability over the life of the loan — 25 years. This last requirement may prove to be a significant barrier to loan approvals under the program.

Chapter 3 - The U.S. motor vehicle manufacturing industry employs about 1 million workers, or about 7.5% of the entire U.S. manufacturing workforce, including those who work in manufacturing parts and bodies, as well as those who assemble motor vehicles. Since 2000, the industry has eliminated about 300,000 manufacturing jobs, but the employment level is still almost as high as in 1990. By comparison, manufacturing in general has suffered a much higher rate of job loss.

The Detroit-based U.S.-owned manufacturers (General Motors, Ford, and Chrysler, collectively known as the "Big Three"), all of which are organized by the United Auto Workers union (UAW), have cut back domestic production by 3 million units since 2000, accounting for all the net employment losses. The shift in consumer preferences from trucks and SUVs to smaller vehicles has accelerated a loss of market share by the Big Three producers and gains for foreign-owned domestic manufacturers and imports. Big Three employment losses were partially offset by new investments by foreign-owned manufacturers in the United States. Today, companies owned by foreign investors produce 28% of all U.S.-made light motor vehicles, up from 11% in 1990.

The patterns of job loss and creation have not been evenly distributed around the country. Forty-four percent of all persons in the industry work in a "heartland auto belt" of three states, Michigan, Ohio, and Indiana, each of which has more than 100,000 persons in the industry. Michigan alone has accounted for more than a third of the net job loss in the industry since 2000. Losses in Ohio and Indiana have been less severe, offset somewhat by foreign investment. Alabama has been the big recent job gainer, adding 15,000 jobs since 2000. Tennessee and Kentucky, now the fourth and fifth largest producing states, have added the most jobs since 1990, and South Carolina has also seen a big net gain. These jobs, mostly non-union, have stretched the "auto belt" more to the South.

New fuel economy standards for automobiles and light trucks, as approved by Congress and signed into law (P.L. 110-140), may encourage greater development of small, fuel efficient cars, but the number of such U.S. plants, even for foreign- owned companies, has declined in recent years. S. 2191, approved at committee level in the Senate in December 2007, would use funds from the auction of emission allowances to support domestic manufacture of fuel-efficient vehicles and components. Congress may also consider the proposed Korea-U.S. Free Trade Agreement, which addresses the current imbalance in automotive trade. The Employee Free Choice Act (H.R. 800), approved by the House, but on which a cloture vote failed in the Senate, could help the UAW organize foreign-owned companies.

In seeking to improve the competitiveness of Big Three assembly operations against both non-union domestic producers and imports, the UAW and the Big Three in 2007 negotiated new contract bargaining agreements. The deals addressed health care costs, wage levels, and other issues.

Chapter 4 - The American automobile industry has serious financial problems. Corporate executives from the Big Three (General Motors, Ford, and Chrysler) have testified before Congress about their need for federal credit (direct loans and guaranteed loans). This chapter examines the Chrysler loan guarantee program for possible insights that could assist Members of Congress in evaluating proposals to provide federal credit assistance.

In 1979, Chrysler applied for federal loan guarantees. In 1979 and 1980, the economy was in recession and the price of oil had unexpectedly increased dramatically. However, at that time there was no financial liquidity crisis, as is the case today. Most of the arguments for and against the proposed Chrysler loan guarantee program are relevant to current proposals for credit assistance to the Big Three. For example, in the 1979 debate, proponents argued that the Chrysler loan guarantee would save many jobs. But opponents contended that the financial capital obtained for Chrysler by the proposed loan guarantee would have been used by other firms to expand their productive facilities, output, and employment. Thus, any Chrysler job losses could be offset by gains at other firms.

Provisions in the Chrysler Loan Guarantee Act of 1979 included the establishment of a Chrysler Loan Guarantee Board, extensive federal oversight of Chrysler's operations, detailed reporting requirements by Chrysler's management, shared sacrifice of parties benefiting from the loan guarantee, and protection of the federal government's interest.

Chrysler used federal loan guarantees to borrow $1.2 billion of the $1.5 billion available and redeemed its guaranteed loans in 1982. Some critics argued that Chrysler was only able to return to profitability because of the imposition by the U.S. government of "voluntary" import quotas on Japanese vehicles. In 1980, the Chrysler loan guarantee was treated as a contingent liability with no initial cost at the time the guarantee was provided. Because Chrysler repaid all of its guaranteed loans, the U.S. government incurred no budgetary cost. Furthermore, the U.S. government received warrants to buy Chrysler stock, which it subsequently sold at auction to Chrysler for $311 million. Thus, it can be argued that the U.S. government made a profit from the loan guarantee program.

Currently, the Federal Credit Reform Act requires that the reported budgetary cost of a credit program equal the estimated subsidy costs to the taxpayer at the time the credit is provided. For proposed legislation establishing a new credit program, the Congressional Budget Office is responsible for making the initial estimate of the subsidy cost. Once legislation has been enacted, the Office of Management and Budget estimates the subsidy cost on the credit program. An appropriation for the annual subsidy cost of each credit program is made into a budget account called a "credit program" account. Thus, under today's budgetary rule, legislation providing direct loans or loan guarantees to assist the automobile industry would require the inclusion of the estimated subsidy cost, which would require an appropriation of budget authority.

The American automobile industry has serious financial problems. Corporate executives from the Big Three (General Motors, Ford, and Chrysler) have testified before Congress about their need for federal credit (direct loans and guaranteed loans). This chapter examines the Chrysler Corporation Loan Guarantee Act of 1979 for possible insights that could assist Congress in evaluating proposals to provide federal credit assistance.

Chapter 5 - The current economic downturn has brought significant financial stress to the auto manufacturing industry. Recent deteriorating financial, real estate, and labor markets have reduced consumer confidence and available credit, and automobile purchases have declined. While auto manufacturers broadly have experienced declining sales in 2008 as the economy has worsened, sales of the "Big 3" (General Motors, Chrysler, and Ford) have also declined relative to those of some other auto manufacturers in recent years because higher gasoline prices have particularly hurt sales of sport utility vehicles.

In addition to causing potential job losses at auto manufacturers, failure of the domestic auto industry would likely adversely affect other sectors. Officials from the Big 3 have requested, and Congress is considering, immediate federal financial assistance.

This testimony discusses principles that can serve as a framework for considering the desirability, nature, scope, and conditions of federal financial assistance. Should Congress decide to provide financial assistance, we also discuss how these principles could be applied in these circumstances. The testimony is based on GAO's extensive body of work on previous federal rescue efforts that dates back to the 1970s.

Chapter 6 - This chapter is edited and excerpted testimony by James McElya before the Committee on Financial Services on November 19, 2008.

Chapter 7 - This chapter is edited and excerpted testimony by Alan R. Mulally before the Committee on Financial Services on November 19, 2008.

Chapter 8 - This chapter is edited and excerpted written testimony by Robert Nardelli before the Committee on Financial Services on November 19, 2008.

Chapter 9 - This chapter is edited and excerpted testimony by Ron Gettelfinger before the Committee on Financial Services on November 19, 2008.

Chapter 10 - This chapter is edited and excerpted testimony by Matthew J. Slaughter before the Committee on Financial Services on November 18, 2008.

Chapter 11 - This chapter is edited and excerpted testimony Felix G. Rohatyn before the Committee on Financial Services on December 5, 2008.

Chapter 12 - This chapter is edited and excerpted testimony by Annette Sykora before the Committee on Financial Services on November 19, 2008.

Chapter 13 - This chapter is edited and excerpted testimony by Rick Wagoner before the Committee on Financial Services on November 19, 2008.

In: The U.S. Auto Industry and the Role of Federal Assistance   ISBN: 978-1-60741-322-6
Editor: James R. Elliot   © 2010 Nova Science Publishers, Inc.

Chapter 1

U.S. MOTOR VEHICLE INDUSTRY: FEDERAL FINANCIAL ASSISTANCE AND RESTRUCTURING

*Stephen Cooney, James M. Bickley, Hinda Chaikind,
Carol A. Petit, Patrick Purcell, Carol Rapaport   and
Gary Shorter*

SUMMARY

On December 19, 2008, President George W. Bush provided financial assistance to General Motors (GM) and Chrysler. These two automakers had testified before Congress that if they did not receive federal financial assistance before the end of the year, they could be forced into bankruptcy. After Congress did not provide the assistance requested, the Treasury Department agreed to provide a total of $13.4 billion to GM and $4 billion to Chrysler from the Troubled Assets Relief Program (TARP), established by the Emergency Economic Stabilization and Recovery Act (EESA, P.L. 110-343). Ford, the third member of the "Detroit 3," testified that it did not need such assistance immediately, though it has said that it could potentially require a line of credit in 2009. The Bush Administration also loaned a further $6 billion under the TARP for General Motors Acceptance Corporation (GMAC), and $1.5 billion for Chrysler Financial, the two manufacturers' respective credit affiliates.

The Detroit 3 have been affected by a long-term decline in their U.S. motor vehicle sales market share, plus the impact of a general decline in U.S. motor vehicle sales in 2008 resulting from a severe constriction of credit related to problems in U.S. and global financial markets. The rise in gasoline prices in mid-2008 caused a sales decline and a structural shift in motor vehicle consumption patterns. Motor vehicle purchases fell substantially in late 2008 despite the subsequent decline in gasoline prices.

A bill to provide up to $25 billion in direct loans from the TARP to auto companies (S. 3688) was introduced in November 2008 by Senate Majority Leader Harry Reid. The Bush Administration instead proposed to make general-purpose loans from a program for advanced technology vehicle production set up under Section 136 of the Energy Independence and

Security Act (EISA, P.L. 110-140). This bill had become law in December 2007, and was funded under P.L. 110-329. In December 2008, Representative Barney Frank introduced H.R. 7321, which would have allowed most of the EISA loan funding to be used to support "bridge loans." This bill was supported by the Democratic leadership of both houses, and the Bush Administration. It passed the House on December 10 by 237-170. The bill was opposed by the Republican leadership in both bodies. Efforts to invoke cloture in the Senate in an attempt to pass the bill failed.

President Bush then provided loans for GM and Chrysler from the TARP, subject to a number of oversight conditions. Eligible companies are to establish an approved restructuring plan by March 31, 2009. They are to target debt reduction through conversion of bonded indebtedness and debt owed for retiree health care to corporate equity. This chapter analyzes the financial solution provisions, including bankruptcies as an alternative, and the impact of the loan provisions on pensions, voluntary employees' beneficiary associations (VEBAs), protection of taxpayers' investment, labor contracts, and executive compensation. Hourly workers are required under the plan to accept contract changes designed to make the companies' workforces more competitive with those of Japanese-owned auto manufacturers in the United States. The United Auto Workers union (UAW) and some Members of Congress have criticized the workforce contract targets as unfair, and may seek to change them under the new Obama Administration.

Completion of the loan package under TARP was allowed in the 111th Congress when S.J.Res. 5, a restrictive measure, was defeated 5 2-42 in the Senate on January 15, 2009. Auto loan provisions would be modified by a House measure (H.R. 384) approved on January 21, 2009, but this measure will have no effect without Senate action.

INTRODUCTION[1]

The Detroit 3 in Crisis[2]

A decline of sales in motor vehicles, which had been evident since 2004, accelerated sharply in late 2008, despite falling gasoline prices. For the year, sales were down to 13.2 million units, a decline of 18%, compared to more than 16 million units sold in 2007 (see section on domestic auto market later in this chapter for details). Consumer spending fell during the summer and fall, with purchases of motor vehicles and parts accounting for most of the decreases in durable goods in October and September.[3] Overall auto sales fell to a 26-year low, although automakers offered aggressive sales incentives.[4] Rapidly declining gas prices failed to boost automotive sales, but, together with incentives, may have caused a short-term shift in consumer demand from cars back to light trucks in December 2008.

In the unfavorable economic circumstances of late 2008, the entire U.S. motor vehicle sector (passenger cars and light trucks, and both domestic and foreign-owned companies) faced difficult times. Almost every manufacturer reported declines for the year.[5] Moreover, the decline accelerated during the latter part of the year. Sales ran about 30-40% lower than in the same month in 2007. While year-over-year sales were 13.2 million units, the annual rate of monthly sales by late 2008 had declined to ten million units or less.

Within an overall down market, the U.S.-owned automakers have been especially hard hit. The "Detroit 3" consist of General Motors (GM), Ford Motor Company, and Chrysler LLC (owned by Cerberus Capital Management LP). For each, annual sales fell by more than 20%. The Japanese, Korean, and European producers, mostly reported lower rates of decline. Toyota, the largest foreign-owned producer, recorded the worst sales performance among them, down by 15.4%.[6] The U.S. market downturn has particularly affected Toyota's U.S. and global output, sales, and profitability.

Many argue that the current situation of the U.S. domestically owned auto industry primarily reflects a structural shift in the Detroit 3's competitive position, which has declined at an accelerating rate during this decade.[7] That decline has been compounded by the worst U.S. economic conditions in several decades. The credit crunch that has dampened general consumer demand for new vehicles has also reduced the ability of the Detroit 3's "captive" credit companies to make loans to many consumers and to dealers for their inventories, an issue that the Treasury Department has also begun to address. The Detroit 3 have much higher pension and retiree health care costs (frequently called "legacy costs") than foreign automakers, and also may be more adversely affected by stricter federal corporate average fuel economy (CAFE) standards than foreign-owned producers, because of their history of sales of less fuel-efficient product fleets.[8]

The cyclical decline in the market has also combined with a rapid shift in early 2008 by consumers from trucks and SUVs back to cars, declining overall sales, and accelerating losses of market shares for the "Detroit Three." The combined shocks of these adverse factors have placed the Detroit 3 business model, which includes a collective bargaining relationship between management and labor, at risk. Congress is facing the possibility that one or more of the unionized, domestically owned motor vehicle companies could go out of business if its restructuring plans do not prove successful.[9]

Legislation was introduced to implement a federal loan program to prevent one or more of the Detroit 3 from falling into bankruptcy, but no bills were approved. Congress in December 2008 left the decision whether and how to assist the Detroit 3 companies to the Bush Administration. On December 19, 2008, President George W. Bush announced a plan to loan $17.4 billion from the Troubled Assets Relief Program (TARP), established by the Emergency Economic Stabilization Act (P.L. 110-343),[10] to GM and Chrysler LLC to prevent any near-term bankruptcy and to help them to restructure as more viable and competitive companies over the longer term.

Organization of This Chapter

This chapter focuses on the current situation faced by the Detroit 3, key aspects of their current crisis, including possible consequences of a failure of one or more companies, and some aspects of legislative actions that have been considered to bridge their financial conditions to a more stable situation. The subjects covered are:

- The impact of the automotive industry on the broader U.S. economy and of potential failure of the Detroit 3 companies;

- Financial issues, including the present conditions affecting credit for automotive consumers and dealers, and legal and financial aspects of government-offered loans to the industry;
- The current situation in the U.S. automotive market, including efforts in 2007 by the Detroit 3 and the United Auto Workers union (UAW) to address problems of long-term competitiveness;
- Issues related to government assistance, and various forms of bankruptcy, should this assistance fail to lead to longer term recovery;
- Legacy issues, specifically pension and health care responsibilities of the Detroit 3; and
- Stipulations that have been imposed on auto manufacturers as conditions of assisting in their restructuring.

Before reviewing these aspects of the situation and specific policy questions, the report will summarize the developments of December 2008. During the month, Congress considered aiding the Detroit 3, but was unable to agree on a plan to assist the companies. Deciding it was necessary to avoid a "disorderly collapse" of the Detroit 3, President Bush announced on December 18, 2008, a plan to aid the two companies closest to immediate bankruptcy, GM and Chrysler, using TARP funds already appropriated by Congress.

AUTO INDUSTRY LOAN DEVELOPMENTS IN DECEMBER 2008[11]

Auto Industry Restructuring Plans

Legislation to provide emergency "bridge loans" to the domestically owned Detroit 3 auto manufacturers ("original equipment manufacturers," OEMs) was introduced on November 17, 2008, by Senate Majority Leader Harry Reid (S. 3688). It would have provided loans to the Detroit 3 by using funds available in the TARP. The industry's need for these loans and their current situation was discussed in a hearing before the Senate Banking Committee on November 18, 2008, with the chief executive officers of the Detroit 3 and UAW president Ronald W. Gettelfinger. The next day, the same witnesses also appeared before the House Financial Services Committee.

Use of TARP funds by the Detroit 3 was opposed by the Bush Administration, as well as by many Members of Congress, including the Republican leadership.[12] The Administration suggested instead using funds already appropriated for the auto industry under a direct loan program operated by the Energy Department (DOE) under the Energy Independence and Security Act (EISA, P.L. 110-140, funded under P.L. 110-329, § 129, as discussed in a previous CRS report[13]). A bipartisan group of senators, led by Senators George Voinovich of Ohio, Christopher Bond of Missouri, and Carl Levin and Debbie Stabenow, both of Michigan, subsequently drafted a compromise proposal, which would have shifted funding to EISA. But the House and Senate leadership on November 21, 2008, demurred on this approach, and suggested that the auto companies instead needed to provide more detailed plans, including how they would use bridge loan funding from the federal government and how they would restructure themselves to insure their long-term competitiveness and viability.

The companies presented their plans to Congress on December 2, 2008. Although each of the Detroit 3 faces serious economic difficulties, financial conditions among the three differ markedly. The following reviews the plans, as summarized in company documents and discussed in Senate Banking and House Financial Services Committee hearings that resumed on December 4-5, 2008. More detailed plans, including confidential corporate information, were provided to the committee leadership and staff, and not made available to the public.

GM Restructuring

GM's leadership has taken the position that the company is already on the right track to achieve long-term competitiveness and viability. This includes "a major transformation of its business model," while "accelerating its plans to produce more fuel-efficient vehicles." However, already that "transformation has consumed a substantial amount of resources and accounts for a major portion of GM's" debt – a total of $62 billion, according to data in the plan. Nevertheless, GM claimed, "the company would not require Government assistance were it not for the dramatic collapse of the U.S. economy, which has devastated the company's current revenues and liquidity."[14]

In its December 2008 congressional testimony GM stated that the company was so close to running low on operating capital that the company had to escalate its request for emergency "bridge loan" lending and credit. This included an immediate $4 billion loan from the government to ensure that the company would remain solvent through the end of 2008. It would need a further $6 billion for the same purpose for the first quarter in 2009. Furthermore, assuming a relatively pessimistic scenario of a U.S. light motor vehicle sales market of 12 million units for 2009, the company requested a total loan facility of $12 billion, plus a backup $6 billion line of government credit, in case things were worse than expected. This made a total government commitment of $18 billion requested by GM through the end of 2009.[15]

GM's restructuring plan includes a substantial future downsizing of the labor force, even in view of large numbers of buyouts that have already occurred. GM has already reduced its total U.S. workforce from 191,000 in 2000 to 96,500 in 2008, a loss of 95,000 jobs. As part of its restructuring plans, it indicated a further elimination of 20,000 to 30,000 more positions by 2012, to include both hourly and salaried employees. A total of nine plants would be closed, from 47 down to 38 U.S. powertrain, stamping, and assembly plants by 2012 – most of these closures have already been announced.[16] GM's plans also include sale or downsizing of four out of their eight current brands, with Hummer, Saab, Saturn, and Pontiac not being considered as "core" future brands.

Chrysler Restructuring

In its restructuring plan, Chrysler requested $7 billion in a "working capital bridge loan" by December 31, 2008. The Chrysler plan stated that its available cash had shrunk from $9.4 billion after the first half of 2008 to an estimated year-end level of $2.5 billion. The company would spend an estimated $11.6 billion in the first quarter of 2009, principally because of $8.0 billion in payments to suppliers and $1.2 billion to "other vendors." Yet, "the first three months of the year are the months with the lowest sales volumes and, hence, the lowest cash flows."[17] In testimony, CEO Robert Nardelli stated that Chrysler's private-equity majority holding company, Cerberus Capital Management LP, had contributed a fresh capital injection of $2 billion in mid-2008, but that it had rejected further capital assistance later in the year.[18]

Chrysler stressed that since acquisition of a majority share by Cerberus in mid-2007, it had taken major steps to reduce costs, streamline operations, and reduce its reliance on truck-based vehicles with low fuel economy ratings (Chrysler has been the most dependent of the Detroit 3 on light truck sales – see **Table 1** in a later section of this chapter). CEO Nardelli had been recruited from outside the auto industry to inject a fresh approach into corporate management. "Four unprofitable vehicle models were discontinued and over $1 billion in unprofitable assets were identified for sale, with more than 70% of those assets disposed of ... [the company] eliminated 1.2 million units of capacity ... [and] separated over 32,000 employees ..."[19] This left the company with 55,000 employees worldwide in 2008, virtually all in North America . According to the company, virtually all of those jobs would be at risk if Chrysler were to go bankrupt, and could not obtain "debtor-in-possession" financing, which the company did not believe would be available .[20]

The Chrysler paper and CEO Nardelli both insisted that Chrysler has a long-term plan for viability as a stand-alone OEM. This included a proposal to bring out electric vehicles, supported by an $8.5 billion request for loans from the DOE loan program established under EISA. It also included some efforts to share manufacturing under joint ventures with such foreign-owned companies as Volkswagen and Nissan-Renault.[21] Many are skeptical of Chrysler's claim that it can continue to operate as an independent manufacturer, as exemplified by an exchange between Senator Robert Corker and Nardelli at the Senate hearing on December 4, 2008.[22] Subsequently, Chrysler and its parent, Cerberus Capital Management, signed a "non-binding" agreement with Italian auto manufacturer Fiat to establish a "global strategic alliance." In exchange, Chrysler gave Fiat "an initial 35% equity interest in Chrysler."[23]

Ford Restructuring

Alone among the Detroit 3, Ford in late 2008 was not applying for immediate government assistance. In part, this was because Ford had already gone to "more receptive capital markets in December 2006 to raise $23.5 billion in liquidity ..." through borrowing secured by virtually all of the company's assets. The company, as part of its restructuring and market repositioning plan under new CEO Alan Mulally, had also sold its Aston Martin, Jaguar, and Land Rover brands and operations, all based in the United Kingdom. It had in late 2008 sold most of its controlling interest in Mazda, an OEM based in Japan, and was considering the "strategic" future of its Swedish subsidiary, Volvo. The focus of CEO Mulally's strategy has been to integrate disparate North American and overseas operations, enabling the company to more readily manufacture for the U.S. market the types of higher fuel economy vehicles that it already designs, produces, and sells overseas (called the "One Ford" strategy by the company).[24] Ford also is counting on $5 billion from the DOE loan program to support a $14 billion plan to reorient its lineup toward more fuel-efficient vehicles.[25]

Nevertheless, Ford was fully supportive of a program of federal assistance for the Detroit 3. Part of the reason that Ford had gone to credit markets earlier was that, "at the time, Ford was viewed as the Detroit automaker most likely to go under."[26] The company reports that it closed 17 plants and "downsized by 12,000 salaried employees and 45,000 hourly employees in North America" since 2005.[27] Ford's own plan stressed that its ability to survive a recession and return to profitability was not only contingent on how well the total market performs, but also on the short- term survival of its domestic competitors, because "Our industry is an interdependent one. We have 80% overlap in supplier networks," plus many dealers also have operations selling GM or Chrysler products. Accordingly, Ford requested a "stand-by" line of credit of up to $9 billion as "a back-stop to be used only if conditions worsen further and only to the extent needed."[28]

On January 29, 2009, Ford announced its 2008 annual and fourth quarter financial results. The company lost a total of $14.6 billion for the year. The net fourth quarter loss was $5.9 billion, with a pre-tax operating loss of $3.6 billion. Nevertheless, while the company announced that it would draw on an outstanding $10 billion line of credit to back up its cash holdings in the first quarter of 2009, Ford continued to state that, "it does not need a bridge loan from the U.S. government." It stated that it had achieved cost and inventory reduction targets, and had stopped the loss of market shares in the United States and Europe.[29]

Congressional Action in December 2008

Following these appeals by the Detroit 3, Congress considered legislation to assist the industry. Initially plans to assist the industry were reportedly blocked by differences between the Bush Administration and many Members of Congress, including Speaker of the House Nancy Pelosi, over whether funding for short-term loans to the Detroit 3 should come from the TARP or from the EISA DOE loan program set up for production of advanced technology vehicles.[30] But this gridlock was soon broken in view of the automakers' urgent needs. The Speaker and Senate Democratic leaders agreed effectively to reprogram the DOE loan money for one or more short- term loans, with a plan to replenish the EISA loan funding after the 111th Congress convened in January 2009. With the likelihood of default by the companies continuing to rise, the amount of budget outlays for the EISA loans ($7.5 billion) was now estimated by the Congressional Budget Office to support $15 billion in direct loans, as opposed to $25 billion authorized under EISA, and $34 billion as requested in early December by the Detroit 3 (including the $9 billion in standby credit requested by Ford).[31]

Chairman Barney Frank of the House Financial Services Committee introduced a bill reflecting this compromise on December 10, 2008 (H.R. 7321). The bill was reportedly supported by the Bush Administration.[32] The legislation passed the House 237-170 on the same day. The legislation as approved authorized a total of $14 billion in direct loans, subject to a number of conditions, funded by $7 billion in budgetary support from the EISA program. The measure also set up a presidential designee (popularly known as a "car czar," although the bill allowed for multiple designees) to oversee compliance by borrowing companies with the terms of the program, including adequate compliance with requirements for meeting commitments to achieve long-term viability and competitiveness. The loans were limited to $14 billion, because the Congressional Budget Office increased the "subsidy cost" (based on the likelihood of default) to 50%, which was higher than its estimate for the EISA loans in September 2008. $500 million of the original EISA budgetary support was reserved for the original purpose of that program, support for advanced vehicle technology production.

Despite the urging of the Bush Administration, H.R. 7321 faced further opposition in getting through the Senate.[33] On December 11, 2008, Minority Leader Mitch McConnell indicated to the Senate that the Republican caucus had studied the House-passed bill, and that they were unable to support it.[34] Efforts were made to craft a new compromise proposal, including conditions that would specify concessions by unions on behalf of the hourly workforce and by bondholders, but were unsuccessful. Majority Leader Reid moved to close debate, for the purpose of achieving a final vote on the House-passed bill. The vote in favor of cloture was 52-35, which was an insufficient majority, and the Senate abandoned further action on the issue.[35]

Presidential Action to Aid the Auto Industry

Following the Senate cloture vote, the White House indicated that, after all, it would consider making loans from the TARP in support of the auto industry. White House Press Secretary Dana Perino stated:

> Under normal economic conditions, we would prefer that markets determine the ultimate fate of private firms. However, given the current weakened state of the U.S. economy, we will consider other options if necessary -- including use of the TARP program to prevent a collapse of troubled automakers. A precipitous collapse of this industry would have a severe impact on our economy, and it would be irresponsible to further weaken and destabilize our economy at this time.[36]

Over the course of the following week, the Bush Administration determined how, and under what conditions, it would provide industry assistance. On December 19, 2008, speaking from the White House, President Bush announced his plan to assist the auto industry. He stated that, while "government has a responsibility not to undermine the private enterprise system ... If we were to allow the free market to take its course now, it would almost certainly lead to disorderly bankruptcy and liquidation for the automakers."[37]

The specific Administration plan was contained in two "term sheets," drawn up by the Treasury Department for GM and Chrysler, the companies in need of immediate assistance. The terms sheets are identical, except for the appendices, which spell out the specific loans provided for each of the two companies.[38] The automakers would be provided with $13.4 billion in loans in December 2008 and January 2009, divided as follows. GM and Chrysler received $4 billion each when the loans closed on December 29, 2008. On January 16, 2009, GM received an additional $5.4 billion. These three loan installments used what remained of the $350 billion first "tranche" of TARP under EESA. Beyond that, the Administration could make no more outlays without seeking approval from Congress to open the second tranche of TARP funds. Thus, a third projected loan of $4 billion to GM, planned by the Bush Administration for February 2009, was made "contingent on Congressional action."[39] This contingency was met on January 15, 2009, when the Senate voted 52-42 to release the second tranche without further conditions.[40] The Chrysler term sheet further specifies that Chrysler's parent holding company must guarantee the first $2 billion of the loan amount. The term sheets for both companies also establish a loan interest rate of 5%, with an additional 5% interest rate penalty on any amount in default.[41]

The Treasury Department made the loans available to Chrysler and GM only under certain "terms and conditions." The overriding condition is that each firm must become "financially viable"; that is, it must have a *positive net value*, taking into account all current and future costs, and *can fully repay the government loan*." "Binding terms and conditions ... mirror those that were supported by a majority of both Houses of Congress ..." They establish oversight rules and security to be obtained by the government in exchange for providing loans. "Additional targets ... were the subject of Congressional negotiations," but were never voted on. These include a requirement to reduce corporate debt by two-thirds, transfer of half of cash contributions promised by companies for an independent hourly employee retiree health care fund to corporate equity, elimination of "jobs bank" rules that were the subject of much congressional discussion, and acceptance by unions of "competitive" wages and work rules.[42]

With respect to Chrysler's deal with Fiat, Chrysler CEO Robert Nardelli stated that, "The potential ... alliance is consistent both with our strategic plan and with the long-term viability plan required under the U.S. Treasury loan." The agreement would be designed to gain for Chrysler access to "all Fiat small-vehicle platforms," as well as to Fiat's international distribution network (Chrysler at present has only limited sales outside of North America). Nardelli further stated that, "It is important to note that no U.S. taxpayer funds would go to Fiat." He also said that Chrysler would continue to seek the remainder of the $7 billion in federal financial support that it had requested.[43]

The companies must submit to a "President's Designee" (the Treasury Department, under the Bush Administration) by March 31, 2009, a detailed restructuring plan indicating the extent to which they have met both financial and competitive labor restructuring targets. Subject to one brief extension allowed, the "Designee" must decide whether to certify that the plan meets all standards set in the term sheet, and, if not, may recall the outstanding loan balance.[44]

These terms and conditions will be discussed in more detail later in this chapter. Overall, they have been the focus of much discussion and debate since the presidential announcement. Some argue that requirements, though unilaterally set by the Bush Administration, are actually weaker than the legislation proposed by it and the Democratic majority, and approved in the House. Although H.R. 7321 did not mandate specific changes in labor contracts, it did provide (Section 8) that if the parties did not reach agreement on a restructuring plan by March 31, 2009, the presidential designee "shall call the loan ... within 30 days ..." In effect, unions, bondholders, and other interests had that window to negotiate a restructuring plan, or, in effect, by statutory law the company would be forced into bankruptcy. Since the Bush plan is set by executive order, it can be subsequently modified by President Obama without further action by Congress.

The UAW believes that plan's conditions for labor contract changes are too prescriptive. President Ron Gettelfinger said that he was "pleased the Bush Administration acted to provide urgently needed bridge loans" to the auto companies, and "to pursue a process for restructuring outside of bankruptcy." But he was "disappointed that [President Bush] has added unfair conditions singling out workers ... We will work with the Obama Administration and the new Congress to ensure these unfair conditions are removed," he said.[45] Senator Debbie Stabenow in a press release said that

[T]he White House has been characterizing the bridge-loan package as simply having goals for worker concessions ... [but] ... These provisions raise serious concerns regarding unfair, punitive conditions being placed on the backs of workers.[46]

On January 21, 2009, the House addressed the auto loans specifically, in Title III of H.R. 384, a bill to release the second tranche of TARP funds. This bill would have required that a restructuring plan must be agreed by all stakeholders, without reference to specific targets and requirements established in December 2008 term sheets for GM and Chrysler. The measure passed 260-166. However, as the Senate had already defeated a resolution to withhold TARP funds, the House action had no direct legal effect, without any further Senate action.[47]

IMPACT ON THE NATIONAL ECONOMY[48]

The question of rescuing one or more of the Detroit 3 automakers comes up at a time of considerable weakness in the overall economy. In the third quarter of 2008, real gross domestic product (GDP) fell by 0.5%, and the Commerce Department advanced estimate for the fourth quarter was a decline of 3.8%.[49] Most economists are not very sanguine about short run prospects either. The *Blue Chip Economic Indicators* consensus forecast was for real GDP to decline by 1.6% for all of 2009 and for the unemployment rate to be above 8% by the end of 2009.[50] Many believe that the consequences of a Detroit 3 company's failure for the national economy would be serious.

National Impact of Detroit 3 Failure

The White House *Fact Sheet* on the loan program for GM and Chrysler estimated that, "the direct costs of American automakers failing and laying off their workers in the near term would result in a more than 1% reduction in real GDP growth and about 1.1 million workers losing their jobs, including workers for auto suppliers and dealers." Economists generally assess that economic growth of at least 2% is required to accommodate a growing labor force and keep the rate of unemployment from rising.

In the third quarter of 2008, the annual-rate value of motor vehicle output was $331.3 billion out of a total annual-rate gross domestic product (GDP) of $14.4 trillion.[51] Motor vehicle production thus represents 2.3% of total output. The total number of workers employed in the manufacture of U.S. autos in 2007, measured on an annual basis, was 859,000. Of those, 186,000 worked in light vehicle assembly, and 673,000 were employed in the manufacture of parts.[52]

Estimates vary of job loss resulting from a failure of one or more Detroit 3 companies and their production. They depend on different models and assumptions. But in every case, the impact on employment is serious.

- The Inforum model at the University of Maryland produced estimates of "peak year" (2011) job loss ranging from 826,000 jobs in event of "retirement" of 20% of Detroit 3 production (a shutdown of Chrysler, for example) to more than 2.2 million peak-year job losses in the event of a 60% Detroit 3 shutdown. However, the study also notes that the higher shutdown level is unlikely over the long term and that the practical worst-case scenario would be a restructuring and downsizing, with a 40% production loss. This would be estimated to result in 1.5 million jobs lost in the peak year, and a net average loss of just under one million jobs per year through 2014, against what employment would otherwise be.[53]

- Anderson Economic Group/BBK, an international business advisory firm with customers in the automotive industry, produced a separate set of estimates with a different methodology. AEG/BBK's worst-case scenario was bankruptcy and eventual liquidation of two of the Detroit 3. In this case, they estimated that more than 1.2 million jobs would be lost in the first year, and nearly 600,000 in the second year. Netting out a small number of persons gaining alternative employment, the AEG/BBK estimate was 1.8 million jobs lost over two years among the OEMs, their suppliers and dealers, and others "indirectly" linked to the industry.[54]

- The Center for Automotive Research (CAR), a research organization with some support from industry, did an economic simulation of a failure of domestic automakers based on two separate sets of assumptions.[55] In the first case it was assumed that the problems of the Detroit 3 automakers led to a permanent 100% decline in the production of domestic automakers in the first year (2009). It was also assumed that the effect of that shock would result in such a large drop in the demand for parts that suppliers would be forced to either liquidate or restructure. It was assumed that the disruption to the parts suppliers would cause domestic production of foreign-owned auto manufacturers to also drop to zero in the first year. In this scenario, the total number of jobs lost in the United States in the first year was estimated to be 2.95 million.[56] That figure includes jobs lost at auto manufacturers, parts suppliers, as well as in the rest of the economy, because of the drop in consumer spending resulting from the direct job losses. In the second year (2010), production at the foreign-owned firms begins to pick up and employment recovers somewhat with the number of jobs lost falling to 2.46 million.

- The second CAR scenario assumes that although in the first year (2009) domestic production of the Detroit 3 automakers drops to zero, auto production recovers to 50% of its former output in the second year and continues at that level. In this scenario, the estimated U.S. job loss in the first year is 2.46 million, falling to 1.50 million in the second year.

Impact Focused on "Auto Alley"

Any loss of output due to the difficulties with U.S. automakers will likely be felt nationwide, but because of the geographic concentration of those firms it will be much greater in some regions than in others. According to Klier and Rubenstein, Michigan accounts for one-quarter of all auto parts.[57] They also point out that there is a corridor between the Great Lakes and the Gulf of Mexico that has become known as "auto alley." In 2008, 43 of 50 auto assembly plants were located in auto alley. Those geographic areas where automakers are concentrated would experience the greatest economic difficulties resulting from any loss of

U.S. auto output. Klier and Rubenstein also estimate that three-quarters of all auto parts suppliers are located within a one day's drive (truck delivery) of Detroit, including those located within the Canadian province of Ontario.[58]

Howard Wial of the Brookings Institution, a Washington, DC-based think tank, has done an analysis of how different U.S. metropolitan areas would be affected if the Detroit 3 companies were to go out of business.[59] Wial's analysis suggests that 50 metropolitan areas rely heavily on Detroit 3-related jobs, measured as the OEMs and suppliers accounting for 1% or more of the area workforce. Though this may seem a small share of total employment, he cites studies to claim that up to twice as many jobs in metro areas are supported by jobs directly in the auto and auto parts industry. These metro areas are almost all clustered in the "auto alley" region noted above, stretching as far south as Tuscaloosa, Alabama, and as far to the northeast as western New York. The only metro area west of St. Louis is Ogden, Utah, and no cities are included on either coast, or in the South, beyond Kentucky, Tennessee, and Alabama. Among the metro areas with the most Detroit 3-related jobs, only the Detroit area itself has more than 100,000 jobs in total that meet this description. The Chicago area is next with about 20,000 jobs. Some smaller cities figure among the top 20 metro areas in Detroit 3-related employment, such as Kokomo, Indiana, where 22% of all jobs are in autos and auto parts. But, Wial says

> There are also many auto and auto parts jobs in Los Angeles, Dallas, and Cincinnati, large metropolitan areas where these industries account for a smaller share of employment. Closures of Detroit 3- related plants in those areas would harm the workers who were laid off but would have less effect on metropolitan area economies.[60]

Conversely, he found that, "In addition, there are 21 metropolitan areas, mainly in the South where at least 1% of total employment is in autos and/or auto parts, but where little or none of that employment is attributable to the Detroit 3 or their suppliers." These metro areas are almost all in the southern states north of Florida and east of the Mississippi River. However, Wial concludes, "If the Detroit 3 disappear then some of [these] metropolitan areas may gain jobs, but they will not gain all of the jobs lost by the Detroit 3."[61]

In conclusion to this section, the consequences of a failure and liquidation of one or more Detroit 3 companies, would be large, and possibly far-reaching in extent.

THE DOMESTIC MOTOR VEHICLE MARKET[62]

Loss of Detroit 3 Market Share

Foreign brands, both imported and produced at U.S. plants, have been gaining market share for decades.[63] As illustrated in **Figure 1**, the Detroit 3's decline relative to the total U.S. market has continued since 2000. From two-thirds of the total U.S. market for passenger cars and light trucks in 2000, the Detroit 3 share declined gradually to 58.2% in 2005. Some of this decline represented aggressive U.S. manufacturing and expansion plans by foreign-owned companies: Toyota, Honda, Nissan, and Hyundai have all opened new assembly plants in the United States since 2000, and more are on the way. While, as noted below in this chapter, some planned foreign- owned plants may be delayed, Toyota is still planning to open a new plant in Mississippi, Kia is building its first plant in Georgia, and Volkswagen, which had closed a U.S. plant in the 1980s, has said that it will continue to build an announced plant in Tennessee. Additionally, a number of the foreign-owned plants have significantly expanded existing facilities.[64]

However, after losing eight points of market share in 2000-2005, the Detroit 3 saw their losses accelerate by an additional 10 points between then and the first three quarters of 2008, to a 48% market share. This loss of market share occurred at the same time as the total market was in decline. Although the U.S. automotive market is cyclical, the decline in sales starting in mid-2008 appears to have been especially abrupt because of the crisis in global credit markets.[65] **Figure 1** indicates that the total domestic light motor vehicle market stabilized at around 17 million sales per year through 2005 (passenger cars and light trucks, which include sport utility vehicles, minivans, and pickup trucks). It dropped about a half-million units in 2006 to 16.5 million, another half-million to just more than 16 million in 2007, then plunged to just 13.2 million in 2008.[66] Car and light truck unit sales by the Detroit 3 fell to just 6.4 million, compared to 11.5 million in 2000, and almost 10 million as late as 2005. More detailed data show that each of the Detroit 3 saw sales decline by nearly one million vehicles or more just since 2005, and each suffered significant market share losses.

Automotive data is usually figured in "units," which means, for example, that an expensive Cadillac Escalade counts the same as an inexpensive Kia Rio. But for the entire industry, average new vehicle transaction prices, after rising from 2004 through 2007, fell steadily in 2008, meaning less "top line" revenue per unit sold.[67] Moreover, **Table 1** illustrates that part of the Detroit 3's problems relate to the continued reliance on truck sales, when light trucks are declining as an overall share of the market. Having become more specialized in larger vehicles, the Detroit 3 have been especially adversely affected by the sharper decline in the sales of such vehicles.

In 2001, "light truck" sales, which include smaller SUVs known as "crossover" utility vehicles (CUVs), were higher than U.S. passenger car sales for the first time. Trucks' lead over cars continued to expand through 2005—9.3 million units to 7.7 million units in that year, for a net margin of 1.6 million. But 2004-2005 saw Hurricanes Ivan, Katrina, and Rita, which temporarily disrupted oil and gas production in the Gulf of Mexico and exacerbated a period of rising fuel prices and volatility that continued through 2008.[68] In 2008 U.S. car and truck sales both fell: car sales by 800,000 versus a two million unit decline in light truck sales. Truck sales were also more than three million units less than the all-time 2005 annual peak. While most foreign-owned manufacturers had also expanded their truck offerings (including SUVs and minivans) in the U.S. market, they have not been as reliant as the Detroit 3 on truck products. By 2008, each of the Detroit 3 still counted on light trucks for a majority of sales (55% for GM, higher levels for Ford and Chrysler), while no foreign-owned competitor did so. Only about a third of foreign-brand companies' sales overall were classified as light trucks.

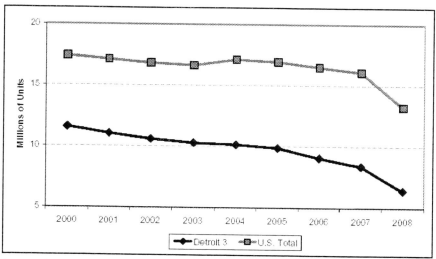

Source: Automotive News Market Data Center (2008 data); *Ward's Automotive Yearbook* (2001-2008).

Figure 1. U.S. Motor Vehicle Sales Passenger Cars and Light Trucks

During the present decade, both market forces and federal regulation have begun to push fuel economy levels upward, leading to a move away from larger, less fuel-efficient vehicles, a market that the Detroit 3 have generally dominated. While the CAFE standard set by the Department of Transportation's National Highway Transportation Safety Administration (NHTSA) for cars has held steady at 27.5 mpg throughout the decade, the actual average of model-year vehicles sold, as measured on a different basis by the Environmental Protection Agency (EPA), has increased from 22.9 mpg to 24.1 mpg, with most of the gain coming in model year (MY) 2007-2008.[69] While the light truck standard held steady at 20.7 mpg through 2004, actual average truck mpg, as measured by EPA, remained less than 17.0 mpg. Both the federal standard and the actual average declined in 2005 for light trucks. The actual average mpg was 18.1 by MY2008.[70]

While the first half of 2008 was characterized by a market shift to more fuel-efficient vehicles in the U.S. market under the influence of high fuel prices, the latter half of the year saw all almost OEMs suffer from declining sales, in the United States and globally. IHS Global Insight estimated that global vehicle production fell by 16% in the fourth quarter of 2008. CSM, an automotive consulting group, estimated that there is now enough worldwide capacity to build 90 million cars a year, but only 66 million will be produced in 2009.[71] Not just the Detroit 3 are affected by this slump. Toyota announced that it would probably record its first annual operating loss in more than 70 years in the fiscal year to March 31, 2009. Honda similarly projected negative results for the second half of its fiscal year. Both companies cited strengthening of the yen against the U.S. dollar to the highest level in 13 years as a major factor in worsening their results. According to the *Financial Times*:

"I would like the government and the Bank of Japan to move a bit more swiftly in ensuring the stability of the exchange rate," [said Honda CEO Takeo Fukui], code for intervening in the market to weaken the currency.[72]

Table 1. Market Shares of U.S. Car and Truck Sales

Manufacturers	2001 Sales (millions of units) Cars	Light Trucks	Total	2001 Market Share (%)	2005 Sales (millions of units) Cars	Light Trucks	Total	2005 Market Share (%)	2008 Sales (millions of units) Cars	Light Trucks	Total	2008 Market Share (%)
GM	2.3	2.6	4.9	28.3	1.8	2.7	4.5	26.3	1.4	1.6	3.0	22.3
Ford	1.5	2.4	3.9	22.9	1.0	2.1	3.1	18.3	0.7	1.3	2.0	15.1
Chrysler	0.6	1.7	2.3	13.3	0.5	1.8	2.3	13.6	0.5	1.0	1.5	11.0
Detroit 3 (total)	**4.4**	**6.7**	**11.0**	**64.5**	**3.3**	**6.6**	**9.9**	**58.2**	**2.5**	**3.9**	**6.4**	**48.4**
Asian Brands	**3.3**	**1.9**	**5.2**	**30.4**	**3.6**	**2.6**	**6.2**	**36.6**	**3.8**	**2.1**	**5.9**	**44.6**
German Brands	**0.8**	**0.1**	**0.9**	**5.0**	**0.7**	**0.1**	**0.8**	**5.0**	**0.7**	**0.2**	**0.9**	**6.5**
Total U.S. Sales[a]	**8.4**	**8.7**	**17.1**	**100.0**	**7.7**	**9.3**	**16.9**	**100.0**	**7.2**	**6.3**	**13.5**	**100.0**

Source: Automotive News Market Data Center (2008 data); *Ward's Automotive Yearbook* (2001-2008).

a. U.S. total includes other specialty manufacturers.

Reaction among Japanese companies in their U.S. plants included temporary production cutbacks, and Toyota's announced delay in completing its new plant in Mississippi to build the Prius hybrid model. Toyota also consolidated production of its full-size Tundra pickup at the San Antonio plant, and temporarily closed one line there. Production cutback and temporary production shutdown announcements in were widespread among Asian OEMs in the United States.[73] On January 6, 2009, Toyota in Japan also announced that it would suspend "production at all 12 of its directly operated domestic plants, which include 4 vehicle assembly plants and also factories that make transmissions, engines and other parts." Another three-day shutdown had already been scheduled for January 2009.[74] Nissan, meanwhile, has converted its truck and SUV line in Mississippi to produce a commercial type of vehicle.[75] Among German-owned manufacturers, Mercedes Benz has offered buyouts to all 4,000 of its production workers in Alabama.[76]

Nor are the Detroit 3 unaffected by negative trends abroad. The German government is reported to have responded to a GM request by offering as much as $2.5 billion in "conditional credit guarantees" to GM's subsidiary Opel, which has manufacturing plants in four German states.[77] The Swedish government is proposing a $3.4 billion emergency aid package for Volvo and Saab, respectively the Swedish-based subsidiaries of Ford and GM.[78] And Canada followed up on President Bush's TARP loan actions with a package of $3.29 billion in emergency loans to GM and Chrysler, including more than $1 billion from the provincial government of Ontario.[79]

Labor Negotiations in 2007 to Address Competitive Issues

Many analysts have commented that, in competing with foreign-owned auto manufacturers, the Detroit 3 are hampered by outdated labor contracts, negotiated with the UAW through decades of collective bargaining.[80] In 2007, each of the Detroit 3 negotiated new collective bargaining agreements with their principal union, the UAW.[81] These agreements provided for transfer of retiree health care in 2010 from the companies to a separate trust, with some board members appointed by the UAW. The trusts are to be established with financial support initially from each of the Detroit 3. The agreements also provided the companies with other flexibility in managing and reducing labor costs, so that they could compete on a footing perceived to be more equal to foreign-owned companies, which are generally non-union in the United States. This included union acceptance of a second, and lower, tier of wages and benefits for new hires by the Detroit 3, under specified circumstances.[82]

But with the auto market declining, there has been little new hiring at the lower wage rate.[83] Even so, wage rate gaps between the Detroit 3 and the international companies may be exaggerated. CAR data quoted in a *Wall Street Journal* article compare standard UAW hourly assembly line worker pay of $26 per hour with $26 per hour at Toyota, $24 at Honda, and $21 at Hyundai. Honda and Kia are starting production line workers at their new plants in Indiana and Georgia, respectively, at a wage of just less than $15 per hour, but this compares with a similar starting "Tier 2" wage for new UAW hires at Ford and GM.[84]

The principal gap remains in the legacy cost burden that the 2007 Detroit 3 contract agreements with the UAW attempted to address. CAR is quoted as calculating that Toyota's hourly total labor cost, including all benefits, is $44 per hour versus $73 at GM.[85] In its December 2008 restructuring plan presented to Congress, Ford attached a table showing that wages and wage- related costs in 2008 were $43 per hour, versus an average of $35 per hour at foreign-owned U.S. auto manufacturers. But Ford's total hourly labor cost was $71, against $49 for the foreign-owned companies. The principal difference was a "legacy cost" – principally projected health care costs for retirees – of $16 per hour, versus comparable foreign companies' costs of $3 per hour. The new UAW contract, by transferring this cost off Ford's books to the VEBA in 2010, would bring the hourly cost burden down to $58 per hour. And, if Ford could replace 20% of its projected workforce with new, entry-level employees, as allowed by contract, they would bring the hourly cost level down to $53.[86]

Another issue addressed in the 2007 contracts and in congressional hearings was pay for laid-off autoworkers and the "jobs bank." Laid-off Detroit 3 production workers receive unemployment compensation from state governments, plus supplementary compensation from company funds that brings their pay close to the base level for one year.[87] After that, if they are still unemployed, they may be eligible to enter the jobs bank, where they may continue to receive almost their full base salary, even if no jobs are available. The terms are now more restrictive under the new contract, and two years is the maximum stay. The jobs bank was declared suspended by the UAW as of December 2008, in an effort to assist the Detroit 3. Elimination of the jobs bank was made an explicit target of the federal loans term sheets signed by GM and Chrysler in December 2008. In January 2009, on the occasion of announcing its annual 2008 financial results, with a large corporate loss, Ford indicated that it and the UAW had agreed to end the jobs bank program at Ford.[88]

The Energy Independence and Security Act of 2007 (EISA)

The new collective bargaining agreements were negotiated and ratified by the time Congress approved, and President Bush signed, a substantial increase in mandated fuel economy in EISA (P.L. 110-140) in December 2007. Although the Detroit 3 were losing money, the new labor agreements, combined with an EISA direct loan program for manufacturing advanced technology vehicles and components, appeared to provide new resources for a transition that would aid the Detroit 3 in achieving improved fuel economy.[89]

By the time Congress considered funding this program in September 2008, the economic climate for the auto sector as a whole, and for the Detroit 3 in particular, had worsened markedly. The downturn in the broader domestic economy reduced sales for virtually all manufacturers in the middle of the year, as consumer confidence declined and credit became harder to obtain. While neither Ford nor GM has been profitable since 2006, the operating losses turned much worse in 2008. After total GM losses of $18.7 billion for the first two quarters, the company reported an adjusted third-quarter loss of $4.2 billion. Ford reported a small net profit in early 2008, but that was offset by an $8.7 billion loss in the second quarter. It had only a small reported net overall loss in the third quarter, but its after-tax operating loss was $3 billion. "Cash burn" (net operating cash loss) for the two companies accelerated to about $7 billion each for the quarter.[90] In testimony before the Senate Banking Committee on November 18, 2008, CEO Robert Nardelli of privately held Chrysler acknowledged that, after losing money in the first half of the year, his company's "cash burn" increased to $3 billion in the latest quarter. At the same hearing, UAW president Ron Gettelfinger testified that of the three companies, GM was in most immediate danger of failure, and Chrysler was next; Ford, having arranged credit during a more favorable period two years earlier, was in less immediate danger.[91]

Representatives of the Detroit 3 reportedly attempted to increase the scale of loans available during legislative consideration of appropriations to fund the EISA direct loan program, as well as to reduce restriction of the EISA loans to production of advanced technology vehicles. But these efforts were unavailing, as Congress maintained the same program rules, when it approved the appropriations in September 2008.[92]

Legislative Efforts to Assist Automakers Prior to December 2008

Following the November 2008 elections, the Bush Administration was asked to consider making funds available to the auto industry from the $700 billion appropriated for relief of the financial sector in the Emergency Economic Stabilization Act (EESA, P.L. 110-343).[93] Secretary of the Treasury Henry Paulson and Senate Minority Leader Mitch McConnell instead urged Congress to assist the automakers by diverting funds from the EISA loan program.[94]

On November 17, 2008, Senate Majority Leader Harry Reid introduced S. 3688, which, in Title II, included a provision allowing $25 billion from the EESA funding to be used as loans to automakers in the United States under certain conditions. On November 18-19, hearings were held before the Senate Banking Committee and the House Financial Services Committee, in which the chief executive officers of the Detroit 3, as well as UAW President Gettelfinger, made the case for immediate assistance to the industry. They were supported by some Members of Congress. Critics of such assistance were also heard.

The industry CEOs stated that they were asking for "bridge loans" to tide them over, during a market decline of unanticipated severity, which had affected all automakers, and an equally unanticipated unavailability of credit from financial markets. The bridge loans would provide time for cost-saving measures, including the transfer of retiree health care responsibilities, to work. That, plus a hoped-for recovery of the domestic auto market by 2010, could allow the Detroit 3 to return to financial stability. As GM CEO G. Richard Wagoner testified:

> [We, in cooperation with the UAW] have taken actions designed to improve GM's liquidity by $20 billion by the end of 2009, and they obviously affect every employee, retiree, dealer, supplier, and investor involved in our company ... I do not agree with those who say we are not doing enough to position GM for success. What exposes us to failure now is not our product lineup, is not our business plan, is not our employees and their willingness to work hard, it is not our long-term strategy. What exposes us to failure now is the global financial crisis, which has severely restricted credit availability and reduced industry sales to the lowest per capita level since World War II.
>
> Our industry, which represents America's real economy, Main Street, needs a bridge to span the financial chasm that has opened before us. We'll use this bridge and we'll use it effectively to pay for essential operations, new vehicles and power trains, parts from our suppliers, wages and benefits for our workers and suppliers, and taxes for state and local governments that help deliver essential services to millions of Americans.[95]

In the hearings, the CEOs revealed how the $25 billion in loans would be divided among their three companies. CEO Wagoner of GM stated that his company would need $10-12 billion to bridge the present period of financial insecurity, while Robert Nardelli of Chrysler said that his company would require $7 billion. CEO Alan Mulally of Ford stated that Ford currently did not have an operating capital shortfall, but would request that $7 billion to $8 billion be reserved in case of eventual cash needs.[96]

Congressional critics of the industry's requests included Senator Richard Shelby, Ranking Member of the Banking Committee, and Representative Spencer Bachus, who holds the same position on the House Financial Services Committee. They argued that to a large extent, the problems of the Detroit 3 were due to the long-term consequences of poor management and labor decisions, which would not be fixed with short-term financial assistance, and that the industry would soon be requesting additional federal support. Moreover, assistance to the auto industry, it was stated, would encourage other industries to also importune the federal government for aid during the present economic downturn.[97]

No action was taken in the Senate on S. 3688 in November 2008. Further developments were deferred until December 2008, after full reports had been presented by the Detroit 3 on their financial condition and restructuring plans.

Employment in the Automotive Sector

Employment in the automotive sector of the U.S. economy includes both manufacturing and services activities, but the latter actually employ more than in manufacturing. As seen in Table 2, in September 2008 the Current Employment Survey of the Department of Labor's Bureau of Labor Statistics estimated that there were about 857,000 persons employed altogether in motor vehicle manufacturing (including heavy trucks, trailers and other vehicles), compared to more than 3.7 million in various service activities.

Since the era of Henry Ford, automotive employment has been a mainstay of U.S. manufacturing employment. But its relative significance has declined in recent years, despite the opening or expansion of foreign-owned assembly and parts facilities. Table 2 examines levels of and changes in automotive employment by both manufacturing and services categories.[98] It presents the latest published data, from September 2008, compared to September 2001, on a seasonally adjusted basis, to measure against a comparable point in the business cycle. Motor vehicle manufacturing employment in 2008 was down about 82,000 jobs, a drop of 30%. However, as pointed out by Thomas Klier and James Rubenstein, as well as in earlier CRS analyses, by far more people are employed in parts manufacturing than in motor vehicle assembly.[99] In September 2008, total employment in all categories of automotive manufacturing was 857,000, down about 30% from 1.2 million in 2001.

Service activities employment directly related to the automotive industry has also declined, but not nearly as significantly as manufacturing employment in the sector. Wholesale distribution of vehicles and parts fell by about 8,500 jobs. Employment at dealers—the largest single North American Industry Classification System category in the sector, with more than one million jobs—fell by 47,500 jobs, or 4%. Employment in retail outlets for automotive parts, accessories, and tires actually grew by 7,600 jobs. The largest decline in automotive services employment since September 2001 has been at gasoline stations, where jobs fell by 87,000, or almost 10%.

Both Ford and GM are consolidating their dealer networks, so that their unit sales per dealer will better approximate the levels recorded, for example, by Toyota and Honda. Each of those companies has roughly 1,000 U.S. dealers, compared to 3,790 dealers for Ford as of 2008, and 6,450 for GM. Yet in terms of market share, GM in 2008 was just over 22%, Toyota just under 17%, Ford about 15%, and Honda nearly even with Chrysler at around 11%. Thus there is no proportionality between numbers of dealers and leading companies' market shares. GM and Ford have already begun to consolidate dealers and reduce their numbers. GM has eliminated more than 1,000 dealers since 2005, and their restructuring plan calls for eliminating 1,800 more, down to a total level of 4,700 by 2012. Ford has eliminated 600 dealers since 2005, but did not indicate a target number for the future.[100]

Paul Taylor, chief economist of the National Automobile Dealers Association, has forecast that, because of economic conditions, there will be a total net loss of about 1,600 dealers in 2008-09. About two-thirds of those closing have been Detroit 3 dealers, he estimated. If this forecast holds, there will be fewer than 20,000 new car dealers in the United States at the end of 2009, compared to 28,000 in 1980.[101] Even if the Detroit 3 succeed in consolidating franchises into larger operations, the implication is that the total number of dealership employees will decline, perhaps dramatically.

Automotive manufacturing employment has also fallen as a share of total employment in manufacturing. While total manufacturing employment has fallen by more than three million jobs since September 2001, employment in motor vehicle manufacturing dropped at an even faster rate, with its share of total manufacturing employment falling from 7.4% to 6.4%. During this period, total automotive sector employment, including services, as shown in **Table 2**, fell from 5.1 million to 4.6 million, while total U.S. employment grew by six million. As a result, automotive employment, including both manufacturing and services, as a share of total U.S. employment, fell from 3.9% to 3.3%.

FINANCIAL ISSUES IN THE AUTO INDUSTRY

Credit Conditions[102]

Credit is the lifeblood of the U.S. auto industry. Credit conditions govern the industry's ability to invest, the ability of its dealers to finance their inventory ("floorplan"), and the ability of dealers, in turn, to sell to individual consumers. The systemic crisis in the U.S. and global financial markets in 2008 has had a severely negative impact on all these aspects of automotive credit.

An auto dealer's floorplan is the financing dealers must have to finance their inventory. A new vehicle dealer will generally buy cars from the OEM, most often in the past on credit provided by the OEM's "captive" financial organization. The dealer will then sell vehicles to customers at a negotiated transaction price. The dealer will be paid, alternatively:

Table 2. U.S. Automotive Employment

	NAICS Code	All Employees ('000s)		
		Sept. 2001	Sept. 2008	Change
Manufacturing:				
Motor Vehicle Mfg.	3361	277.8	196.0	-81.8
Motor Vehicle Bodies and Trailers	3362	155.7	128.7	-27.0
Motor Vehicle Parts	3363	767.6	531.9	-235.7
Total Motor Vehicle Mfg.		**1,201.1**	**856.6**	**-344.5**
Services:				
Wholesale Distribution	4231	348.6	340.1	-8.5
Auto Dealers	4411	1,227.8	1,180.3	-47.5
Auto Pts., Accessories & Tires	4413	496.9	504.5	7.6
Gasoline Stations	4470	921.2	833.9	-87.3
Auto Repair & Maintenance	8111	902.2	864.1	-38.1
Total Services		**3,896.7**	**3,722.9**	**173.8**
Total Automotive Employment		**5,097.8**	**4,579.5**	**-518.3**

Source: Dept. of Labor. Bureau of Labor Statistics. *Current Employment Survey* (November 22, 2008).
Note: Monthly survey data may differ from annual figures cited earlier. "Services" total does not necessarily include all NAICS auto-related categories.

- in cash by the customer;
- through a financial transaction by the OEM captive credit organization; or
- through a third party loan to a customer from a bank, credit union, or finance company.

Each of the Detroit 3 has traditionally operated with a captive credit organization for both floorplan financing and consumer credit: General Motors Acceptance Corporation (GMAC), Ford Motor Credit and Chrysler Financial, respectively. Floorplan financing has generally been provided for dealers by these credit organizations at favorable (better than prime) interest rates.[103] Dealers have also been financially encouraged to refer customers to the captive finance organizations. For much of the period since 2000, a very large share of each of these OEM's corporate profits has been accounted for by its captive financial organization.

But the financial performance of the three credit organizations has progressively deteriorated. According to *Automotive News*:

> Standard & Poor's has assigned subinvestment-grade ratings to all three finance arms. Ford Credit and GMAC are rated B- with a credit watch of negative. Chrysler Financial has an S&P rating of CCC+ with a negative outlook ...[104]

This means that the financial arms have found it much more difficult to raise capital to lend to dealers or customers. GMAC, in particular, had virtually ceased lending except to customers with the highest credit scores, and stopped supporting domestic leasing altogether. All three companies have had to raise interest rates on floorplan financing, in many cases forcing dealers or customers to use third-party lending.[105]

Two of the three captive credit organizations are now controlled by the private equity hedge fund Cerberus Capital Management. Cerberus acquired Chrysler's credit arm with its acquisition of a controlling share (80.1%) of the auto manufacturing operation in 2007. Earlier, it had bought a 51% stake in GMAC. GMAC has been particularly affected by the global credit squeeze and subprime lending, as it had become a major player in mortgage lending through its Residential Capital (ResCap) division. The latter has been primarily responsible for GMAC's multibillion- dollar losses in 2008.[106] However, unlike the situation in subprime home mortgages, Detroit 3 CEOs at the November 18, 2008, Senate Banking Committee hearing on the domestic auto industry said that there had not been a major rise in delinquencies among their automotive credit borrowers.[107]

Ford Motor Credit remains 100% owned by Ford Motor Company. It has sought to offset negative reports on credit availability by widely advertising that Ford consumer credit is still available. It has raised floorplan financing rates by 0.5% in view of higher borrowing costs, but has also waived the increase for dealers that meet overall sales targets.[108] CEO Alan Mulally testified before the House Financial Services Committee on December 5, 2008, that Ford Motor Credit still supported "77% of all wholesale financing.[109]"

The Japanese OEMs are also affected by the financial crisis. Traditionally weaker than the U.S. companies' financial arms and more reliant on third-party consumer lending by banks, they have become much more competitive in recent years. Notably, Toyota has inaugurated an aggressive "Saved by Zero" consumer lending campaign that features 0% loans for qualified buyers on most models. Nissan has followed suit.[110] Even so, the Japan-based car companies saw monthly sales declines in late 2008 of about 30% or more, compared to sales one year earlier.

Customers and dealers have alternatively sought to finance deals through banks, but the banks have also reduced their consumer lending.[111] Dealers have sought alternative inventory funding sources from community banks, which generally have funds to loan, and which have not been as severely affected by the subprime mortgage crisis as the money center banks. The local banks may offer more attractive financing rates than the OEMs, but for many dealers, they do not have the scale to cover a dealer's floorplan.[112] On the other hand, GM and Ford have told Congress that they have explicitly planned to consolidate and reduce their numbers of dealers.

Credit has thus been more difficult for the Detroit 3, their dealers, and their customers. Former U.S. Senator from Michigan and Bush Administration cabinet member Spencer Abraham has written that an estimated $700 billion to $800 billion in auto loan exposure "is currently thrashing around our financial system." He has further stated that securities tied to auto loans account for more than 25% of all asset-backed securities, with large holdings by insurance companies, mutual funds, and pension funds, as well as banks.[113]

GMAC on November 20, 2008, applied to become a bank holding company, in order to make itself eligible to obtain new capital from the EESA financial relief package described in a section above.[114] With some difficulty, GMAC achieved this transition on December 24, 2008.[115] On December 29, 2008, the Treasury Department announced that it was making a $5 billion investment in GMAC, through a purchase of "senior preferred equity." These funds also came from the TARP program. In addition, the agency also loaned $1 billion to GM itself, with the funds to be used to increase its investment in GMAC. These funds increased GMAC's liquidity, allowing it to continue to support dealer floorplans and to liberalize significantly its credit requirements for consumers.[116] On January 16, 2009, the Treasury announced that it had agreed to make a $1.5 billion loan to Chrysler Financial.[117] Meanwhile, earlier in December 2008, the Federal Reserve Board announced that auto dealers could participate in a new $200 billion "term asset-backed securities loan facility" to finance inventory.[118]

Aside from consumer and dealer credit, another issue has been the unavailability of capital for major Detroit 3 investment projects. Delphi is GM's former parts-making subsidiary, now an independent company, but still linked to GM by a supplier relationship and labor contracts through the UAW and other unions. It has been operating in bankruptcy since 2005, and was unable to exit as planned in 2008 because a private investor group backed out of a deal to buy its securities for $2.5 billion.[119] GM's plan to acquire Chrysler and merge the two companies, which was widely reported in October 2008, was similarly withdrawn when the companies could not find sufficient funds, including proposed federal financial support, for the deal.[120]

Bush Administration's Financial Plan to Assist Automakers[121]

On December 19, 2009, President George W. Bush announced his plan to provide credit assistance to U.S. automobile manufacturers. He stated that "In the midst of a financial crisis and a recession, allowing the U.S. auto industry to collapse is not a responsible course of action."[122] His plan would provide General Motors and Chrysler with loans for a three month window allowing them to develop plans to restructure into viable companies.[123] "This restructuring will require meaningful concessions from all involved in the auto industry – management, labor unions, creditors, bondholders, dealers, and suppliers."[124]

GM received up to $13.40 billion in subsidized loans: $4.0 billion on December 29, 2008, $5.4 billion on January 16, 2009, and $4.0 billion on February 17, 2009 (contingent of congressional action).[125] Chrysler received $4 billion on December 29, 2008.[126] The loans were issued by Treasury through authority provided for the TARP under EESA.

By February 17, 2009, top executives at General Motors and Chrysler would be required to submit restructuring plans to achieve and sustain their long-term viability, international competitiveness and energy efficiency of the companies and their subsidiaries.[127] On or before March 31, 2009, each company must submit a report detailing the progress it has made in implementing its restructuring plan.[128]

Stakeholders' Concessions

Each major stakeholder would be required to make concessions in order for General Motors and Chrysler to receive financial assistance.[129]

The Union

The Bush plan is similar to the plan in H.R. 7321, the *Auto Industry Financing and Restructuring Act*, which was passed by the House.[130] The primary difference is the requirement that U.S. employees of General Motors and Chrysler accept reductions in their compensation to an equivalent level of employees in foreign transplants in the United States. The president of the UAW opposes these additional union concessions.

Union Concessions

- "Compensation Reductions": The corporations' restructuring plans will include a reduction in compensation of their U.S. employees to an equivalent level paid by foreign transplants in the United States by no later than December 31, 2009.
- "Severance Rationalization": Payment to idled U.S. employees of the corporations or their subsidies, other than customary severance pay, would be eliminated.
- "Work Rule Modifications": Work rules would be changed in a manner that is competitive with foreign transplants in the United States.
- "VEBA Modifications": Not less than one-half of companies contributions to a new union-administered healthcare fund will be paid in shares of the respective corporation. VEBA is an abbreviation for "voluntary employees beneficiary association."

Investors

- "Bond Exchange": Outstanding unsecured public indebtedness (other than pension and employee benefits obligations) must be reduced by not less than two-thirds through a debt-for-equity exchange.
- No dividends permitted while government loans remain unpaid.

Management

- Benefits plans must be modified or terminated (including golden parachute agreements).
- Limits are imposed on the annual executive compensation of the CEO and the four highest compensated officers (other than the CEO), which are deductible as a business expense. These limits are one-half of the amount (or $500,000 per year) stated in Section 162(m)(5) of the IRS Code.
- The 25 most highly compensated employees (the "Senior Employees") cannot receive or accrue any bonus or executive compensation except as approved by the President's Designee.
- Management of Chrysler and General Motors must report "material transactions" (any asset sale, investment, contract, or commitment) of more than $100 million to the President's Designee for review and approval.
- Private passenger aircraft will be divested.
- Chrysler and General Motors shall maintain and implement a comprehensive written policy on corporate expenses ("Expense Policy"). Any material deviations for the expense policy shall promptly be reported to the President's Designee.

Dealers/Suppliers

- New agreements to lower costs.
- New agreements to reduce capacity.

Treasury Stock Warrants

In return for providing loans to General Motors and Chrysler, the U.S. Treasury receives warrants to purchase common shares of each company. The exercise price per share is the 15 day trailing average price determined as of December 2, 2008. The total number of warrants equals to 20% of the maximum loan amount divided by the exercise price per share. A "warrant limit" is set, however, at 20% of the issued and outstanding common shares. The warrants have a perpetual term and are immediately exercisable, in whole or in part, at 100% of their issue price plus all accrued and unpaid dividends.[131]

FINANCIAL SOLUTIONS: BRIDGE LOANS AND RESTRUCTURING[132]

In late 2008, when the Detroit 3 executives requested federal financial assistance, they dismissed the possibility of filing for reorganization under the Bankruptcy Code. They asserted that such a filing would inevitably lead to liquidation rather than reorganization because consumers would not purchase a car from a company in bankruptcy. A survey by CNW Marketing Research reportedly indicated that 80% of consumers said that concerns about warranty coverage and replacement parts would make them unlikely to buy a car from a company operating in bankruptcy reorganization. However, two later surveys—including another by CNW—indicated that this reluctance could be reduced or neutralized if the government were backing the reorganization.[133] Currently, none of the Detroit 3 has filed a bankruptcy petition, but both GM and Chrysler each recently received some immediate financial assistance from the federal government. GM received additional federal assistance in January 2009 and is scheduled to receive another loan in February 2009. Repayment of the loans is due December 29, 2011, but would be accelerated if certain conditions are not met within the first four months of 2009.[134] If one of the loans is accelerated, the affected automaker might have no option other than filing for bankruptcy. This section will look at the terms for the loans as they involve protection of the loan amounts, the restructuring plan, and the restructuring targets. It will also outline basic options available under the Bankruptcy Code if the companies are not able to successfully restructure outside of Chapter 11 reorganization.

Federal Bridge Loans

On January 21, 2009, the House passed H.R. 384. Title III of that bill proposed adding a new title (as Title IV) to EESA. Some of the bill's provisions could allow additional financial assistance to the automakers currently or potentially receiving federal loans. The terms and protections provided in this assistance differ in some ways from those discussed below. As this bill will have no legal effect , unless it is taken up by the Senate, analysis of the changes are beyond the scope of this chapter.

Collateral and Other Protections

On December 29, 2008, GM and Chrysler each received a loan of $4 billion. Under the terms of the loans, the federal government receives collateral for the loans in the form of first-priority liens on all unencumbered assets and junior liens on all encumbered assets. This provision appears to provide greater protection for the taxpayer dollars that were loaned to the automakers than would otherwise exist in the event of a bankruptcy filing. Additional protections include: (1) Mandatory prepayments of the net cash proceeds from certain transactions, such as sales of any collateral outside the normal course of business;[135] (2) Warrants to purchase common shares of the automaker;[136] (3) Additional guarantors and pledges of collateral from subsidiaries, etc.;[137] and (4) Conversion of the loan to debtor-in-possession (DIP) financing if the automaker is in bankruptcy. In addition to restrictions on executive compensation discussed later in this chapter, the terms of the loans also restrict expenses and "material transactions."[138]

Although the terms of the loans are intended to provide protection for taxpayer funds, the protection provided by these terms may not be sufficient to ensure repayment of the loan amount. A lien provides protection only to the extent that the property that is subject to that lien has sufficient value to cover the lien. Likewise, the mandatory prepayment requirement will result in early repayments only when the collateral sold outside the ordinary course of business has sufficient value to equal or exceed all liens against it. Warrants to purchase stock provide protection only to the extent that there is either a market for the warrant or value to the stock that exceeds the warrant price; however, if the automakers are able to successfully restructure, the warrants may allow the government, and thus the taxpayers, to benefit financially from the loan agreements.

The terms of the loan impose first-priority liens only against otherwise unencumbered assets. For other assets, the terms grant the United States only a junior lien. A junior lien provides protection only to the extent that the asset has sufficient value to cover the junior lien *and* all liens that are senior to it. The extent to which either GM or Chrysler has any significant assets that are not encumbered has been questioned.[139] There is also some question about the value of any of the collateral, encumbered or unencumbered, to anyone other than the automaker who currently owns it or to a party who wanted to buy the entire operation as a going concern. Thus, the liens may not fully secure the money that has been loaned to GM and Chrysler.

The warrants to buy common stock may be exercised at a relatively low cost. The number of warrants is determined by dividing 20% of the maximum loan value by the exercise price of the warrants. However, the warrants exercised cannot be higher than 20% of the issued and outstanding common equity interests before the warrants are exercised. The ability to either buy common stock or sell warrants (as with Chrysler warrants in 1983) has value only if the automakers remain in business and their stock value increases above the warrant price.

Each of the loans requires guarantors. For the Chrysler loan, CarCo Intermediate HoldCo I and all direct and indirect domestic subsidiaries are guarantors of the loan on a joint and several basis, meaning that any one of them may be responsible for the entire loan. Additionally, half of the Chrysler loan amount must be guaranteed by FinCo Intermediate HoldCo LC and DaimlerChysler Financial Services Americas LLC. GM's domestic subsidiaries are guarantors of the GM loans, again on a joint and several basis. Additionally, the terms specify that any successor entity of GM would also be a guarantor of the loan, thus preventing sale of GM free and clear of the debt obligation.

The loans also have conditions precedent that are specific to each automaker and involve pledges of inventory, real estate, or membership interests to the U.S. government to provide another layer of protection for the loans.[140]

One protective provision of the loans anticipates the possibility of an automaker's bankruptcy. If a bankruptcy petition is filed, the terms of the loan allow the government to convert the existing loans to "DIP" financing. "DIP" financing provides the debtor-in-possession (or the trustee in a Chapter 7 case) with sufficient funds to meet continuing expenses while the business is either reorganized or liquidated. Generally, DIP financing is a post-petition obligation that enjoys a high priority for being repaid from the bankruptcy estate or under the reorganization plan. In contrast, the government loans are being made while the companies are still operating outside of bankruptcy protection, and the loans are pre-petition debts.[141] One of the purposes of bankruptcy protection is to provide debtors relief from pre-petition debts. This provision in the terms of the loans seems to go against that purpose as well as the purpose for DIP financing. It may also make it more difficult to arrange true DIP financing to use during reorganization.

Accelerated Repayment Provisions

Although the expiration date for the loans is December, 29, 2011, the loans made to GM and Chrysler could become due early in the second quarter of 2009 or possibly even earlier. Under the terms of the loans, the entire outstanding amount of the loans could become due upon an "event of default," as defined in the term sheets.[142] Additionally, if the restructuring plan report submitted by the automakers fails to meet the required standards and is not approved by the President's Designee, the loan would automatically be accelerated and amounts not "invested in or loaned to the Borrower's principal financial subsidiaries"[143] would become due within 30 days.

Restructuring Outside of Bankruptcy

As a condition of the financial assistance, GM and Chrysler must each submit a restructuring plan designed to achieve certain goals. Additionally, they must "use their best efforts to achieve ... [restructuring] targets."[144] The goals involve financial viability and vehicle production. The targets involve a "Bond Exchange,"[145] "Labor Modifications,"[146] and "VEBA Modifications."[147] For these restructuring targets, each company must submit to the President's Designee agreements that have been signed by company representatives and applicable representatives of the affected groups.[148]

One of the advantages of reorganizing under the Bankruptcy Code is the ability to modify creditors' claims without the agreement of all of the affected creditors. Outside of bankruptcy, the automakers will not have this advantage as they attempt to design a restructuring plan and achieve sufficient cooperation from creditors to allow the plan to succeed. An additional advantage to reorganization in Chapter 11 is the ability to reject most executory contracts and leases. Without §365 of the Bankruptcy Code, automakers may be unable to terminate franchise arrangements with their dealerships without a significantly greater cost than they would incur if reorganizing in Chapter 11.

Among the restructuring targets are several modifications to existing collective bargaining agreements (CBAs) that govern wages, work rules, and benefits, including retiree health benefits. The targets may or may not involve terms that union members will be willing to accept. Chapter 11 of the Bankruptcy Code includes two code sections that allow the Bankruptcy Court to approve a debtor's request to reject or modify CBAs when the debtor and union have been unable to reach a negotiated agreement and the Court finds that the debtor's proposals have been rejected without good cause.[149] This provision does not exist outside of bankruptcy. Presumably, the union workers are concerned with the continued survival of the automakers and will be willing to negotiate with the automakers if they believe that the CBA must be changed to ensure the company's survival. However, in the non-bankruptcy environment there is no judge to evaluate the balance of equities to determine whether the union members are being asked to make disproportionate sacrifices to aid the company's survival. Further, there appears to be no provision for transparency that would allow all creditors to evaluate the restructuring plan as a whole and their place in it.

Bankruptcy Procedures in Case Restructuring Fails

Most domestic corporations have two choices when filing bankruptcy: Chapter 7[150] or Chapter 11.[151] Chapter 7 involves liquidation, effectively ending the corporation's existence. Chapter 11 involves reorganization, generally allowing the company to modify contract obligations and debts so it can be financially viable and continue its operations long-term. However, some cases filed under Chapter 11 result in liquidation.

Under the Bankruptcy Clause of the U.S. Constitution,[152] Congress may create sections of the Bankruptcy Code (shortened in this part of the report to simply "the Code") to address issues of a particular type of industry or entity so long as the laws are uniform rather than for a specific, named debtor. In the past, during times of financial turmoil, Congress has modified the existing bankruptcy law. Examples include Chapter 9: municipalities (11 U.S.C. § 901 *et seq*); Subchapter IV of Chapter 11: railroads (11 U.S.C. §§ 1161-1174), and Chapter 12: farmers and fishermen (11 U.S.C. § 1201 *et seq*). Congress has the power to modify the Code to customize reorganization for the automotive industry.[153] Therefore, the following discussion of Chapters 7 and 11 generally describes the characteristics of these two chapters of the existing Code, but should not be interpreted as constraining Congress's ability to enact laws that would modify the provisions of these chapters as they apply to the automotive industry or to create an additional chapter of the Code that is applicable to the automotive industry.

Chapter 7

In Chapter 7 of the Bankruptcy Code,[154] a trustee is chosen to represent and administer the bankruptcy estate.[155] The trustee takes over the company's assets, sells them, and distributes the proceeds to the creditors who have presented valid claims. There is a hierarchy to the distribution of the proceeds.[156] Secured creditors generally will receive payment up to the amount of their secured interest. Unsecured creditors include those with priority claims and those with non- priority claims. Priority claims are paid in the order of priority so long as there are funds available.[157] When the funds are depleted, no more claims are paid even if they are priority claims. After all priority claims are paid, remaining funds are distributed on a pro rata basis to the remaining unsecured creditors.

Chapter 11

Chapter 11 of the Bankruptcy Code provides companies with a way to continue in business while at the same time receiving protection from creditors. It also provides them with opportunities to modify debts and contracts[158] in a way that enhances the company's possibilities of recovering from financial troubles. It is generally believed that a business is worth more as a going concern than as an assortment of assets that are sold separately. Survival of the company benefits creditors, employees, and the community in which the business is located. In most cases, the company retains its management. Generally, a trustee is appointed only when management is removed "for cause."[159] However, even when a trustee is not appointed, the company may decide to turn operation of the business over to a "turnaround specialist" who has experience in guiding companies through Chapter 11 and into solvency.[160]

The reorganization plan is the key to a Chapter 11 bankruptcy. The plan is a proposal, generally by the debtor-in-possession (DIP), as to how the valid claims of each class of creditors are going to be resolved.[161] To be confirmed, the plan must be agreed to by at least one impaired class of claims. Additionally, each holder of a claim in an impaired class must accept the plan unless the amount received under the plan is no less than the amount that would have been received under Chapter 7.[162] In a standard Chapter 11 bankruptcy, the plan proposal and negotiation with the creditors takes place after the company has filed for bankruptcy. In a prepackaged Chapter 11, the company does not file for bankruptcy until negotiations with creditors have resulted in a confirmable plan that is presented when filing the bankruptcy case. This may have the effect of reducing uncertainty about the company's future. Negotiating a prepackaged Chapter 11 does take some time, so it is unclear to what extent a "prepack" would benefit the automakers. In their requests for government financial assistance the automakers said they were rapidly running out of operating capital. The assistance they received was less than requested. It is possible that conditioning receipt of additional government assistance on a prepackaged agreement among the creditors might encourage creditors to quickly reach negotiated modifications with debtor companies. An additional benefit to a prepack is the elimination, in some cases, of the need for arranging "DIP financing."

DIP financing involves agreements to provide funds to a debtor-in-possession (DIP) to allow it to meet expenses incurred during reorganization. If suppliers have refused to continue shipments without prepayment, DIP financing can provide the means of making the prepayment. In some cases, simply having the loan agreements is sufficient to restore supplier's confidence and willingness to ship without prepayment. If one or more of the Detroit 3 filed under Chapter 11, it is possible that government loans could provide the DIP financing. The DIP financing lender can enjoy the highest protection available in a Chapter 11 bankruptcy. When used for current operating expenses, the financing is an administrative expense under 11 U.S.C. § 503(b)(1) and would be a priority claim under 11 U.S.C. § 507(a)(2).[163]

Section 507 priorities are important in a Chapter 11 bankruptcy and must be addressed in the reorganization plan, but Chapter 11 provides greater flexibility in the payment of these claims than does Chapter 7. The holders may agree either to modify their claims or to accept alternative payment arrangements rather than receiving full payment before other unsecured claims are paid. If there is no such agreement, the Code prescribes treatment for each priority claim that must be met for the plan to be confirmed. However, some of the statutory treatments allow deferred payments or installment payments of amounts due.[164] This added flexibility for resolving priority claims may increase the amounts available to pay other unsecured claims. It may also make it possible for the company to meet its operations expenses both short-term and long-term.

PENSION AND HEALTH CARE ISSUES

Pensions and Pension Insurance[165]

The Pension Benefit Guaranty Corporation

Pension benefits provided under qualified defined benefit plans are insured up to certain limits by the Pension Benefit Guaranty Corporation (PBGC), a government corporation established by the Employee Retirement Income Security Act of 1974 (ERISA, P.L. 93-406). In 2008, the PBGC insured the pensions of approximately 44 million workers and retirees in more than 29,000 private-sector defined benefit pension plans. The PBGC does not insure pension benefits provided by state and local governments or benefits under defined contribution plans, such as 401(k) plans. The maximum pension benefit guaranteed by the PBGC is set by law and adjusted annually. For plans that terminate in 2009, workers who retire at age 65 can receive up to $4,500 a month ($54,000 a year). The guarantee is lower for those who retire early or when there is a benefit for a survivor. The guarantee is higher for those who retire after age 65.

The PBGC receives no funds from general tax revenues. The PBGC collects insurance premiums from employers that sponsor insured pension plans, earns money from investments, and receives funds from pension plans it takes over. When the PBGC takes over a pension plan, it assumes responsibility for future benefit payments to the plan's participants, up to the limits set in law. In general, the PBGC takes over only plans that are underfunded and that the employer is not expected to be able to fully fund because it has filed for bankruptcy or is experiencing serious financial difficulties that put its ability to fund its pension obligations at risk. Consequently, in most cases in which the PBGC takes over a pension plan, it assumes pension liabilities that are greater than the assets held by the pension plan it has taken over. In recent years, the PBGC has taken over several large pension plans that were significantly underfunded. As a result, the PBGC's liabilities exceed its assets.

According to the most recent annual report of the PBGC, its insurance program for single-employer plans had assets of $61.6 billion against liabilities of $72.3 billion on September 30, 2008. If the current economic downturn were to result in the termination of several large defined benefit plans with significant underfunding, the PBGC's deficit could grow rapidly. Although ERISA does not provide for supplementing the PBGC's income with general tax revenues, it is likely that if the PBGC were unable to meet its financial obligations to the participants whose pensions it has taken over, there would be considerable political pressure on Congress to provide the PBGC with the financial resources necessary for it to continue to pay benefits to retirees and their surviving dependents.

In order to qualify for the tax exemptions and deferrals that Congress has authorized for employer-sponsored retirement plans, defined benefit plans must meet certain requirements established under ERISA and the Internal Revenue Code (IRC). One requirement is that the plans must be "fully funded," i.e., the plan's assets must equal or exceed its liabilities. In most cases, the sponsor of a plan that is underfunded is required to make additional contributions to the plan that would amortize the underfunding in seven years or less.[166] In addition to meeting the funding requirements of ERISA and the IRC, companies that sponsor defined benefit plans must report certain information about the plans annually to the Internal Revenue Service. This information is available to the public, but the financial data is often out of date by the time it is released to the public. Publicly traded companies must report information about their pension plans to the Securities and Exchange Commission (SEC). These reports are generally available to the public immediately.

Funded Status of Auto Manufacturers Pension Plans

GM, Ford, and Chrysler each maintain one or more defined benefit pension plans for workers employed in the United States.[167] The companies have separate plans for union members and nonunion workers. According to the information filed by GM and Ford with the SEC in February 2008, both companies' plans for U.S. employees had assets in excess of plan liabilities at yearend 2007. GM reported a pension surplus of $18.8 billion and Ford reported a pension surplus of $1.3 billion (see Table 3). GM's pension surplus was equal to about 22% of its pension plan liabilities, while Ford's surplus was much smaller, amounting to 2.8% of its pension liabilities. As a privately-held company, Chrysler is not subject to the same SEC reporting requirements as are GM and Ford. Current information about Chrysler's pension plans was not available at the time this CRS report was written.[168]

Several factors have affected the funding status of the automakers' pension plans going forward. Among the most important of these factors are:

- Stock prices fell sharply in 2008, depressing the value of pension fund assets. This would tend to reduce pension surpluses and increase pension deficits.
- Long-term interest rates rose during 2008, reducing pension plan liabilities. This would tend to increase pension surpluses and reduce pension deficits.
- Plan participants have accrued an additional year of pension benefits.
- Plan sponsors have, in some cases, made contributions to their pension plans.
- Certain one-time events may have occurred including plan amendments to raise or lower future benefit accruals, the sale or acquisition of businesses with pension liabilities, and the expiration or initiation of collective bargaining agreements.

Table 3. Funded Status of General Motors and Ford Pension Plans for U.S. Employees, Year-end 2007 (amounts in millions of dollars)

	General Motors	Ford Motor Co.
Benefit obligation (plan liabilities)	$85,277	$44,493
Fair value of plan assets	104,070	45,759
Surplus or (Deficit)	18,793	1,266
Surplus (Deficit) as a percentage of liabilities	*22.0%*	*2.8%*
Estimated allocation of plan assets		
Equity securities	26%	51%
Debt securities	52%	46%
Real estate, private equity, and other assets	22%	3%

Source: Company filings of Form 10-K with the Securities and Exchange Commission, Feb. 2008.

GM Pension Fund

In its most recent quarterly filing with the SEC, GM noted several factors that reduced its pension surplus, including

- investment losses of $6.3 billion in its pension plan asset portfolio;
- recording a $2.7 billion liability related to a settlement agreement with the United Auto Workers (UAW) related to retiree medical care;
- recording a $2.7 billion liability due to the increase in the monthly pension benefit paid to salaried employees as compensation for the elimination of post-65 healthcare benefits;
- the transfer of $2.1 billion of Delphi Corporation pension liabilities to GM; and
- recording a $2.0 billion cost due to special workforce attrition programs for union members.

GM reported in November 2008 that its plan for hourly workers was underfunded by $500 million as of September 30 and that its plan for salaried employees was overfunded as of June 30. The plans were overfunded on a combined basis. GM stated that it did not expect to have to make any contributions to its defined benefit plans for 2008.[169]

Ford Pension Fund

The two most significant factors affecting the funding status of Ford's pension plans since year-end 2007 are the decline in the stock market and in the increase in long-term interest rates. Based on the estimated percentage of Ford's pension plan assets invested in stocks, if its pension fund assets performed as the major market indices did in 2008, Ford's pension assets invested in equities would have lost $8.2 billion to $9.4 billion in value through the first eleven months of 2008. This would represent 18% to 20% of the value of assets held by Ford's U.S. pension plans at year-end 2007. The effect of the decline in asset prices was offset to some extent by the rise in long-term interest rates in 2008.[170] Rising interest rates reduce the present value of pension liabilities. In its most recent 10-K filing with the SEC, Ford estimated that an increase of 0.25% in interest rates would reduce its pension liabilities by 2.3%. Ford estimated that with an increase in the discount rate of 1.0% in 2008, its pension liabilities would have fallen by $4.1 billion. This would represent a 9.2% decline in Ford's year-end 2007 pension liabilities.

In its SEC filing for the third quarter of 2008, Ford stated that during the first nine months of 2008, it "contributed $1.9 billion to our worldwide pension plans," and that the company expected to contribute an additional $300 million in 2008. Although the statement did not specify how much of this contribution was made to its U.S. plans, less than 10% of Ford's pension contributions in 2007 and less than 15% of its contributions in 2006 were made to its U.S. defined benefit plans.

PBGC Actions in Late 2008 and Early 2009

In a November 2008 interview with *The Wall Street Journal*, PBGC Director Charles Millard characterized the current funding of the automakers' plans as "OK," but he said that the agency is concerned that the cost of funding early retirement incentives could cause financial difficulties for their pension plans in future years.[171] During the week of November

24, the PBGC sent letters to General Motors, Ford, and Chrysler stating the agency's concern that early retirement incentives offered to employees could adversely affect the funding of their pension plans, and asking the companies to inform the PBGC of the costs of their buyout and early retirement programs.[172] The PBGC is concerned that buyout and early retirement programs were not fully accounted for when the automakers estimated their pension liabilities, and that these programs could "undermine the state of the plans."[173]

PBGC Director Millard added, in a separate November 2008 statement, that if an automaker were to initiate a termination of a pension plan while in bankruptcy, the agency would oppose the termination.[174] According to Mr. Millard's public statements, the PBGC would argue in federal court that the companies' should maintain their defined benefit pension plans.[175]

In January 2009, the PBGC clarified and somewhat altered the tenor of its earlier comments on the pension plans of GM, Ford, and Chrysler. While they are "well funded" according to the accounting procedures of the Securities and Exchange Commission, their pensions were collectively underfunded by as much as $41 billion according to the accounting rules followed by the PBGC when a plan terminates.[176] The PBGC estimates that if all three automakers were to declare bankruptcy and terminate their pension plans, the agency would pay out $13 billion of the $41 billion shortfall to plan participants and beneficiaries. The remainder represents benefits that PBGC could not pay because of legal limits on the benefits that are insured by the PBGC.

The PBGC has estimated that GM's plans are underfunded by $20 billion (20%) on a termination basis. Chrysler's plans would be $9.3 billion (34%) underfunded if they were terminated. Ford's plans are estimated to have an $11.7 billion (27%) deficit under the under termination accounting rules. Outgoing PBGC Director Millard noted that if the companies were financially healthy and were able to meet all of their future funding obligations, the current underfunded status of their pension plans would not necessarily pose a risk to the PBGC. However, the possibility that one or more of the companies will file for bankruptcy protection and terminate their pension plans poses a financial risk for the PBGC. Millard stated that as of January 2009, the risk to the PBGC "is significantly greater than it was six or seven months ago."[177]

Health Care Issues[178]

If an automaker files for bankruptcy, health care coverage for both active and retired workers and their families could be at risk. The risk differs depending on whether the bankruptcy is a liquidation under Chapter 7 or a bankruptcy reorganization under Chapter 11, whether individuals are still working or retired, and whether they are covered by a collective bargaining agreement. Individuals' options for obtaining alternative coverage, either private or public, also differ; factors such as age or Medicare eligibility, income, and family circumstances could be important. The 111th Congress might consider broad health care reforms that could provide further options at some point in the future.

The future funding status for retiree health insurance for workers covered by the UAW's collective bargaining agreement may be uncertain. During the 2007 contract negotiations, each of the three firms reached separate agreements with the UAW to contribute a percentage of their projected retiree health liabilities to a Voluntary Employees' Beneficiary Association. Following their initial VEBA contributions in 2007, the firms agreed to make additional contributions to the VEBA trust beginning in 2008. In total, the Detroit 3 contributions are projected to fund 64% of their future retiree health obligations.[179] Before January 1, 2010, the automakers remain responsible for funding retiree health. By 2010, the VEBA will be managed by an independent board of trustees appointed by the UAW and the court.[180] The automakers will have no funding responsibilities after this point.

However, the size of the actual 2008 to 2010 contribution to the VEBA could depend on the financial conditions of the Detroit 3. For example, under Chapter 11, the Detroit 3 and the UAW may renegotiate health insurance benefits during the reorganization process. In addition, increasing the share of funding of the VEBA from stock could affect the value of its funds.

Bankruptcy filing could also threaten health plans for union workers and nonunion workers and retirees.[181] Under a liquidation, there would presumably be no health plans remaining for any former workers or retirees. In the event of a bankruptcy reorganization under Chapter 11, if a firm continues to provide health benefits to its workers, certain individuals would be entitled to purchase health benefits through COBRA (Title X of the Consolidated Omnibus Budget Reconciliation Act of 1985, P.L. 99-272).

Under COBRA, employers who offer health insurance must offer the option of continued health insurance coverage at group rates to qualified employees and their families who are faced with loss of coverage due termination of employment, a reduction in hours, or certain other events. Employers are permitted to charge the covered beneficiary 100% of the premium (both the portion paid by the employee and the portion paid by the employer, if any), plus an additional 2% administrative fee. The continued coverage for the employee and the employee's spouse and dependent children must continue for 18 months.

A retiree may have access to COBRA coverage in the event that a former employer terminates the retiree health plan as a result of a bankruptcy reorganization under Chapter 11.[182] This option would only be available to those retirees who are receiving retiree health insurance. In this case, the COBRA coverage can continue until the death of the retiree. The retiree's spouse and dependent children may purchase COBRA coverage from the former employer for 36 months after the retiree's death. However, beginning on January 1, 2009, GM was to follow the lead of Ford and Chrysler, and stop providing non-union retirees with health benefits once they become eligible for Medicare at age 65. Instead, retirees will receive additional funds which they may choose to use to purchase Medicare supplemental policies. These individuals would not qualify for COBRA, as they will no longer be receiving health insurance.

The 111th Congress may consider broad health care reforms that could help some autoworkers, either active or retired, and their family members to obtain and pay for health care coverage. While it is unclear when specific broad health care reform proposals will be developed, let alone whether they will be adopted, the possibility of reforms might be taken into account as policy makers consider the financial future of the auto industry and its workers. Additionally, the stimulus bills currently being considered by Congress offer assistance for health care coverage to certain individuals who lose their jobs.

STIPULATIONS AND CONDITIONS ON TARP LOANS TO THE AUTO INDUSTRY

Most supporters and advocates of assistance to the Detroit 3 through a program of federal direct loans have acknowledged that such assistance may be accompanied by conditions placed by Congress on the Detroit 3 and their management. In the 110th Congress, S. 3688 and H.R. 7321 both addressed this issue, and in similar ways. In the 111th Congress, the House also addressed these conditions in H.R. 384: in §409 specifically for the auto industry, and in § 102 for all recipients of TARP funds more generally. But none of these measures has been enacted into law.

The present report has already included an outline of the Bush Administration's conditions and stipulations placed on the loans planned for GM and Chrysler, especially relating to loan repayment and financial oversight. The following section concludes the report by reviewing in more detail:

- Restrictions on executive privileges and compensation;
- Requirements in company restructuring plans;
- Restructuring targets required of the companies, including competitive pay and benefits for the hourly workforce.

Executive Privileges and Compensation[183]

Until the facility is repaid in full and the U.S. Treasury no longer owns any of their equity securities, the following restrictions on executive privileges and compensation will apply to GM and Chrysler. Such standards generally apply to the treatment of the chief executive officer, chief financial officer, and the next three most highly compensated executive officers. A number of the requirement derive from Section 111(b) of the EESA and subsequent Treasury Department interpretive guidelines, while others do not.

Required Compliance with the Overall Executive Compensation Requirements in Section 111(b) of the EESA. Both companies are subject to the overarching executive compensation and corporate governance requirements established in Section 111(b) of the EESA and the Treasury Department guidelines for companies involved in the TARP's Systematically Significant Failing Institutions' (SSFI) program.[184] Briefly, the section in the EESA requires participating institutions to ensure that their five most senior executive officers, including the CEO: 1) do not take unnecessary and excessive risks that threaten the value of the company; 2) are subject to provisions that allow for the company's recovery or the clawback of any bonus or incentive compensation paid to them that is based on financial statements of such things such as earnings that are later proven to be materially inaccurate; and 3) are not allowed to receive golden parachute payment from the company during the time in which the Secretary of the Treasury holds an equity stake in the company.

Strictures on the Provision of Golden Parachutes. Both companies are required to modify or change the benefit plans, arrangements and agreements, including golden parachute agreements for all senior officials to the extent necessary to be in compliance with the aforementioned Section 111(b) of the EESA and applicable guidelines.

Golden parachutes are defined in the relevant Treasury Department interpretation as payments of more than three times an executive's average base compensation from a firm over the five most recent years in the event of the official's involuntary termination, or bankruptcy or receivership of a financial institution. It is the definition of a golden parachute that the department has used for tax purposes for many years, and it is the applicable definition for the financial firms that are participating in the EESA's TARP Capital Purchase Program.[185] Explaining the rationale for the proscription in the EESA, a Treasury Department official observed that " ... our key focus is that we do not want to reward poor performance ... "[186]

However, there are some concerns that the provision sets too high a level of reward to have much impact. Some executive compensation consultants stress that it is uncommon for executive severance payments to reach the size that would trigger the provision's parameters. They note that such relatively large payments do not normally occur unless an executive is released without cause immediately after a "change in control" situation, usually involving a corporate takeover.[187] Echoing that view, in a letter of October 29, 2008, to Treasury Secretary Henry Paulson, Senate Majority Leader Harry Reid and House Speaker Nancy Pelosi said "... [G]iven the level of public outrage over these compensation schemes.... We would urge you, in particular, to consider the possibility of further restrictions on the use of 'golden parachutes' at such [participating] institutions ... "[188]

Under the compensation strictures outlined in Treasury guidelines for participants in the EESA's SSFI program, GM and Chrysler are subject to more restrictive criteria on golden parachute payments: any compensation that is paid by reason of an involuntary termination from employment or in connection with bankruptcy, insolvency, or receivership is subject to golden parachute treatment even if the total amount of such compensation is less than three times an executive's average taxable compensation during the five most recent years.

Required Compliance with Executive Compensation Corporate Limits on Tax Deduction. Both companies must comply with the limits on annual executive compensation tax deductions imposed by Section 1 62(m)(5) of the Internal Revenue Code of 1986.

In 1993, in response to outrage at executive pay levels, P.L. 103-66 added section 162(m), titled "Certain Excessive Employee Remuneration," to the Internal Revenue Code. It imposes a $1 million cap on the corporate tax deductibility of compensation that applies to the CEO and the four next highest-paid officers of publicly-traded firms. (Pay itself is not capped, only the deduction of pay from corporate income.) Key compensation categories excluded by the law from the $1 million deduction limit include: 1) commission-based remuneration; 2) performance-based compensation that meet outside director and majority shareholder approval; 3) payments to tax- qualified retirement plans (including salary reduction contributions); and 4) amounts excludable from the employee's gross income.

The EESA amended Section 162(m) to provide for Section 162(m)(5), which generally requires firms participating in the EESA's Capital Purchase Program (CPP) to agree to senior executive pay deduction limitations of $500,000, a halving of Section 162(m)' s $1 million deduction limit. Unlike Section 162(m), it also applies to firms that are not publicly traded. Under the terms of the loan agreements, GM and Chrysler would also be subject to such terms.

Limitations on the Executive Pay Arrangements that Would Encourage the Taking of Unnecessary and Excessive Risks. This provision elaborates on the overarching proscription on both companies making compensation arrangements for their senior executives that would encourage them "to take unnecessary and excessive risks" found in Section 111 (b) of the EESA. To comply, the principal executive officer of GM and Chrysler are required to certify in writing, under penalty of perjury, to the Treasury Department's Chief Compliance Officer that their compensation committees have consulted with their senior risk officials and determined that such senior executive pay schemes would not encourage the taking of unnecessary and excessive risks that would pose a threat to their companies' values.

An argument could be made that the provision's operative phrase, "... take unnecessary and excessive risks.... " is quite vague, potentially resulting in considerable interpretative leeway. There is a widely held view that one of the contributing causes of the financial crisis that led to the enactment of the EESA was the managerial compensation structure at Wall Street firms: many think that their pay packages overly emphasized short-term incentives such as bonuses, helping to encourage often reckless and harmful behavior driven by the pursuit of short term corporate profits.[189] Concerns over the relationship between managerial incentive compensation and exceptional risk taking appears, however, to be largely confined to specific parts of the financial sector such as the investment banking sector and hedge funds. In addition, a number of compensation consultants have observed that while the use of uncapped annual incentive pay has been a significant feature of many financial service firms, the practice is said to be generally atypical outside of the sector.[190]

To the extent that legitimate concerns over excessive risk taking do exist, there is a vigorous debate over the extent to which members of corporate boards, are able to act independently of senior management's influence.[191] Similar concerns could be raised about the ability of senior risk managers to maintain their detachment from top management as they also help to arbitrate on top executive pay arrangements under the terms of the agreements. Such concerns might be especially germane to Chrysler, which is owned by a private equity firm. Some research on the quality of corporate board governance at private equity firms found that such boards tend to be heavily influenced by and at times controlled by the principal investors of the equity firm.[192]

Within the motor vehicle industry, the provision also raises a fundamental policy question: to what extent would the discouragement of risk-taking behavior also result in the discouragement of potentially beneficial, innovative, and entrepreneurial behavior? For example, in late 2007, General Motors announced that it hoped to start selling cars powered by hydrogen fuel-cells by 2011.[193] If an automaker began embarking on the development of such technology, under the "excessive risk" provision should such undertakings be seen as excessive risk taking or potentially beneficial and innovative entrepreneurship?

A Ban on the Provision of Incentive Compensation to the 25 Highest Paid Officials. Neither company can provide bonuses or incentive compensation packages to the 25 most highly compensated employees (including the senior executive officers) except as authorized by the President's Designee.

Studies on corporate compensation describe executive bonuses as a popular type of variable incentive pay normally given as a once-a-year payment tied to some short-term performance goals. These can range from judgments on executive performance by a corporate board, to levels of company profits or company sectoral market share. After the EESA's enactment, there was concern expressed both in and out of Congress over reports that executives at financial firms participating in the EESA were receiving what many perceived to be excessively large bonuses, an issue not specifically addressed in the law's restrictions on executive pay. A central concern was that participating companies were using EESA funding to pay for bonuses, a charge that firm executives denied. Among those in Congress expressing concerns was Representative Henry Waxman, then Chairman of the House Oversight Committee, who indicated the funds "might be used for extravagant pensions or bonuses or dividends or any other purpose, inconsistent with what the Congress intended."[194]

Some executives in recent years have received substantial bonuses in the automobile industry. In 2007, Ford reported that CEO Allan Mulally received $2 million in base salary, and $4 million in bonuses (he had also received $18.5 million in bonuses in 2006). Ford also reported that the next four highest paid officials received between $1 million and $780,000 in base salary and between $708,000 and $439,000 in bonuses. However, in response to the industry crisis at the end of 2008, Ford eliminated merit increases and bonuses for all salaried workers in 2009. Its senior executives will receive no salary increases at all. The company has suspended its 401(k) match program, and eliminated or restricted other benefits for salaried employees.[195]

General Motors reported that the 2007 base salary paid to its top five officials ranged from CEO G. Richard Wagoner's $1.56 million down to $825,000, but none of the GM officials received bonuses in 2007. According to the data presented in its restructuring plan, CEO Wagoner and president and chief operating officer (COO) F.A. Henderson each received total compensation of just less than $2 million in 2007, as stock options for the company have been "under water" (less than the target price) since 1999. Top-level salaries were reduced as much as 50% in 2007. GM's 401(k) matching contribution was eliminated in 2008 for all salaried employees, and there was a reduction or elimination of other benefits.[196] As of January 1, 2009, the salary of GM's CEO was reduced to a nominal $1 per year, as was the annual retainer for all board members. The company president's salary was reduced by 30%, and the other three top officers, including executive vice- chairman Robert Lutz, took 20% salary cuts.[197]

There are news reports that Chrysler, which as a privately owned company is not required to disclose data on executive compensation, has contractual agreements to pay what originally totaled $30 million in retention bonuses (reportedly reduced because some of the officials left) to about 50 executives, to be paid out in August 2009. The retention bonuses were crafted by Chrysler's former parent, DaimlerChrysler, as it was preparing to sell Chrysler to Cerberus Capital Management, its current owner. Three of Chrysler's top paid executives, CEO Robert Nardelli, president James Press, and vice-chairman Tom LaSorda, are reportedly not participating in the plan. However, according to Daimler filings, in 2007, Mr. LaSorda received a $15.7 million bonus for his help in Chrysler's sale to Cerberus.[198]

A Chrysler official justified the bonuses because of the need to ensure potential buyers that key company executives would remain in place after the sale, while acknowledging that they had become a source of controversy.[199] Nonetheless, the official also emphasized that it was important to keep in mind that the bonuses had been crafted by DaimlerChrysler, the company's former owner, and that they appear to have been effective in keeping its executive talent in place.[200] Subsequently, as stated in testimony before Congress , CEO Nardelli has agreed to a salary of $1 for both 2008 and 2009.[201]

An argument could be made that the provision's proscription on incentive pay could significantly narrow the types of compensation arrangements that would generally be available for the top five executives. It could thus potentially remove significant parts of executive pay package features from compensation committee consideration as they carry out the earlier provision requiring them to ensure that the pay packages do not encourage excessive and unnecessary risk taking.

A Ban on Compensation Plans that Would Encourage Earnings Manipulation. Neither company can adopt or maintain compensation plans that would encourage manipulation of their reported earnings to enhance the compensation of any of their employees.

This provision is not part of Section 111 (b) of the EESA. Earnings manipulation, often referred to as earnings management, is an umbrella term that is used to encompass everything from earnings "smoothing" to outright accounting fraud. Investors, analysts, and auditors disapprove of such actions, because it makes reported corporate earnings less reliable as a measure of firm performance. A perceived epidemic of earnings management was a significant impetus behind the enactment of the Sarbanes-Oxley Act of 2002 (SOX, P.L. 107-204), which contained a broad range of corporate governance and accounting reforms.

Publicly traded companies have a long history of using stock options as a major component of executive compensation; the strategy's central objective is aligning an executives' personal interests with those of shareholders. In 2007, Ford reported that its stock option awards to its top five senior executives ranged between $2.49 million and $7.51 million. General Motors reported that its option awards to its top five executives ranged from $534,000 to $3.77 million.

There is a growing body of research that has found that executive stock options can have negative consequences with respect to encouraging a greater tendency toward earnings manipulation. For example, one empirical study found statistical evidence that earnings manipulation is more likely where stock options play a larger role in CEO compensation.[202] Another study concluded that CEOs were more apt to manipulate firm earnings when they had more out-of-the-money stock options[203] and lower holdings of conventional company stock.[204] Jack Dolmat-Connell, president of Dolmat-Connell & Partners, an executive-compensation consulting firm, reportedly observed, "While I think that options are an extremely good driver of performance, there's no downside to them from the executive's standpoint... [Y]ou have to have someone with unethical standards who gets lots of stock options for misrepresentation and fraud to occur. If you give someone with strong ethical standards lots of options, nothing is likely to happen."[205]

Thus, it could be argued that to faithfully implement the provision's "prohibition on any compensation plan that could encourage manipulation of the reported earnings" of a recipient firm, companies would have to ensure that executive stock option packages were tailored properly to balance their positive incentive attributes with their potential for encouraging inappropriate behavior. This may assume that the process is conducted with a minimum of executive influence and bias, which, as noted earlier, could be questioned.

A Prohibition on Altering Previously Imposed Restrictions on Executive Benefit Plans. Both companies must not alter the suspensions and the restrictions on company contributions to senior executive benefit plans that were either in place by, or that had been initiated by, the closing date of the agreement.

Clawbacks of Executive Bonuses, Etc. The Treasury Department reserves the right at any time during the period of the loans to require either company to clawback any bonuses or other compensation, including golden parachutes, paid to any of their senior executives that are in violation of any of the aforementioned requirements.

The provision appears to be an expansion of the executive clawback provision in Section 111(b) of the EESA. That provision approaches the recoupment of executive bonuses and incentives in a somewhat different fashion than does an earlier provision in SOX. SOX and its clawback provision were collective responses to the widespread corporate misstatements of corporate earnings that were widely observed in the preceding years. SOX's clawback provision only applies to the CEO and the chief financial officer (CFO) of publicly traded companies. The clawback provision in the GM and Chrysler agreements would also apply to privately held firms (like Chrysler) and the top five senior officers, including the CEO and the CFO. And unlike the provision in SOX, it would not limit the recovery period and covers not only material inaccuracies related to financial reporting, but also material inaccuracies related to other performance metrics used to award bonuses and incentive compensation. Reports indicate that the Securities and Exchange Commission (SEC) has rarely prosecuted violations of Sarbanes-Oxley's clawback provision. Possibly, this is because executives often settle financial misstatement cases without admitting wrongdoing, thus avoiding the triggering the provision, and because of how the pivotal concept of "misconduct" is interpreted.[206]

The expanded clawback provisions in the GM and Chrysler agreements also appear to provide for the broad-based punitive threat of Department of Treasury-initiated clawbacks of top executive bonuses or other forms of compensation in the event that there are violations of any of the agreements' aforementioned requirements on executive pay.

Other Restructuring Plan Conditions[207]

Restructuring Plan Requirements

The term sheets for GM and Chrysler require them to submit by February 17, 2009, a plan to "achieve and sustain ... long-term viability, international competitiveness and energy efficiency . . . " This must include "specific actions to ensure:

- Federal loan repayment under applicable terms and conditions;
- Ability of the company both to meet all applicable federal fuel economy and emission requirements, and to begin manufacturing advanced technology vehicles, as specified in the EISA direct loan program;[208]
- Achievement by the companies of a positive net value;
- Rationalization of "costs, capitalization, and capacity" with respect to workforce, suppliers, and dealer networks; and,
- Competitive "product mix and cost structure."

The companies will be required to produce monthly and annual statements on meeting these restructuring requirements. In addition, the term sheets required the companies to use their best efforts to achieve the following "targets:"

Restructuring Plan Targets

"Bond Exchange"

Reduction of unsecured debt by two-thirds (excluding pension and employee benefit obligations) by conversion of debt into equity or by other means.

"Labor Modifications"

- "Compensation Reduction." Reduce total compensation, including wages and benefits, by the end of 2009 to an average equivalent to those of Toyota, Honda, and Nissan in the United States, as certified by the Secretary of Labor.
- "Severance Rationalization." Eliminate payment of any compensation or benefits to fired, furloughed, laid off, or idled employees, beyond "customary" severance pay;
- "Work Rule Modification." By the end of 2009 apply work rules "in a manner competitive" with the three Japanese-owned companies in the United States named above.

With respect to labor contract modifications and other provisions under collective bargaining agreements covering the hourly workforce, "if any labor union or collective bargaining unit shall engage in a strike or other work stoppage," it has been defined as an "event of default" in the "loan and security agreements" signed by the recipient companies as a condition of receiving the loans from the Treasury Department.[209]

"VEBA Modification"

Convert one-half of the value of each future corporate contribution to the planned VEBA for retiree health care, due by January 1, 2010, to company stock holdings.

Each company is required by February 17, 2009, to submit term sheets signed by representatives of the company and, respectively, bondholders, unions, and VEBA representatives. That is to be followed up by full approval of the terms by the respective groups, and certification by the President's designee, with such variation as may be allowed. Failing completion of this process, the designee could require full loan repayment in 30 days.[210]

Proposed Changes to Stipulations and Conditions in H.R. 384

By contrast with the prescriptive requirements and targets in President Bush's loan term sheets, the House in H.R. 384 gave only a general assignment to the "President's designee" to achieve a plan negotiated by "interested parties" (including employees and retirees of the manufacturer, trade unions, suppliers, dealers, and shareholders). This plan should address: repayment of federal loans; statutory fuel economy and emissions requirements and targets; achievement of positive company net value; rationalization of cost and capacity with respect to workforce, suppliers, and dealers; debt restructuring; and, a "competitive" product mix and cost structure.

End Notes

[1] This section was written by Stephen Cooney, Resources, Science and Industry Division. He also coordinated the report.

[2] The "Detroit Three" comprise General Motors (GM), Ford Motor Company, and Chrysler LLC.

[3] U.S. Department of Commerce. Bureau of Economic Analysis. News release, "Personal Income and Outlays," October 2008.

[4] *Detroit News*, "Auto Sales Plummet to 26-Year Low" (December 3, 2008); *Financial Times*, "Incentives Rise as Carmakers Fight To Get Buyers Behind the Wheel," January 7, 2009.

[5] Subaru (owned by Fuji Heavy Industries of Japan) was the only brand to gain sales in the U.S. market in 2008, about 500 vehicles (+0.3%) ahead of the previous year.

[6] Sales data from *Automotive News* market data website.

[7] This is especially the theme of a critical book written about the U.S. auto industry, by Michelene Maynard, *The End of Detroit: How the Big Three Lost Their Grip on the American Car Market*, New York: Doubleday, 2003. The issue has been examined by in its historical context in CRS Report RL32883, *U.S. Automotive Industry: Recent History and Issues*, by Stephen Cooney and Brent D. Yacobucci.

[8] On this point, see also CRS Report RL34743, *Federal Loans to the Auto Industry Under the Energy Independence and Security Act*, by Stephen Cooney and Brent D. Yacobucci, pp. 2-4.

[9] While cars may have outsold trucks over the course of 2008, it is not yet clear whether the decline in fuel prices at the end of the year will cause a longer term swing of consumer sentiment back from cars to SUVs and other truck-type vehicles; *Business Week*, "The SUV Is Rising from the Dead," December 8, 2008, p. 63.

[10] The basics of this legislation are discussed in CRS Report RS22963, *Financial Market Intervention*, by Edward V. Murphy and Baird Webel.

[11] This section was written by Stephen Cooney of the Resources, Science, and Industry Division.

[12] Opposition was expressed on and off the floor of Congress by, among others, John Kyl (Senate Minority Whip), Senate Banking Ranking Member Richard Shelby, Senator Lamar Alexander, House Majority Leader John Boehner, House Financial Services Ranking Member Spencer Bachus, and Representative Jim Cooper; all quoted variously in *Detroit News*, "Auto Aid Debate Heats Up," and "Congress Starts Talks on Auto Loans," November 17, 2008; "Blitz Starts for Big 3 Aid as Reid Introduces Bill to Tap $700B Bailout;" and, "Political Titans Clash in Auto Loan War," November 18, 2008.

[13] See CRS Report RL34743, *Federal Loans to the Auto Industry Under the Energy Independence and Security Act*, by Stephen Cooney and Brent D. Yacobucci, for the analysis, history, and funding of this legislation.

[14] General Motors Corporation. *Restructuring Plan for Long-Term Viability*, December 2, 2008, p. 2; debt level based on Table 4.

[15] *GM Restructuring Plan*, p. 2.

[16] These data are from *GM Restructuring Plan*, Table 6, labeled "Manufacturing Improvements" – indicating that the proportional difference between number of plant closures versus personnel reductions is to be accounted for through technology and efficiency improvements.

[17] Chrysler LLC. *Chrysler's Plan for Short-Term and Long-Term Viability*, December 2, 2008, pp. 3-4.

[18] U.S. Senate. Committee on Banking, Housing, and Urban Affairs. Hearing, December 4, 2008, *The State of the Domestic Automobile Industry: Part II*. Testimony of Robert Nardelli. For press coverage, see *Detroit Free Press*, "Help from Cerberus Unlikely," December 6, 2008.

[19] *Chrysler's Plan*, pp. 2-3.

[20] *Chrysler's Plan*, pp. 11-12. On "debtor-in-possession" financing, see the section below that explains bankruptcy rules.

[21] *Chrysler's Plan*, pp. 6-7. A planned joint venture with China's Chery auto manufacturing firm has been cancelled, however.

[22] Senate Banking Committee hearing, December 4, 2008.

[23] Chrysler LLC, "Fiat Group, Chrysler LLC, and Cerberus Capital Management LP Announce Plans for a Global Strategic Alliance," news release, January 20, 2009.

[24] This approach is summarized in its *Ford Motor Company Business Plan*, December 2, 2008, pp. 7-8.

[25] *Ford Business Plan*, p. 30.

[26] Sholnn Freeman, "A Temporary Reprieve: Ford, Others Must Still Negotiate Rough Road," *Washington Post*, December 20, 2008, p. D3.

[27] *Ford Business Plan*, p. 9.

[28] *Ford Business Plan*, p. 2.

[29] Ford Motor Co. News release," "Ford Reports 4th Quarter Net Loss of $5.9 Billion ...," January 29, 2009.

[30] *Bloomberg.com*, "Bush, Pelosi Deadlocked over Bailout for Automakers," December 4, 2008.

[31] *Detroit Free Press*, "Pelosi Drops Opposition to Tapping Plant Aid," (December 6, 2008).

[32] *Detroit News*, "Dems, White House Agree to $15B Auto Bailout," December 10, 2008.

[33] See advocacy for the bill by Secretary of Commerce Carlos M. Gutierrez, "A Bridge Detroit Needs," *Washington Post*, December 11, 2008, p. A25; Republican opposition, particularly from Banking Committee Ranking Member Richard Shelby is noted in *ibid.*, "Auto Bailout Clears House, but Faces Hurdles in Senate," p. A1.

[34] *Congressional Record* (December 11, 2008), pp. S 10895-96.

[35] Floor action on the measure was summarized by the Majority Leader in *Congressional Record*, December 11, 2008, pp. S10922-31. He credited Sens. Robert Corker and Christopher Dodd with leading the effort to produce a compromise. The move to close debate was made on an unrelated legislative item, H.R. 7005. The Chairman and Ranking Member of the Finance Committee, Sens. Max Baucus and Charles Grassley, respectively, announced their joint opposition to H.R. 7321 because of inclusion of a provision unrelated to the auto industry, which would have required the U.S. government to act as guarantor for "sale-in, lease-out" transactions engaged in by some public transportation authorities; see *ibid.*, pp. S 10909-11.

[36] White House. Press Briefing, December 12, 2008, p. 1.

[37] White House. Office of the Press Secretary. "President Bush Discusses Administration's Plan to Assist Automakers," December 19, 2008.

[38] The term sheets are available on Treasury's website: http://www.treas.gov/press/releases/hp1333.htm. For a general discussion of rules TARP rules under EESA, see CRS Report RL34730, *The Emergency Economic Stabilization Act and Current Financial Turmoil: Issues and Analysis*, by Baird Webel and Edward V. Murphy.

[39] GM term sheet, Appendix A.

[40] Resolution of disapproval, S.J.Res. 5, introduced by Sen. David Vitter and nine cosponsors, defeated by 52-42 (January 15, 2009).

[41] U.S. Department of the Treasury. *Indicative Summary of Terms for Secured Term Loan Facility*, December 19, 2008, "Appendix A" in both GM and Chrysler term sheets.

[42] White House. Office of the Press Secretary. *Fact Sheet: Financing Assistance to Facilitate the Restructuring of Auto Manufacturers to Attain Financial Viability*, December 19, 2008. Emphases in original.

[43] Letter of Chrysler CEO Robert Nardelli "to all Chrysler employees, dealers, suppliers, and other stakeholders," January 23, 2009.

[44] Treasury, *Summary of Terms*, p. 7.

[45] International Union, United Automobile, Aerospace & Agricultural Implement Workers of America (UAW). Press release, "UAW Applauds Auto Loans, But Says Workers Must Not Be Singled Out for Unfair Conditions," December 19, 2008.

[46] Office of Sen. Stabenow. Press release, "Stabenow Statement on Provisions in Auto Rescue Package," Dec. 19, 2008.

[47] See comments to the press by House Financial Services Committee Chairman Barney Frank, quoted in *Washington Post*, "House Urges Tighter Rules for Bailout Beneficiaries," January 22, 2009.

[48] This section was written by Stephen Cooney, Resources, Science, and Industry Division.

[49] U.S. Department of Commerce. Bureau of Economic Analysis. News release on "Gross Domestic product," January 30, 2009.

[50] *Blue Chip Economic Indicators*, Aspen Publishers, January 10, 2008. The Blue Chip forecast is an average of about 50 separate forecasts.

[51] Department of Commerce, Bureau of Economic Analysis.

[52] Thomas H. Klier and James M. Rubenstein, "Who Really Made Your Car?," *Chicago Fed Letter*, Federal Reserve Bank of Chicago, October 2008. See also **Table 2** below in this chapter.

[53] University of Maryland. Inforum Economic Summary, *Potential Job Losses from Restructuring the U.S. Auto Industry*, December 16, 2008.

[54] Anderson Economic Group/BBK. *Automaker Bankruptcy Would Cost Taxpayers Four Times More Than Amount of Federal Bridge Loans*, December 8, 2008.

[55] David Cole, et al., *CAR Research Memorandum: The Impact on the U.S. Economy of a Major Contraction of the Detroit Three Automakers*, Center for Automotive Research, November 4, 2008.

[56] Jeffrey Werling in the Maryland Inforum study (p. 3) stated, regarding the CAR top number, "It seems implausible that 100% of U.S. auto production would be idled. Yet the most widely cited total job loss figure, 'up to 3 million,' is based on such an unrealistic assumption." Toyota and Honda, for example, are already reportedly planning modifications to their "just-in-time" supply chain models in order to ameliorate the effects of supplier bankruptcies; see, *Detroit News*, "Toyota May Modify Supply Chain," December 30, 2008. The figure of 3 million could be taken, however, as an estimate of the total number of jobs that could be at risk.

[57] Klier and Rubenstein, "Who Really Made Your Car?," (October 2008 article). Also discussed more fully in their book, *Who Really Made Your Car? Restructuring and Geographic Change in the Auto Industry* (Kalamazoo, MI: Upjohn Institute, 2008).

[58] Klier and Rubenstein, *Who Really Made Your Car?*, chapters 5-6. For a state-by-state analysis of automotive manufacturing jobs, see CRS Report RL34297, *Motor Vehicle Manufacturing Employment: National and State Trends and Issues*, by Stephen Cooney, especially Figure 5 and Table 1.

[59] Howard Wial, "How a Metro Nation Would Feel the Loss of the Detroit Three Automakers," *Metropolitan Policy Program at Brookings*, December 12, 2008.

[60] Wial, "Loss of Detroit Three," p. 3.

[61] Wial, "Loss of Detroit Three," p. 4.

[62] This section was written by Stephen Cooney, Resources, Science, and Industry Division.

[63] CRS Report RL32883, *U.S. Automotive Industry: Recent History and Issues*, by Stephen Cooney and Brent D. Yacobucci, esp. Figure 9 and Table 3.

[64] *Automotive News*, "Transplant Expansions: Onward Ho!" December 1, 2008, p. 3.

[65] Ray Windecker, former research and analysis manager for Ford Motor Co., has pointed out that in past cycles, sales declines at the trough were 30% or higher, and between 1978 and 1982 the net decline in annual vehicle sales was 4.5 million units; "A Rough Ride Is Nothing New for Autos," *Automotive News*, November 10, 2008, p. 14. By comparison, the fall in total light motor vehicle sales from a peak of about 17.0 million units in 2005 to 13.2 million units in 2008, represents a decline of 3.8 million units or 22% (data from *Ward's Motor Vehicle Facts & Figures, 2008*, and unpublished data provided by Ward's). However, the fall in monthly sales in late 2008 to an annual rate of about 10.0 million units indicates that we may not yet have seen the trough of this cycle.

[66] For the third quarter, the annual rate of sales was even lower, and, owing to lower-than-average income and credit ratings among their customers, Detroit 3 companies only commanded 42% of the domestic retail market; *Detroit Free Press*, "Credit Crunch Hits Buyers of Detroit 3" (October 26, 2008).

[67] *Detroit Free Press*, "Vehicle Transaction Prices Continue Falling" (October 28, 2008).

[68] On recent trends, see CRS Report RL34625, *Gasoline and Oil Prices*, by Robert Pirog.

[69] EPA's numbers, which are used on the window stickers of new cars and trucks, are downgraded from the CAFE test to better reflect in-use fuel economy. For example, the CAFE test is limited to 55 miles per hour, and does not include the use of air conditioning or other accessories.

[70] For more details, see CRS Report RL34743, *Federal Loans to the Auto Industry Under the Energy Independence and Security Act*, by Stephen Cooney and Brent D. Yacobucci.

[71] Sources quoted in *New York Times*, "Car Slump Jolts Toyota, Halting 70 Years of Gain," December 23, 2008, p. 1.

[72] Quoted by Jonathan Soble, "Honda Cuts Expenses Amid Further Downturn," *Financial Times*, December 18, 2008; see also *Wall St. Journal*, "Corporate News: Honda Slashes Outlook for Full-Year Sales, Profit," December 18, 2008, p. B3; Associated Press, "Toyota Projects First Loss in 70 Years," December 22, 2008. While Japanese domestic auto sales fell to the lowest levels in 20 years in 2007-08, a cheap yen level of about 120 to the dollar and strong exports allowed Japanese production to reach an all-time high in early 2008. But the dollar's fall to less then 90 yen and a global growth slowdown has led to falling auto company profits, production and exports; *Business Week*, "How the Strong Yen Has Weakened Japan," January 19, 2009, pp. 50-51.

[73] *Automotive News*, "Honda, Toyota, Others Whack N.A. Output," December 15, 2008, p. 8.

[74] *New York Times*, "Toyota to Shut Factories for 11 Days," January 6, 2009.

[75] *Automotive News*, "Nissan to Sell Small Commercial Vehicles in U.S.," December 15, 2008, p. 24.

[76] *Tuscaloosa News*, "Mercedes Offers Buyouts to Vance Plant Employees," October 31, 2008.

[77] Bloomberg.com, "Germany Offers GM's Opel As Much As $2.5 Billion," January 9, 2009.

[78] *Detroit Free Press*, "Sweden Gives Volvo, Saab Billions in Aid," December 11, 2008.

[79] *Detroit Free Press*, "Canada Takes Steps To Aid Auto Industry," December 21, 2008.

[80] This issue was reviewed in CRS Report RL32883, *U.S. Automotive Industry: Recent History and Issues*, by Stephen Cooney and Brent D. Yacobucci, pp. 37-43; and, CRS Report RL33169, *Comparing Automotive and Steel Industry Legacy Cost Issues*, by Stephen Cooney.

[81] This included Chrysler, which had become newly independent from German parent Daimler after Cerberus, a hedge fund, bought an 80% share of the company.

[82] These agreements are described in CRS Report RL34297, *Motor Vehicle Manufacturing Employment: National and State Trends and Issues*, by Stephen Cooney, pp. 25-32.

[83] *Washington Post*, "Bankruptcy Could Offer GM More Flexibility" (November 29, 2008), p. D1.

[84] *Wall St. Journal*, "America's Other Auto Industry," December 1, 2008, p. A22; *Automotive News*, "Transplant Wages Are a Moving Target," December 15, 2008, p. 3.

[85] *Wall St. Journal*, "America's Other Auto Industry."

[86] *Ford Business Plan*, Appendix 2.

[87] Communication to CRS from UAW, December 17, 2008.

[88] Ford Motor Co. news release, January 29, 2009.

[89] Details of the direct loan program are discussed in CRS Report RL34743, *Federal Loans to the Auto Industry Under the Energy Independence and Security Act*, by Stephen Cooney and Brent D. Yacobucci, pp. 14-24.

[90] *Automotive News*, "Cash Burn Rates Threaten GM, Ford" (November 10, 2008).

[91] See hearing citation below.

[92] See CRS Report RL34743, *Federal Loans to the Auto Industry Under the Energy Independence and Security Act*, by Stephen Cooney and Brent D. Yacobucci, pp. 10-11, 17.

[93] Speaker of the House Nancy Pelosi and Senate Majority Leader Harry Reid, Letter to Secretary of the Treasury Henry M. Paulson (November 8, 2008).

[94] *Financial Times* (*FT.com*), "Paulson Rejects TARP Aid for US Carmakers" (November 12, 2008); *Bloomberg.com*, "Paulson Urges Congress to Approve Automaker Funding" (November 13, 2008); and "Democrats, Bush Deadlocked over Expanding Aid to U.S. Carmakers" (November 19, 2008).

[95] U.S. Senate. Committee on Banking, Housing, and Urban Affairs. Hearing. *Examining the State of the Domestic Auto Industry* (November 18, 2008), Testimony of G. Richard Wagoner.

[96] Senate Banking Committee hearing, November 18. The total level of requests was raised to $34 billion in subsequent business plans formally submitted by the three companies to Congress on December 2, 2008 (as summarized in *Washington Post*, "Auto Giants Ratchet Up Pleas for Aid" (December 3, 2008), p. A1.

[97] See their respective statements in the Senate Banking Committee hearing (December 4, 2008) and the House Financial Services Committee hearing (December 5, 2008), on the domestic auto industry.

[98] The table uses the Bureau of Labor Statistics *Current Employment Survey*, in order to estimate the most recent data available.

[99] Thomas Klier and James Rubenstein, *Who Really Made Your Car?* (Kalamazoo, MI: W.E. Upjohn Institute, 2008). A detailed CRS analysis of U.S. automotive manufacturing employment trends, nationally and by state, is in CRS Report RL34297, *Motor Vehicle Manufacturing Employment: National and State Trends and Issues*, by Stephen Cooney, pp. 1-20.

[100] *GM Restructuring Plan*, pp. 18-19; *Ford Business Plan*, p. 11.

[101] *Automotive News*, "Economy Decimates Dealerships," December 15, 2008, p. 1.

[102] This subsection was written by Stephen Cooney, Resources, Science, and Industry Division.

[103] For example, "As recently as September 30, [2008,] GMAC provided dealer inventory financing for 80% of GM vehicles worldwide." *Automotive News* , "A GMAC Failure Could Doom Dealers," December 15, 2008, p. 31.

[104] *Automotive News*, "Advantage, Ford: Mulally Likes Owning Ford Credit" (November 3, 2008) p. 8.

[105] *Automotive News*, "The Scramble for Credit" (Oct 27, 2008); CRS interview with Patrick Calpin, National Automobile Dealers Association (November 10, 2008).

[106] *Financial Times*, "GMAC Losses Add to GM Woes;" *Detroit News*, "GMAC Posts $2.52 Quarterly Loss" (both stories November 5, 2008).

[107] Comments at the hearing from G. Richard Wagoner (GM) and Robert Nardelli (Chrysler).

[108] *Automotive News*, "Advantage, Ford".

[109] U.S. House. Committee on Financial Services. Hearing, *Auto Industry Stabilization Plans* (December 5, 2008), discussion between Alan Mulally and Rep. Paul Hodes.

[110] *Automotive News*, "To Match Toyota, Nissan Offers 0% Loans" (November 3, 2008), p. 43.

[111] *Detroit News*, "Big Banks Back Off Consumer Car Loans" (November 10, 2008).

[112] "Scramble for Credit;" NADA interview.

[113] Spencer Abraham, "A Cure for the Coming Crisis in Auto Finance," *Financial Times* (November 3, 2008).

[114] *Detroit News*, "GMAC Files with Fed for Bank Holding Status" (November 20, 2008).

[115] Associated Press (*Durham [NC] Herald-Sun*), "Fed: GMAC OK to Seek Bailout Money," December 25, 2008, p. 1.

[116] U.S. Department of the Treasury. Press release, "Treasury Announces TARP Investment in GMAC," December 29, 2008. See also attached term sheet and GM commitment letter. The easing of GMAC's credit requirements for consumers is discussed in *Detroit Free Press*, "GMAC To Offer More Loans in Wake of Aid," December 30, 2008; and *Washington Post*, "GM Aims To Drive Sales with Incentives," December 31, 2008. According to press analysis, because investors' bonded indebtedness has been converted to equity, GM and Cerberus may lose financial control of GMAC; see *Detroit News*, "Feds Invest $6B in GMAC;" *Detroit Free Press*, "$6B for GMAC; Aid Planned for Other Auto Finance Companies,;" and, *Washington Post*, "GMAC To Get $6 Billion Lifeline," all December 30, 2008.

[117] U.S. Department of the Treasury. Press release, "Treasury Announces TARP Investments in Chrysler Financial," January 16, 2009.

[118] National Automobile Dealers Association. Press release, "Federal Reserve Approves NADA-Backed Initiative Aimed at Increasing Inventory Financing," December 22, 2008.

[119] *Detroit Free Press*, "Delphi's Fate Still Tied to GM's" (November 14, 2008).

[120] *Detroit Free Press*, "GM's Efforts to Merge with Chrysler Put on Hold for Now" (November 8, 2008).

[121] This subsection was written by James Bickley of the Government and Finance Division. More detail on pensions, health care, executive and labor compensation, and some other issues is provided in subsequent sections of the report.

[122] "President Bush Discusses Administration's Plan to Assist Automakers," White House Press Release, Dec. 19, 2008, p. 1. Available at [http://www.whitehouse.gov/news/release/2008/12/20081219.html], visited Dec. 19, 2008.

[123] Ibid.

[124] Ibid.

[125] U.S. Treasury, "Indicative Summary of Terms for Secured Term Loan Facility" [for General Motors], Dec. 19, 2008, p. 14 [Appendix A]. Available at [http://www.ustrea.gov/press/releases/hp1333.htm], visited Dec. 19, 2008.

[126] U.S. Treasury, "Indicative Summary of Terms for Secured Term Loan Facility" [for Chrysler], Dec. 19, 2008, p. 14 [Appendix A]. Available at [http://www.ustrea.gov/press/releases/hp1333.htm], visited Dec. 19, 2008.

[127] Ibid., p. 5.

[128] Ibid., p. 6.

[129] This section on concessions is based on "Indicative Summary of Terms for Secured Term Loan Facility" [for General Motors and Chrysler]; and Daniel Dombey and Bernard Simon, "Bush Bails Out Detroit with $17 Billion Package," *Financial Times*, December 19, 2008, pp. 1-2.

[130] "President Bush Discusses Administration's Plan to Assist Automakers," p. 2.

[131] U.S. Treasury, "Indicative Summary of Terms for Secured Term Loan Facility," pp. 11-13.

[132] This section was written by Carol A. Pettit of the American Law Division.

[133] John D. Stoll, "Chapter 11 May Not Deter Some Car Buyers," *Wall Street Journal*, December 17, 2008, p. B3. He reports that a Merrill Lynch study indicated 90% of car buyers might buy a car from an automaker in bankruptcy, while a CNW Marketing Research survey indicated 48% would consider it.

[134] The companies' Restructuring Plan Reports must be reviewed by the President's Designee and certified no later than April 30, 2009 to avoid automatic acceleration of the loans' maturity. GM and Chrysler term sheets, p. 7.

[135] *See* Term Sheets, pp. 2-3.

[136] *See* Term Sheets, pp. 11-12.

[137] *See* Chrysler Term Sheet, App. A (requiring consent by majority of holders of Chrysler LLC first lien and second lien indebtedness to pledge MOPAR Parts Inventory and some real estate collateral to the government as Lender); GM Term Sheet, App. A (requiring consent by the common holders of Class A and Class C Membership Interests of GMAC LLC to pledge Class B Membership Interests as well as Preferred Membership Interests to the government as Lender).

[138] *See* Term Sheets, pp. 4-5.

[139] *See* Adam Levitin, "More on the Auto Bailouts," *Credit Slips*, December 20, 2008, at http://www.creditslips.org/creditslips/2008/12/more-on-the-auto-bailouts.html; Adam Levitin, "Auto Bailout," *Credit Slips*, December 19, 2008, at http://www.creditslips.org/creditslips/2008/12/auto-bailout.html.

[140] Term Sheets, App. A.

[141] Whether a court would honor the pre-petition contract provision to convert the government loans to DIP financing following a bankruptcy filing is beyond the scope of this chapter. If a court were to honor the provision, the debtor might encounter more difficulty arranging additional DIP financing to carry it through its reorganization.

[142] Term Sheets, p. 10.

[143] Term Sheets, p. 7.

[144] Term Sheets, p. 5.

[145] Term Sheets p. 5.

[146] Term Sheets, p. 6.

[147] Term Sheets, p. 6.

[148] Term Sheets p. 6.

[149] *See* 11 U.S.C. §§ 1113, 1114.

[150] 11 U.S.C. § 701 *et seq.*

[151] 11 U.S.C. § 1101 *et seq.*

[152] Art. I, sec. 8, cl.4.

[153] Since the Bankruptcy Clause empowers Congress to enact "*uniform* laws," modifications could be industry-specific, but not company-specific.

[154] The Bankruptcy Code is 11 U.S.C. § 101 *et seq.*

[155] The "trustee" of the bankruptcy estate is different from the U.S. Trustee, who is a member of the U.S. Trustee Program and appointed by the U.S. Attorney General. A private trustee, who represents a bankruptcy estate, is either appointed by the U.S. Trustee or elected by the creditors. 11 U.S.C. §§ 701-703.

[156] *See* 11 U.S.C. § 726.

[157] *See* 11 U.S.C. § 507.

[158] Most executory contracts can be accepted or rejected, with the court's approval, under 11 U.S.C. § 365. Modification of collective bargaining agreements (CBAs) is subject to greater limitation under 11 U.S.C. § 1113. Similarly limited is modification of retiree health benefits under 11 U.S.C. § 1114.

[159] "Cause" generally involves fraud, dishonesty, incompetence, or mismanagement. *See* 11 U.S.C. § 1104. Note, however, that under the Railroad Reorganization Act, a trustee *must* be appointed. 11 U.S.C. § 1163.

[160] An example of such a specialist in the automotive industry is Robert S. Miller, who has been leading parts-maker Delphi through its bankruptcy since 2005. He earlier led Bethlehem Steel through its Chapter 11 bankruptcy and its sale to the International Steel Group (eventually, the company was acquired by ArcelorMittal Steel).

[161] *See* 11 U.S.C. § 1123 (Contents of Plan).

[162] *See* 11 U.S.C. § 1129 (Confirmation of Plan).

[163] Greater protection may be available to DIP lenders if credit cannot be obtained without such protection. *See* 11 U.S.C. § 364(c), (d).

[164] *See* 11 U.S.C. § 1129(a)(9).

[165] This subsection was written by Patrick Purcell of the Domestic Social Policy Division.

[166] For a more detailed description of the funding requirements for defined benefit plans, see CRS Report RL34443, *Summary of the Employee Retirement Income Security Act (ERISA)*, by Patrick Purcell and Jennifer Staman.

[167] ERISA governs only pensions provided to workers employed in the United States.

[168] According to information filed by Chrysler on the IRS Form 5500 for 2005, its pension liabilities at that time totaled approximately $15.8 billion and its assets were valued at about $15.0 billion.

[169] "General Motors Corp. does not expect to have to make any pension contributions to meet minimum funding requirements in the next three to four years, even though its funded status declined in the first nine months of 2008 because of negative investment returns and recent employee-related cutbacks, according to its third-quarter financial report Friday, November 7." "GM Doesn't Foresee Required Pension Contributions," *Workforce Management*, November 11, 2008.

[170] Watson Wyatt reported that as of September 30, discount rates had increased by about 1 percentage point since yearend 2007, and that yields on AA rated corporate bonds had risen by almost 80 basis points from the end of September to mid-November.

[171] Early retirement programs could result in pensions being paid earlier than was originally forecast, creating an unfunded liability for the plans.

[172] *Detroit Free Press*, "Agency Concerned about Detroit 3 Buyout Costs" (November 29, 2008).

[173] *Wall St. Journal*, "Pension Agency Sounds Alarm on Big Three," (November 28, 2008).

[174] "Federal Pension Agency Asks Automakers for Details on Buyouts," *Bloomberg News*, November 28, 2008.

[175] *New York Times*, "GM's Pension Fund Stays Afloat, Against the Odds" (November 25, 2008).

[176] This is known as the "termination liability," for which the PBGC may ultimately become responsible. "Agency Raises Concerns About Car Makers' Pensions," *Wall St. Journal*, January 9, 2009.

[177] *Detroit News*, "Big 3 Pension Gap Grows," January 10, 2009.

[178] This subsection was written by Carol Rapaport, Janemarie Mulvey, and Hinda Chaikind of the Domestic Social Policy Division.

[179] GM and Ford Investor Presentations, *UA W. Chrysler Report*, 2007.

[180] There is pending litigation including possible appeals or court challenges that could potentially affect the VEBA terms and conditions.

[181] One option for subsidizing the purchase of health insurance, that could be available although is unlikely at this time for the Detroit 3 workers, is the Health Coverage Tax Credit (HCTC) for certain categories of affected workers. The HCTC covers 65% of the premium for qualified health insurance purchased by an eligible taxpayer. For further information on the HCTC see CRS Report RL32620, *Health Coverage Tax Credit Authorized by the Trade Act of 2002*, by Bernadette Fernandez.

[182] If the retiree coverage is eliminated and it differs from coverage offered to active employees, "presumably the obligation can be satisfied if the affected retirees are offered coverage similar to that provided to active employees," according to the American Bar association, Joint Committee of Employee Benefits (Employee Benefits in Bankruptcy: COBRA Health Continuation Coverage Rules. Teleconference/Live Audio Webcast, May 12, 2004).

[183] This subsection was written by Gary Shorter, Government and Finance Division.

[184] U.S. Department of the Treasury Notice 2008-PSSFI.

[185] This definition is much broader than the popular definition of a golden parachute, which is severance payment to an executive in the event that a company undergoes a change in control.

[186] Chris Isidore, "Golden Parachutes Here to Stay," *CNNMoney.com*, (September 29, 2008).

[187] Theo Francis, "Bank Rescue: Making Wall Street Pay?," *Business Week*, October 15, 2008.

[188] "Letter from Senate Majority Leader Harry Reid and House Speaker Nancy Pelosi to Treasury Secretary Henry Paulson (October 29, 2008).

[189] For example, see Robert Samuelson, "Wall Street Ignored Risk to Gain Short-Term Riches, *Washington Post*, September 18, 2008.

[190] "Bank Rescue: Making Wall Street Pay?," *Business Week*, October 16, 2008.

[191] *USA Today*, "GM Pushes the Pedal on Hydrogen Fuel-Cell Power" (November 5, 2007).

[192] John England, Vickie Williams, "Private Equity: Redrawing the Rules of Executive Compensation," *Towers Perrin online*, (July 7, 2008).

[193] *USA Today*, "GM Pushes the Pedal on Hydrogen Fuel-Cell Power."

[194] "Frank Warns Banks Against Misuse of Bailout Funds," *NPR 's All Things Considered* (October 31, 2008).

[195] *Ford Business Plan*, pp. 12 and 27, and Appendix 1.

[196] *GM Restructuring Plan*, p. 31.

[197] Senate banking Committee hearing, December 4, 2008, testimony of G. Richard Wagoner, and additional information provided to CRS by GM on January 22, 2009.

[198] Tom Walsh and Tim Higgins, "Chrysler Leaders Get Millions," *Detroit Free Press*, November 13, 2008.

[199] Ibid.

[200] See the debate discussed in Gene J. Puskar, "Chrysler Leaders Get Millions," *USA Today* (November 14, 2008).

[201] Confirmed to CRS in communication from Chrysler LLC, January 23, 2009.

[202] Gary K. Meek, Ramesh P. Rao, and Christopher J. Skousen, "Evidence on Factors Affecting the Relationship Between CEO Stock Option Compensation and Earnings Management," *Review of Accounting & Finance*, Vol. 6, Issue 3, 2007, p. 304.

[203] This is a stock option that would be worthless if it expired today due to the fallen current market price of the underlying stock.

[204] Xiaomeng Zhang, Kathryn M Bartol, Ken G Smith, Michael D Pfarrer, and Dmitry M Khanin, "CEOS on the Edge: Earnings Manipulation and Stock-Based Incentive Misalignment," *Academy of Management Journal*, April 2008, p. 241.

[205] David Shadovitz, "The Risks of Stock Options," *Human Resource Executive Online* (July 25, 2007).

[206] Peter Galuszka, "What Are Compensation 'Clawbacks'?," *Bnet Briefing*, 2008.

[207] This subsection was written by Stephen Cooney, Resources, Science, and Industry Division.

[208] Requirements for eligibility under this program are described in CRS Report RL34743, *Federal Loans to the Auto Industry Under the Energy Independence and Security Act*, by Stephen Cooney and Brent D. Yacobucci.

[209] U.S. Securities and Exchange Commission. Form 8-K filed by General Motors Corporation, December 31, 2008, p. 60. A similar provision is reportedly in the loan agreement signed by Chrysler LLC, a privately held company. This provision was first noted by the press: *Wall St. Journal*, "Bailout Pact of GM, U.S. Would Block a UAW Strike;" *Detroit News*, "Strikes Would Imperil Bailout Funding,;" *Detroit Free Press*, "UAW Strike Would Kill Auto Loans," all January 9, 2009. Commentators quoted in the stories noted that strikes were in any case highly unlikely in view of the financial conditions of the automakers.

[210] These conditions are summarized from Treasury, GM and Chrysler *Term Sheets*, pp. 5-7.

In: The U.S. Auto Industry and the Role of Federal Assistance   ISBN: 978-1-60741-322-6
Editor: James R. Elliot   © 2010 Nova Science Publishers, Inc.

Chapter 2

FEDERAL LOANS TO THE AUTO INDUSTRY UNDER THE ENERGY INDEPENDENCE AND SECURITY ACT

Stephen Cooney and Brent D. Yacobucci

SUMMARY

U.S. automakers are facing a myriad of unfavorable conditions, including a worsening economy and credit crunch that have dampened consumers' demand for new vehicles, high legacy costs, increased competition from foreign automakers, and stricter Corporate Average Fuel Economy (CAFE) standards. The last concern — the regulatory cost of higher fuel economy standards — led Congress to consider various federal programs, including grants and loans, to help automakers with the increased cost to comply with the new standards.

In December 2007, the Energy Independence and Security Act of 2007 (P.L. 110-140) authorized a program to provide loans to automakers and parts suppliers for the production of fuel-efficient cars and light trucks. The law authorized up to $25 billion in total loans. However, funds were not appropriated for the loan program until September 30, 2008, when the Consolidated Security, Disaster Assistance, and Continuing Appropriations Act (P.L. 110-329) was enacted. This act appropriated $7.5 billion to cover the subsidy cost of up to $25 billion total in loans, as well as $10 million for program implementation. The act further directed the Department of Energy (DOE) to implement an interim final rule within 60 days of enactment — this deadline would be November 29, 2008.

On November 5, 2008, DOE announced an interim final rule for the program. The rule will be effective the date it is published in the *Federal Register* (when this will happen is unclear). Once published, DOE will have a 30-day public comment period on the interim rule before issuing the final rule for the program. Loan funds will be separated into tranches, with applications for each tranche due every 90 days, until all loan authority has been expended. The application deadline for the first tranche is either the effective date of the program (the day it is published in the *Federal Register*), or December 31, 2008 — the rulemaking documents are contradictory on this point.

To qualify for a loan, an automaker must have an average fleet fuel economy no lower than that in Model Year 2005. Also, eligible facilities (either vehicle assembly or part making) must be located in the United States. Specific projects must result in the production of vehicles that achieve at least 25% higher fuel economy than Model Year 2005 models with similar size and performance. Further, applicants must be able to demonstrate their financial viability over the life of the loan — 25 years. This last requirement may prove to be a significant barrier to loan approvals under the program.

INTRODUCTION

Congress has approved, and the President has signed into law, two legislative provisions that authorize and fund a program to provide as much as $25 billion in direct loans to automotive manufacturers in the United States, and their suppliers. These measures are in § 136 of the Energy Independence and Security Act (EISA) of 2007 (P.L. 110-140, which became law on December 19, 2007) and §129 of the Consolidated Security, Disaster Assistance, and Continuing Appropriations Act (P.L. 110-329, signed into law on September 30, 2008). The first measure authorizes the loan program at the level stated, and establishes the purposes for which such loans may be used. The second measure appropriates $7.51 billion to cover the subsidy and administrative costs of the program and directs that the loans should be made by the Federal Financing Bank. It further establishes an expedited timetable, so that the Department of Energy (DOE) should write an "interim final rule" for administering the program within 60 days after enactment.[1] On November 5, 2008, DOE announced its interim final rule implementing the program, although the rule has not yet been published in the *Federal Register*.[2]

This program has been widely misinterpreted as a broad "bailout" of U.S.-based domestic motor vehicle manufacturers. Already losing money when the authorizing legislation was passed in late 2007, the U.S.-owned "Big Three" nameplate companies based in Detroit (henceforth the "Detroit 3") — General Motors (GM), Ford Motor Company, and Chrysler LLC — have seen substantial increases in losses since then. Many commentators noted that this increased the urgency for Congress to approve appropriations legislation to fund a program to assist the domestic companies. For example, the *Washington Post* headlined an article reporting on possible delays in administering the EISA loans, "Lifeline for Automakers Dangles Just Out of Reach."[3] While automakers and their supporters in Congress have reportedly called for a larger program, with a broader range of possible industry uses, the language in these laws indicates the intent of Congress that the loans are for the purpose of enabling the U.S. auto industry to produce more fuel-efficient vehicles.

One of the major provisions in EISA mandated an increase in corporate average fuel economy ("CAFE") standards. Title I of the law is labeled "Energy Security Through Improved Vehicle Fuel Economy." Its first subtitle is "Increased Corporate Average Fuel Economy Standards," and the short title is the "Ten-in-Ten Fuel Economy Act," a label used by supporters of a dramatic increase in U.S. CAFE standards.[4] The new law established a corporate average fuel economy (CAFE) target of 35 miles per gallon (mpg) by model year (MY) 2020 for the combined passenger automobile and light truck fleet, as opposed to

MY2008 standards of 27.5 mpg for cars and a lower standard, 22.5 mpg, for light trucks. The law further requires "maximum feasible" increases from 2021 through 2030.[5]

Compliance Costs May Fall Most Heavily on Detroit 3

During the debate on this legislation, representatives of the U.S. motor vehicle manufacturing industry, including unions representing production workers, emphasized that these would be very difficult targets for the industry to achieve. They pointed to an earlier estimate by the National Highway Traffic Safety Administration (NHTSA) of the Department of Transportation (DOT) that to increase fuel economy standards by four percent per year, as had been suggested by the Bush Administration, would cost motor vehicle manufacturers $114 billion. The bulk of this cost (about $85 billion, according to the NHTSA estimate) would be borne by the Detroit 3.[6] These companies are still responsible for the majority of the motor vehicles manufactured in the United States, despite high levels of U.S. investment in recent decades by many foreign-owned producers.

Moreover, since at least the 1980s, the Detroit 3 have tended to specialize more in larger consumer vehicles, such as pickup trucks and sport utility vehicles (SUVs), which have relatively low fuel economy ratings. Thus, it was anticipated that the requirement to achieve substantial improvements in CAFE for these manufacturers would be more difficult than for most foreign-based manufacturers, whose domestic markets have historically featured smaller, more fuel-efficient vehicles, which they are then able to import into the U.S. market.

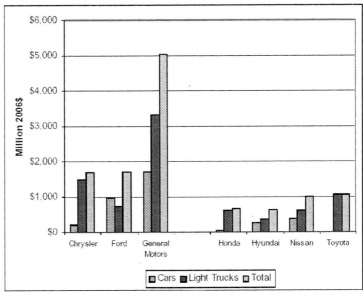

Source: CRS Analysis of National Highway Traffic Safety Administration (NHTSA), *Preliminary Regulatory Impact Analysis: Corporate Average Fuel Economy for MY2011- 2015 Passenger Cars and Light Trucks* (April 2008).

Figure 1. Total Estimated Incremental Costs in Model Year 2015 for Selected Manufacturers Under the Proposed CAFE Rule

However, it should be noted that proposed car and light truck standards for model years 2011 through 2015 shift the burden from a "straight-line" average — where all automakers must meet the same numerical average — to a size-based standard — where each automaker will have a different fuel economy target, and those automakers that produce smaller vehicles will face a higher target. In NHTSA's Preliminary Regulatory Impact Analysis (PRIA) for the proposed rule, the Agency found that total costs for cars and light trucks for the Detroit 3 were significantly higher than for the major Japanese automakers (Honda, Hyundai, Nissan, and Toyota.[7] (See Figure 1.) That said, in some cases, NHTSA found that under the proposed rule, Detroit 3 automakers faced lower per-vehicle costs. (See Figure 2.) For example, NHTSA estimated that Chrysler would face lower per- vehicle costs for its passenger cars than Hyundai or Nissan. Likewise, Ford may face lower per-vehicle costs for its light trucks than any of the Japanese automakers, and lower total costs for its light trucks than Toyota.

The next part of this chapter will analyze how shifting market trends have disfavored the Detroit 3, as foreign-based manufacturers, especially from Asia, have gained increased U.S. market shares since 2000. This trend has accelerated during a period of gasoline price increases and volatility since 2005. Market conditions for the Detroit 3 in 2008 worsened markedly, even by comparison with most other auto manufacturers, with the economic downturn and credit market crisis that occurred.

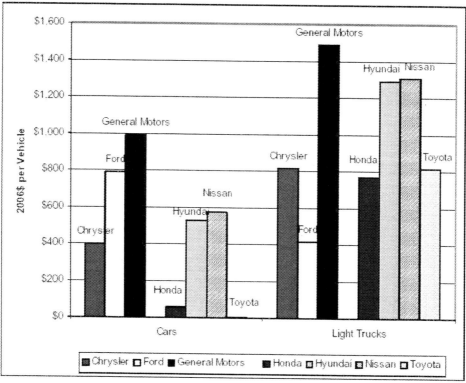

Source: CRS Analysis of National Highway Traffic Safety Administration (NHTSA), *Preliminary Regulatory Impact Analysis: Corporate Average Fuel Economy for MY2011- 2015 Passenger Cars and Light Trucks* (April 2008).

Figure 2. Estimated Per-Vehicle Incremental Costs in Model Year 2015 for Selected Manufacturers Under the Proposed CAFE Rule

Congress Seeks to Assist Technological Change

Congress ultimately decided that the mandate to increase CAFE standards created both a significant technological challenge for the domestic automotive industry and a potential competitive disadvantage for the older-established, domestically based Detroit 3, who were already struggling with market changes and their inherited wage cost and benefits structure.[8] Having established higher CAFÉ standards, P.L. 110-140 in Subtitle B of Title I ("Improved Vehicle Technology") added a number of provisions to encourage and help pay for the costs of transitioning motor vehicle manufacturing in the United States to achievement of higher fuel economy. These provisions include:

- Section 132, which amends Section 712 of the Energy Policy Act of 2005 ("EPAct 2005," 42 U.S.C. 16062) to require the Department of Energy (DOE) to create a grant program to "encourage domestic production and sales of efficient hybrid and advanced diesel vehicles and components ...";
- Section 134, which authorizes loan guarantees for production of fuel efficient vehicles or parts of such vehicles;
- Section 135, which requires establishment of a DOE program to provide loan guarantees for manufacturing advanced vehicle batteries and battery systems;
- Section 136, which authorizes a DOE "Advanced Technology Vehicles Manufacturing Incentive Program" — this includes both a grant program and, as subsection (d), the direct loan program that is the principal subject of this chapter;
- In addition, §112 under Subtitle A of the law requires that 50% of the fines paid by companies that fail to meet CAFE standards be set aside to carry out a grant program to manufacturers for producing advanced technology vehicles and components.

These newly authorized or expanded programs join other efforts which have been embarked on in the past by the U.S. government to promote advanced or alternative vehicle technology development. From these EISA initiatives, only the direct loan program under § 136(d) has so far received any funding at a level significant enough to make a difference in the competitive and highly expensive world of motor vehicle manufacturing.[9] Thus, while this chapter will further review other new and existing programs to develop advanced vehicle technologies, the principal focus will be on the direct loan program, which has been approved and funded by Congress at a high level, and awaits implementation by DOE.

THE DETROIT 3: AN ECONOMIC COLLAPSE?

U.S. automakers are facing a myriad of unfavorable conditions, including a worsening economy and credit crunch that have dampened consumers' demand for new vehicles, high legacy costs, increased competition from foreign automakers, and stricter federal CAFE standards. The $25 billion loan program authorized in Section 136 of EISA was arguably established to help automakers address the last concern — the regulatory cost of higher fuel economy standards — but some observers believe that $25 billion may not be enough to address the more systemic concerns facing the industry.

The major Detroit-based auto manufacturers were formerly known as the "Big 3." They are not any more, because by 2007, one Japanese company, Toyota, outsold two of the Detroit companies, Ford and Chrysler, in the United States, their own home market. In addition, by the first nine months of 2008, Honda had roughly equaled Chrysler in domestic U.S. motor vehicle sales.

This has not been merely a loss of some companies' competitive position to others, a normal shift in the marketplace. The loss of market shares, combined with the cyclical decline in the market and the sudden change in consumer preferences from trucks back to cars, has led to huge losses for the former "Big 3." It has put their entire business model, based on a collective bargaining relationship between management and labor, at risk. As a consequence, the issue faced by Congress, when it authorized and funded the direct loan program, was that the unionized, domestically owned motor vehicle industry might not be in a position to contribute to the national goal of reducing rates of petroleum demand by developing alternative technology vehicles. Along with other unfavorable conditions for the Detroit 3, some conclude that the mandate to improve fuel economy at the levels required could force one or more of the Detroit 3 out of the business.

The major market shifts did not happen overnight. As reported earlier by CRS,[10] foreign brands, both imported and produced at U.S. plants, have been gaining market share for decades. As illustrated in Figure 3, this trend has continued since 2000. However, the slope through 2005 was rather gentle: from two-thirds of the total U.S. market for passenger cars and light trucks in 2000, the Detroit 3 share declined gradually to 5 8.2% in 2005. Some of this decline represented aggressive U.S. manufacturing and expansion plans by foreign-owned companies: Toyota, Honda, Nissan, and Hyundai have all opened new assembly plants in the United States since 2000, and more are on the way.

However, after losing eight points of market share in 2000-2005, the Detroit 3 saw their losses accelerate by an additional 10 points, to an annual level of just over 48% market share, between then and the first three quarters of 2008. This occurred while the total market itself was declining. The U.S. automotive market is notoriously cyclical. Auto manufacturers have gross sales of more than a half-trillion dollars annually. Motor vehicles are consumers' number one discretionary purchase (excluding housing), and their sales have both a cause and effect relationship with the domestic economy. Figure 3 indicates that the total domestic light vehicle (auto and truck) market stabilized at around 17 million sales per year through 2005. It dropped about a half-million units in 2006 to 16.5 million, another half-million to just more than 16 million in 2007, then to an annual rate of just 14.4 million in the first three- quarters of 2008.[11] The annual rate of car and truck sales by the Detroit 3 fell to less than seven million, compared to 11.5 million in 2000, and almost 10 million as late as 2005. More detailed data show that each of the Detroit 3 saw sales decline by about one million vehicles or more, and each suffered significant market share losses.

Automotive data is usually figured in "units," which means, for example, that an expensive Cadillac Escalade counts the same as an inexpensive Kia Rio. But for the entire industry, average new vehicle transaction prices, after rising from 2004 through 2007, fell steadily in 2008, meaning less "top line" revenue per unit sold.[12] Moreover, **Table 1** illustrates that part of the Detroit 3's problems relate to the continued reliance on truck sales, when trucks are declining as an overall share of the market. Having become more specialized in larger vehicles, the Detroit 3 have been especially adversely affected by the sharper decline in the sales of such vehicles.

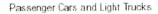

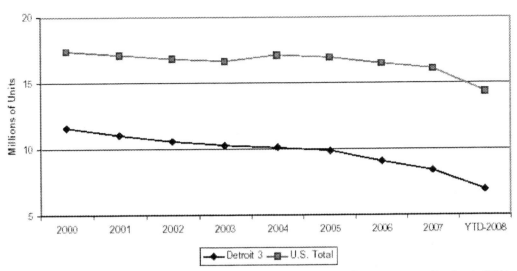

Sources: Automotive News Market Data Center (2008 data); *Ward's Automotive Yearbook* (2001-2008).

Figure 3. U.S. Motor Vehicle Sales

In 2001, "light truck" sales, which include pickups, SUVs, minivans, and smaller SUVs known as "crossover" utility vehicles (CUVs), were higher than U.S. passenger car sales for the first time. Trucks' lead over cars continued to expand through 2005 — 9.3 million units to 7.7 million units in that year, for a net margin of 1.6 million. But 2004-2005 saw Hurricanes Ivan, Katrina, and Rita, which shut down substantial portions of oil and gas production in the Gulf of Mexico and exacerbated a period of rising fuel prices and volatility that has continued through 2008.[13] Through the first nine months of 2008, U.S. car sales were actually up slightly at an annual rate over the previous year, but truck sales were almost a million less than cars, down by almost two million units over the previous year, and almost three million units less than the all-time 2005 annual peak. While most foreign- owned manufacturers had also expanded their truck offerings (including SUVs and minivans) in the U.S. market, they have not been as reliant as the Detroit 3 on truck products. By 2008, each of the Detroit 3 still counted truck products for the vast majority of sales (60%), while no foreign-owned competitor did so. Only about a third of foreign-owned companies' sales overall were classified as trucks.

Figure 4 illustrates how both the market and federal regulation has already begun to push fuel economy levels upward in the present decade, leading to a move away from larger, less fuel-efficient vehicles in which the Detroit 3 have generally dominated the market. While the NHTSA CAFE standard for cars has held steady at 27.5 mpg throughout the decade, the actual average of model-year vehicles sold, as measured on a different basis by the Environmental Protection Agency (EPA), has increased from 22.9 mpg to 24.1 mpg, with most of the gain coming in MY2007- 2008.[14] While the light truck standard held steady at 20.7 mpg through 2004, actual average truck mpg, as measured by EPA, remained less than 17.0 mpg, and declined slightly on a net basis. For light trucks, both the CAFE standard and the market have moved upward since then, with an actual average mpg of 18.1 by MY2008.

Table 1. Market Shares of U.S. Car and Truck Sales

Manufacturers	Sales (millions of units)							
	2001		2005		2007		2008 (Jan.-Sept. Annualized Rate)	
	Cars	Light Trucks	Cars	Light Trucks	Cars	Light Trucks	Cars	Light Trucks
GM	2.3	2.6	1.8	2.7	1.5	2.3	1.5	1.7
Ford	1.5	2.4	1.0	2.1	0.8	1.7	0.8	1.3
Chrysler	0.6	1.7	0.5	1.8	0.6	1.5	0.5	1.1
Detroit 3 (tot.)	**4.4**	**6.7**	**3.3**	**6.6**	**2.9**	**5.5**	**2.8**	**4.1**
Asian Brands	**3.3**	**1.9**	**3.6**	**2.6**	**4.0**	**2.8**	**4.1**	**2.3**
Ger. Brands[a]	**0.8**	**0.1**	**0.7**	**0.1**	**0.7**	**0.2**	**0.7**	**0.2**
Total U.S. Sales	**8.4**	**8.7**	**7.7**	**9.3**	**7.6**	**8.5**	**7.7**	**6.6**

Sources: As for Figure 1.

a. BMW, Volkswagen/Audi and Mercedes Benz brand of Daimler AG only. U.S. total includes other specialty manufacturers.

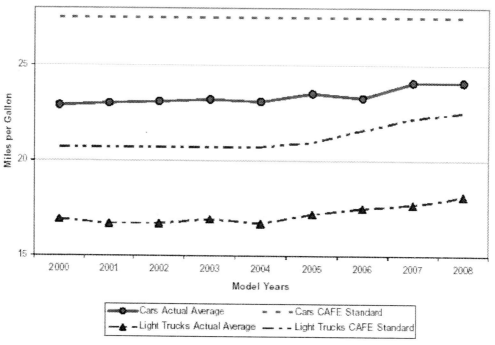

Source: CAFE standards from U.S. Dept. of Transportation. National Highway Traffic Safety Administration, Summary of Fuel Economy Performance (Mar. 2008); actual average data from U.S. Environmental Protection Agency. Light-Duty Automotive Technology and Fuel Economy Trends: 1975 Through 2008 (EPA420-R-08-015, Sept. 2008), Tables C-5 and C-6.

Note: EPA estimated in-use fuel economy is less than manufacturers ratings under CAFE system.

Figure 4. U.S. New Car and Truck Fuel Economy (All Manufacturers)

The Detroit 3 have indicated a commitment to producing a greater share of fuel efficient, advanced technology vehicles as part of their fleets going forward, but the cost of such changes raises doubts about their financial ability to contribute to this national goal over the longer term. In 2007, each of the Detroit 3 negotiated new collective bargaining agreements with their principal union, the United Auto Workers (UAW).[15] These agreements provided for transfer of retiree health care in 2010 from the companies to the UAW, with financial support initially from each of the Detroit 3. The agreements also provided the companies with other flexibility in managing and reducing labor costs, so that they could compete on a footing perceived to be more equal to foreign-owned companies, which are generally non-union in the United States.[16] These new agreements were negotiated and ratified by the time Congress approved EISA in December 2007. Although the Detroit 3 were losing money, the new labor agreements, combined with the direct loan program, appeared to provide a transition that would especially aid the Detroit 3 in achieving improved fuel economy.

By the time Congress considered funding this program in September 2008, the economic climate for the Detroit 3 had worsened markedly. The broader domestic economy reduced sales for virtually all manufacturers in the middle of the year, as consumer confidence declined and credit was harder to obtain. While neither Ford nor GM has been profitable at least since 2006, the operating losses turned much worse in the first half of 2008. GM's total losses for the first two quarters were $18.7 billion.[17] Ford reported a small net profit in early 2008, but that was offset by an $8.7 billion loss in the second quarter, after its net losses for 2006-2007 had totaled more than $15 billion.[18] Representatives of the Detroit 3 reportedly urged doubling the scale of available lending to $50 billion, as well as broadening the purposes for which the loans could be used.[19] The overall U.S. and global credit market crisis made further borrowing by these companies, whose bonds are in "junk" status, both difficult and expensive. Writing in the *Detroit Free Press*, Justin Hyde reported:

> Because of their weak finances, Detroit automakers can borrow money today only at high interest rates — close to the average 13% that consumers pay on credit cards. If funded, the government loans would provide money at interest rates just above what the ·U.S. Treasury pays to borrow — about 4% to 5%. That could save the automakers hundreds of millions of dollars.[20]

Nevertheless, Congress did not substantially amend the direct loan plan authorized in EISA, when it approved funding for the program in the Continuing Resolution. The purpose is not a general rescue or bailout of the domestic automotive companies. Rather, it remains to promote investments by all domestic manufacturers, but especially the Detroit 3 in older plants, to assist them in bringing to the market a more fuel efficient line of products. The main change in the funding legislation, as noted earlier, was to require an interim final program to be put in place by DOE before the end of 2008, which would essentially put the program on the same time track as required in the original EISA.[21]

RELATED INITIATIVES IN SUPPORT OF ADVANCED TECHNOLOGY VEHICLES

Over the past few decades, the federal government has undertaken several key initiatives to support the development and deployment of advanced technology vehicles, either through legislation or through executive action. These include federal R&D programs on new vehicles and tax incentives for the purchase of new vehicles and the installation of alternative fuel refueling infrastructure.

The Partnership for a New Generation of Vehicles (PNGV)

The Partnership for a New Generation of Vehicles (PNGV) was a cooperative research initiative between the Clinton Administration and the Detroit 3.[22] It was financed by private contributions and the re-channeling of research funds for ongoing federal programs. The goals of the initiative were to improve domestic manufacturing capabilities and to develop prototypes of a mid-sized family car with three times the fuel economy of a comparable 1994 model. All three manufacturers developed concept cars, but there were problems with the development of production prototypes. Questions have been raised about the success of the initiative, especially since there was no requirement for automakers to actually produce the new vehicles. Further, since that time the Detroit 3's sales of advanced vehicles, particularly hybrid-electric vehicles, have lagged those of Honda and Toyota. In 2002, the George W. Bush Administration replaced the PNGV initiative with a new initiative focused largely on fuel cell vehicles.

FreedomCAR and the President's Hydrogen Fuel Initiative

In 2002, President George W. Bush announced the Freedom Cooperative Automotive Research (FreedomCAR) initiative to replace the earlier PNGV initiative, and to promote cooperative research between the federal government and the Detroit 3 on the development of fuel cell vehicles. In 2003, the Bush Administration announced the President's Hydrogen Fuel Initiative, aimed at reducing the costs of producing hydrogen fuel for transportation and stationary applications.[23] These two initiatives refocused federal vehicles and fuel research funding — mainly DOE funding — on the development of fuel cell vehicles and hydrogen for transportation applications. However, funding for hybrids and other advanced vehicles was not entirely eliminated, and that research is ongoing. These two initiatives aim to make hydrogen fuel competitive with gasoline and to bring down the cost of fuel cell vehicles, which are currently prohibitively expensive. From FY2003 through FY2008, DOE has spent nearly $2 billion on these initiatives.

Tax Incentives for New Vehicles and Alternative Fuel Infrastructure

The Energy Policy Act of 2005 (P.L. 109-58) established tax credits for the purchase of new alternative fuel and advanced technology vehicles. Eligible vehicles include hybrids, advanced lean-burn (diesel) vehicles, fuel cell vehicles, and alternative fuel vehicles including natural gas vehicles.[24] Tax credits may vary depending on the type of technology, the vehicle's fuel economy, and the weight of the vehicle. For example, light-duty hybrid vehicles can qualify for a tax credit of up to $3,400, while a heavy-duty hybrid could qualify for a credit of as much as $15,000.[25]

The Emergency Economic Stabilization Act (EESA, P.L. 110-343) expanded these tax credits to include plug-in vehicles, with credits of up to $7,500 for light- duty vehicles and up to $15,000 for heavy-duty vehicles.[26] According to an analysis in the *Detroit News*, the Chevrolet Volt plug-in electric vehicle being developed by GM would qualify for the maximum $7,500 tax credit.[27] The tax credit may be critical to GM marketing plans for the Volt, as its selling price may have to be as high as $40,000 — and analysts were unsure whether many could be sold at such an elevated price. The tax credit could serve to bring the vehicle down into a more affordable range.

EPAct 2005 also established a tax credit for the installation of alternative fuel infrastructure, including credits of up to $30,000 for retail infrastructure and up to $1,000 for residential installations.[28] Eligible fuels included biodiesel, ethanol, hydrogen, liquefied petroleum gas (LPG), and natural gas. EESA extended these credits through the end of 2010, and expanded them to include systems to recharge electric vehicles.[29]

Proposed Grant Program in the Enhanced Energy Security Act of 2006

The specific parameters, definitions, and restrictions that govern the direct loan program, as it was authorized in December 2007, are generally derived from an earlier piece of legislation in the 109th Congress, the Enhanced Energy Security Act of 2006 (S. 2747). This was introduced on May 4, 2006, by Senator Jeff Bingaman; the bill eventually attracted 12 cosponsors. It was a broad-based bill aimed at an overall reduction of U.S. energy dependence on foreign oil imports. The bill included §208, "Deployment of New Technologies to Reduce Oil Use in Transportation."

Subsection (b) of S. 2747 would have established an "Advanced Technology Vehicles Manufacturing Incentive Program," that has features similar or identical to §136 of P.L. 110-140. Besides the identical title, these features include:

- A grant program to pay motor vehicle manufacturers and component suppliers "not more than 30% of the cost of reequipping or expanding an existing manufacturing facility in the United States to produce qualifying" advanced technology vehicles or components, and "engineering integration" to accomplish such purpose;
- Part of the definition of "advanced technology vehicle," namely the requirements that a qualifying vehicle must meet current and future EPA emission standards, and must have "at least 125% of the base year fuel economy for its weight class;"

- Production of components may be qualified if they are "specially designed for advanced technology vehicles," and "installed for the purpose of meeting the performance requirements ...;"
- An "improvement" provision to insure that, for an automobile manufacturer to receive an award, its average fuel economy for the most recent data year are no less than its average for MY2002.

While some other qualifying provisions in S. 2747 were subsequently dropped, notably a restriction to limit eligible vehicles to "hybrid" or "advanced lean burn technology" modes, and some were further modified, this is essentially the grant program that was carried forward as §136 of P.L. 110-140 in the 110th Congress.

ADVANCED TECHNOLOGY VEHICLE LOAN AND GRANT PROGRAMS IN EISA

Establishment of a Direct Loan Program

The direct loan program enacted in EISA was based on a grant program originally proposed in S. 2747 in the 109th Congress.[30] (note above). S. 2747 provided the framework for §136 of the law approved in December 2007.

Direct Loan Program

Subsection (d) authorizes DOE to establish, "not later than 1 year after the date of enactment" a "program to provide a total of not more than $25,000,000,000 in loans to eligible individuals and entities ... for the costs and activities described" elsewhere in the section. DOE is required also to set the specific standards for eligibility, under the terms of the definitions and requirements of § 136. Further provisions of the subsection set forth rules for labor compensation on construction projects, financial viability of loan recipients, and repayment periods. On this last issue, subsection (d) provides that loan repayment could be stretched out for the "projected life ... of the eligible project," or a maximum of 25 years. It further stipulates that the initial repayment of loans can be deferred up to five years after projects begin operations. Facilities, equipment, and "engineering integration" covered by these loans must be completed and in service no later than the end of 2020.

In selecting an eligible project, DOE must require that the project is "financially viable without the receipt of additional Federal funding" (subsection (d)(3)(A)). In an earlier program, the Emergency Steel Loan Guarantee program, which was designed as an economic assistance program for that industry, many companies were unable to use the benefits, because they could not meet a financial viability test. There were efforts to modify the conditions through legislation, but they did not succeed.[31] DOE is required in this law to establish these and other eligibility criteria.

Loans May Cover Full Costs of Project[32]

Because the direct loan program was inserted into a section of EISA originally intended to include only the grant program, there is some confusion resulting from the cross-references within § 136. Most notably, this confusion has occurred over whether or not loans are for full costs of projects, or whether they are limited to 30% of project costs. This is because subsection (d)(1) defines the loans to cover the "costs of activities described in subsection (b)." The introduction to subsection (b) states that DOE "shall provide facility funding *awards* [emphasis added] under this section to [recipients] to pay not more than 30% of the cost ..." However, subsection (d) only refers back to the earlier subsection for the purpose of using the same description of eligible projects (subsection (b)(1-2)). Senator Bingaman made this clear on the floor, in discussing the subsequent appropriations provision:

> ... I have been told that there may be some confusion about the terms of the loans as the provision creating the loan program references the "activities" that are the subject of a grant program also authorized in the same section of EISA. The grant program is limited to 30 percent of the costs of a facility. This is a fairly typical cost share for grant programs. Some have raised the question as to whether this 30 percent cap should also apply to the loan program. That is not the way I read the language of the law and was certainly not our intent in writing the provision. Moreover, I would argue that it would dramatically limit the effectiveness of the program as it would require companies to go to tight credit markets for 70 percent of their financing, precisely the problem we were seeking to remedy with the creation of the loan program.[33]

Subsequent joint and separate references to loans and grants ("awards") in subsections (e) through (h) of § 136 further make it clear that they are to be considered separately — sometimes the same rules apply to both, and sometimes they do not.

Priority for Older Plants and Definition of an Eligible Facility

Congress added at subsection (g) of 136 of EISA a provision ordering DOE to give "priority to those facilities that are oldest or have been in existence for at least 20 years. Such facilities can currently be sitting idle." This provision has been described as an indirect way of requiring that loans be reserved for union-organized automakers. As the *Wall Street Journal* wrote in a critical editorial:

> We're told the low-interest loan proposal would give priority to the "oldest" plants — which is another way of saying those plants organized by the United Auto Workers.[34]

There are two important qualifications that should be stated about this provision, however. First, subsection (g) applies only to DOE "in making awards or loans to those manufacturers that have existing facilities...." This is an important qualification, because subsection (b)(1), in defining eligible activities, includes "reequipping, expanding, or *establishing* [emphasis added] a manufacturing facility...." A facility to be established cannot, by definition, be 20 years old. Furthermore, subsection (g) only requires a priority, not an absolute limitation or prohibition based on the age of factories. Finally, as a matter of factual accuracy, Honda, Nissan, and Toyota all have plants operating in the United States, not organized by the UAW, which are more than 20 years old.[35]

Defining Advanced Technology Vehicles and Components

As opposed to the earlier model for a grant program in S. 2747, the definition of a "qualified" advanced technology vehicle has been loosened. As noted above, the earlier bill was directed to hybrid or "advanced lean burn" technologies. This prescription has been removed from the legislation entirely. Subsection (a)(1) establishes only three conditions for determining what is "advanced technology." Two of the conditions relate to compliance with present and future EPA emissions rules.

Thus, the critical condition is the third one, set in (a)(1)(C). It requires that qualified vehicles must achieve 25% more fuel economy than the average "base year combined fuel economy for vehicles with substantially similar attributes." The law does not specify how the "base year" is determined when an application is made, and whether DOE should use the size-based "attribute" classes that have been established for fuel economy standards by NHTSA, or devise some other method. Nor does the law specify that the subject project alone should be responsible for the 25% gain over the class average, only that the resulting vehicle be 25% above average. "Combined fuel economy" is already established under statutory law, with an additional qualification for "plug-in" electric vehicles (subsection (a)(2)).

Subsections (a) and (b) together clarify that suppliers may be recipients of direct loans. "Activities" eligible for direct loans in subsection (b)(1)(B) include production of "qualifying components." By subsection (a)(4)(A-B), DOE is directed to insure that such components are "designed for advanced technology vehicles ... and installed for the purpose of meeting [their] performance requirements...." How that is to be determined is left to regulation.

Requirement for Improvement

Subsection (e) establishes a standard for improving fuel economy that would apply broadly in determining the eligibility of companies receiving either loans or grants. A manufacturer's fleet must show improvement in its adjusted average fuel economy in the latest year for which data are available over that manufacturer's average for all light-duty vehicles in MY2005. This is an anti-backsliding provision, which prevents a manufacturer from building a fleet that is less fuel-efficient overall, but nevertheless being able to "cherry pick" a low-interest federal loan for a specific product or project.

Small Manufacturers Set-Aside Does Not Apply to Loans

Subsection (h) establishes a set-aside for vehicle or component manufacturers that employ less than 500 people. However, this provision applies only to 10% of the awards made under the grant program, which is so far unfunded. The limitation does not apply to the direct loan program established in subsection (d).

Funding the Direct Loan Program

After the direct loans provision became law as part of EISA, Congress was still required to budget funding for the program. For a loan program, budget rules require funding of the "subsidy cost," that is, the difference estimated by the Congressional Budget Office (CBO) between the interest rate available in the financial market and the interest rate charged by the

Federal Government to the borrower. Another interpretation of this gap is the likelihood of default, as the market rate builds in an assumption of risk.

During the congressional debates and discussions on EISA, an informal estimate of $3.75 billion was used for the subsidy cost, but no formal CBO estimate was ever provided, because no budgetary outlay was required for the direct loan authorization. When Members called for funding of the program to be included in an appropriations package toward the end of the Second Session of the 110th Congress, this was the amount they referenced.[36]

Funding for the direct loan provision in subsection 136(d) of EISA was included as §129 of Division A in the Consolidated Security, Disaster Assistance, and Continuing Appropriations Act of 2009 that was approved by both houses of Congress in September 2008. It was signed into law by President Bush on September 30, 2008, as P.L.110-329.

Because market conditions had become parlous for the Detroit 3 companies in the intervening months after the passage of EISA, CBO now scored the subsidy cost of the loan program at $7.5 billion, reflecting market estimates of a 30% chance of industry defaulting on the loans. A further $10 million was added to the budget outlay to cover administrative expenses (subsection (a)).

The only substantive change to the program was the requirement in subsection 129(c) that DOE issue an "interim final rule" within 60 days of the enactment of the Continuing Appropriations Resolution. The same subsection also amended EISA to mandate that a program administrator be hired, at a salary grade not to exceed the GS- 15 on the government pay scale. On October 24, 2008, the *Detroit News* reported that the Bush Administration had appointed Lachlan Seward, a senior Treasury Department official, who had experience in the 1980 Chrysler loan guarantee program and in a loan guarantee program for U.S. airlines following the 2001 terrorist attacks, to manage the loan program.[37]

Using Federal Loan Programs to Assist in Auto Industry Restructuring

The timing and availability of loans to the U.S. automotive industry have become major issues. The intent of Congress in approving a direct loan program in EISA in December 2007 was to assist in the development of "advanced technology" programs with the goal of improving U.S. fuel economy. But the availability of $25 billion in low-interest loans has made the program a key potential source of federal funding for the Detroit 3 for the broader purpose of saving one or more companies from bankruptcy.

Even before the appropriation for the EISA loans was approved, an issue developed over how quickly loans could be disbursed to the beleaguered auto industry. Having failed to increase or broaden the purposes of the loan program during the appropriation process, the Detroit 3 and their congressional supporters were stunned to learn that there could be considerable delays in disbursement of loans. In response to an inquiry from House Energy and Commerce Committee Chair John Dingell, Secretary of Energy Samuel W. Bodman wrote:

> In light of the legal and administrative requirements with which [DOE] must comply, we anticipate that it would take at least six to 18 months or more, after necessary funds are appropriated, before any section 136 loans could be issued and funds disbursed.[38]

In his letter, Bodman cited a number of statutory requirements, which Congress had not waived, as constraining DOE from rapid approval of loans and disbursement of funds. These included a need to allow a public comment period, a requirement to lay program rules before Congress for at least 60 days under the terms of the Congressional Review Act,[39] assessment of projects under the National Environmental Policy Act,[40] and financial review of projects with the Office of Management and Budget.[41] After Senator Debbie Stabenow of Michigan had stated that the auto industry could receive loans by the end of the year, a DOE spokeswoman said, "We have significant doubts about whether distribution of loans by January 2009 is realistic."[42]

Representative Dingell and other Members of Congress, particularly from auto industry states urged that DOE rethink its position and consider means of speeding up loan approvals. These responses included commitments from both the Republican and Democratic presidential candidates to seek to expedite loan approvals.[43] Later, Michigan Senator Carl Levin said that he might seek doubling the loan program to $50 billion as part of an economic stimulus plan Congress could consider after the November 2008 elections.[44]

By late October 2008, the EISA loans were being considered as part of a package of federal assistance, which could be used to aid the largest of the Detroit 3, GM, in a possible takeover of the smallest company in the group, Chrysler LLC. Chrysler's privately held majority owner, Cerberus Capital Management LP, was reportedly interested in exiting the automotive manufacturing business. Plans were reportedly being considered for GM to acquire the Chrysler operations and possibly trading to Cerberus its remaining minority stake in their jointly owned General Motors Acceptance Corporation. As both companies were experiencing declining cash balances and credit markets for auto industry loans remained closed, GM could need some type of capital infusion from public sources to complete the deal. The goal would be to salvage some parts of Chrysler's operations and brands, close down others, and achieve operational, production and management synergies. Although a DOE spokeswoman opined that federal aid in direct support of a merger "would be more appropriate for separate legislation," assistance from the direct loan program could be used to help the merged company develop competitive ongoing projects, such as the Chevrolet Volt plug-in hybrid, to comply with EISA fuel economy mandates, while other assistance would support company consolidation and restructuring.[45]

Through late October 2008 the EISA loans remained part — but only a part — of a GM-Cerberus plan for federal assistance in restructuring the Detroit 3. When the EISA itself was passed — and possibly as late as the congressional approval of appropriations in September 2008 — loans to enhance production of advanced technology vehicles and components were not considered in the context of a major industry restructuring. This has now changed, not only with the widely discussed possibility of a GM-Chrysler merger,[46] but also the crisis in financial markets linked to subprime lending — which may include consumer auto loans. A package for the Detroit 3 — including Ford as well as the GM-Chrysler combination — might also include financial assistance for General Motors Acceptance Corporation, as well as Ford Motor Credit and Chrysler Financial. Such assistance may depend on those operations becoming qualified as banks under the terms of the Troubled Assets Relief Program established under the Emergency Economic Stabilization Act of 2008 (EESA, P.L. 110-343).[47] Some estimates are that GM would need at least $10 billion from outside sources not currently available, in order to undertake a merger with Chrysler and a rationalization of operations. This could require some funds through EISA, recapitalization of credit operations through EESA, and even beyond these existing instruments, direct federal financial support for the transaction.[48]

DOE's Interim Final Rule Implementing the Program

On November 5, 2008, DOE announced an interim final rule to implement the loan program. This is despite previous comments by Secretary Bodman that a quick turnaround on the rulemaking process was unlikely.[49] Apparently, many of the Secretary's concerns have been addressed, including review under the National Environmental Policy Act (NEPA). The interim final rule will be effective on the date it is published in the *Federal Register*, and there will be a 30-day period for public comment.

Schedule for Comment, Application, Approval, and Repayment

DOE has provided for a comment period of 30 days after publication in the *Federal Register* for public comments on the rule. While this is shorter than the comment period for most major rulemakings, it is consistent with DOE's belief that Congress wanted the Department to act as quickly as possible to implement the program.

In the interim final rule, DOE will award loans in tranches, with applications for each tranche evaluated every 90 days, as long as loan authority remains. However, the language in the Summary, Introduction and Background, and Application Submission sections of the Supplementary Information on the rulemaking is contradictory. In some places, it states that the deadline for loan applications for the first tranche is December 31, 2008; in others, the deadline is defined as the effective date of the interim rule (i.e. the date it is published in the *Federal Register*). There is no apparent reference to this deadline in the amendments to the *Code of Federal Regulations* (CFR) at the end of the rulemaking document. In a fact sheet on the rule published by DOE's Office of Public Affairs, DOE states that the deadline is December 31, 200 8.[50] Presumably, that was DOE's intent, despite the conflicting language in the rulemaking.

After applications are received, DOE will evaluate those applications and will approve and close on loans from each tranche before considering applications from the next tranche. However, DOE gave no specific time frame for the evaluation and approval process for the loans, and states that "DOE may make decisions on such applications and close loans with respect to such applications at any time."[51]

Once a loan has been closed, it must be fully repaid within 25 years, or if the facility subject to the loan is closed before that, the date of closure. Borrowers may have up to five years after the facility begins operation to begin payment of the principal; interest payments may not be deferred.

Key Project Requirements

For each project, EISA requires that the new vehicle achieve at least 25% higher fuel economy than the average "in the base year" of "vehicles with substantially similar attributes." However, the statute defined neither "base year," nor "substantially similar attributes." For the base year, DOE determined that for all applications, the base year would be Model Year 2005, because this is one of the most recent years for which CAFE compliance data are available. Further, under EISA, this is also the model year on which automaker eligibility is predicated; to be eligible to submit an application under the program, an automaker must have a CAFE average in its most recent model year equal to or higher than its average in 2005.

For the criterion of "substantially similar attributes," DOE devised a system that includes the vehicle's size or weight class, and its performance. For passenger cars, size classes include two-seaters, subcompact, compact, mid-size, and large sedans, and small, mid-size, and large wagons. Truck classes are based on function and weight, and include small and standard pickups, passenger, cargo, and mini-vans, and sport utility vehicles (SUVs). Further, most passenger cars are divided into standard and "performance" vehicles, with different average fuel economy ratings. DOE's rationale for separating out performance cars is that they are substantially different from non-performance vehicles:

> Performance vehicles generally have lower fuel economy ratings than non-performance vehicles in the same EPA class. Also, different fuel economy technologies may be applicable to performance as opposed to non-performance vehicles (i.e., additional aerodynamic improvements may not be available for performance vehicles).[52]

In determining which vehicles were standard or performance vehicles, DOE plotted the ratio of peak horsepower to curb weight for each vehicle. In cases where vehicles in the same size class had significant differences in power-to-weight ratio, DOE identified break points for each class, with vehicles above that break point considered as performance vehicles. In its determination, DOE separated most car classes — and no truck classes — into standard and performance.

From Model Year 2005 data for vehicle attributes and CAFE ratings, DOE developed a table of average fuel economy by class and target fuel economy under the program (See **Table 2**).

Selection Criteria for Loan Program — Financial Solvency

In evaluating loan applications, DOE has identified four key criteria: the technical merit of the vehicles (or components), program factors such as economic development and geographic diversity, the risk of the loan, and priority for existing facilities 20 years old or older:

> (b) Evaluation criteria. Applications that are determined to be eligible pursuant to paragraph (a) of this section shall be subject to a substantive review by DOE based upon factors that include, but are not limited to, the following:

(1) The technical merit of the proposed advanced technology vehicles or qualifying components, with greater weight given for factors including, but not limited to:

(i) Improved vehicle fuel economy above that required for an advanced technology vehicle;

(ii) Potential contributions to improved fuel economy of the U.S. light-duty vehicle fleet;

(iii) Likely reductions in petroleum use by the U.S. light-duty fleet; and

(iv) Promotion of use of advanced fuel (e.g., E-85, ultra-low sulfur diesel).

(2) Technical Program Factors such as economic development and diversity in technology, company, risk, and geographic location.

(3) The adequacy of the proposed provisions to protect the Government, including sufficiency of Security, the priority of the lien position in the Security, and the percentage of the project to be financed with the loan.

(4) In making loans to those manufacturers that have existing facilities, priority will be given to those facilities that are oldest or have been in existence for at least 20 years even if such facilities are idle at the time of application.[53]

Among other considerations, the interim final rule requires that DOE consider "financial projections demonstrating the applicant's solvency through the period of time that the loan is outstanding."Also for a manufacturer to be eligible, EISA requires that the recipient "financially viable without the receipt of additional Federal funding associated with the proposed project."[54] In interpreting this statutory language, DOE may have made it more difficult for automakers to take advantage of the loan program and any other future support for the auto industry:

Table 2. Fuel Economy Averages and Program Requirements by Vehicle Class

Vehicle Class	Power / Weight	2005 Fuel Economy Average	2005 mpg x 125%
Two-Seater	< 0.121	25.3	31.6
Two-Seater Performance	≥ 0.121	22.2	27.8
Minicompact Sedan	< 0.088	29.3	36.7
Minicompact Performance Sedan	≥ 0.088	22.4	28.0
Subcompact Sedan	< 0.082	29.6	37.0
Subcompact Performance Sedan	≥ 0.082	22.8	28.5
Compact Sedan	< 0.073	33.8	42.2
Compact Performance Sedan	≥ 0.073	23.6	29.5
Mid-Size Sedan	< 0.085	29.4	36.7
Mid-Size Performance Sedan	≥ 0.085	23.1	28.9
Large Sedan	n/a	26.2	32.7
Small Wagon	n/a	32.7	40.8
Mid-Size and Large Wagons	n/a	26.7	33.4
Small and Standard Pickups	n/a	19.7	24.6
Minivan	n/a	24.3	30.4
Passenger Van	n/a	19.0	23.8
Cargo Van	n/a	24.2	30.2
Sport Utility Vehicle	n/a	21.8	27.2

Source: U.S. Department of Energy, *Advanced Technology Vehicles Manufacturing Incentive Program: Interim Final Rule; Request for Comment* (November 5, 2008), p. 27.

In today's interim final rule, the Department interprets the term "additional Federal funding" to mean any loan, grant, guarantee, insurance, payment, rebate, subsidy, credit, tax benefit, or any other form of direct or indirect assistance from the Federal government, or any agency or instrumentality thereof, other than the proceeds of a loan approved under section 136, that is, or is expected to be made available with respect to, the project or activities for which the loan is sought under section 136, and is to be received by the applicant after entering into an Agreement with DOE.[55]

As part of this determination, for a loan, an applicant must demonstrate "a net present value which is positive, taking all costs, existing and future, into account."

Because of the auto industry's current challenges, some automakers may be unable to demonstrate to DOE their solvency and the viability of fuel economy improvement projects. These financial solvency and viability requirements may prove to be a significant barrier to the approval of loan applications.

End Notes

[1] Quoted from P.L. 110-329 §129(c)(2).

[2] U.S. Department of Energy, *Advanced Technology Vehicles Manufacturing Incentive Program: Interim Final Rule; Request for Comment* (November 5, 2008).

[3] *Washington Post* (October 22, 2008), p. A1.

[4] P.L. 110-140 §101.

[5] P.L. 110-140 § 102(b)(2)(A-B). The revised CAFE standards and the debate on the legislation are summarized in CRS Report RL33413, *Automobile and Light Truck Fuel Economy: The CAFE Standards*, by Brent D. Yacobucci and Robert Bamberger. See also CRS Report RL34297, *Motor Vehicle Manufacturing Employment: National and State Trends and Issues*, by Stephen Cooney, pp. 33-34.

[6] *Detroit News*, " Fuel Plan Would Cost Big Three" (March 1, 2007).

[7] National Highway Traffic Safety Administration (NHTSA), *Preliminary Regulatory Impact Analysis: Corporate Average Fuel Economy for MY2011-2015 Passenger Cars and Light Trucks* (April 2008).

[8] These issues have been extensively explored elsewhere by CRS. See the following reports: CRS Report RL34297, *Motor Vehicle Manufacturing Employment: National and State Trends and Issues*, by Stephen Cooney; CRS Report RL32883, *U.S. Automotive Industry: Policy Overview and Recent History*, by Stephen Cooney and Brent D. Yacobucci; and CRS Report RL33 169, *Comparing Automotive and Steel Industry Legacy Costs*, by Stephen Cooney.

[9] Two illustrative anecdotes: Toyota, widely acknowledged as an efficiency leader in automotive manufacturing, budgeted $850 million to build a new, greenfield truck plant in San Antonio, TX; final cost — more than $1.2 billion. Ford shut down two plants in New Jersey and consolidated truck manufacturing on the East Coast in Norfolk, VA, where they invested $350 million in revamping an existing plant. Two years later, they decided to close it down. By comparison, the highest ever annual fine ever paid by a company for failing to meet CAFE standards was $30 million, and the total of such fines for 2006 was less than $50 million (see *Green Car Advisor*, based on NHTSA data release, January 3, 2008). Even if $50 million was collected from CAFE penalties each year for ten years, the total amount would still only represent about 2% of the $25 billion authorized for the Section 136 loan program.

[10] CRS Report RL32883, esp. Figure 9 and Table 3.

[11] For the third quarter, the annual rate of sales was even lower, and, owing to lower-thanaverage income and credit ratings among their customers, Detroit 3 companies only commanded 42% of the domestic retail market; *Detroit Free Press*, "Credit Crunch Hits Buyers of Detroit 3" (October 26, 2008).

[12] *Detroit Free Press*, "Vehicle Transaction Prices Continue Falling" (October 28, 2008).

[13] On recent trends, see CRS Report RL34625, *Gasoline and Oil Prices,* by Robert Pirog.

[14] EPA's numbers, which are used on the window stickers of new cars and trucks, are downgraded from the CAFE test to better reflect in-use fuel economy. For example, the CAFE test is limited to 55 miles per hour, and does not include the use of air conditioning or other accessories.

[15] This included Chrysler, which had become newly independent from German parent Daimler after Cerberus, a hedge fund, bought an 80% share of the company.

[16] These agreements are described in CRS Report RL34297, pp. 25-32.

[17] GM quarterly reports on *Mergent.com*. The total annual loss in 2007 was reported as $39 billion, but this was primarily caused by a writedown of unuseable tax credits because of continuing losses going forward.

[18] Ford data on *ibid*. Chrysler LLC, as a private company, does not report its losses publicly. However, following public reports by Daimler AG on losses in its remaining minority stake, Chrysler has confirmed at least $1.1 billion in losses through the first half of 2008; *Detroit Free Press*, "Chrysler Announces Cuts, Explains Loss" (October 23, 2008).

[19] *Bloomberg.com*, "GM, Ford Seek $50 Billion in U.S. Loans, Doubling First Request" (August 22, 2008); *Detroit News*, "Big 3 Seek $50B in Fed Loans" (August 23, 2008); *Detroit Free Press*, "Auto Industry to Blitz for Aid" (August 23, 2008).

[20] Justin Hyde in *ibid*.

[21] EISA, signed into law on December 19, 2007, requires in § 136(d)(1) that "Not later than 1 year after the date of enactment of this Act, the Secretary [of Energy] shall carry out a program to provide not more than $25,000,000,000 in loans...."

[22] For more information on PNGV, see CRS Report RS20852, *The Partnership for a New Generation of Vehicles: Status and Issues*, by Brent D. Yacobucci.

[23] For more information on these initiatives, see CRS Report RS2 1442, *Hydrogen and Fuel Cell Vehicle R&D: FreedomCAR and the President's Hydrogen Fuel Initiative*.

[24] P.L. 110-58, §1341.

[25] For more information see CRS Report RS22558, *Tax Credits for Hybrid Vehicles*, by Salvatore Lazzari; and CRS Report RS22351, *Tax Incentives for Alternative Fuel and Advanced Technology Vehicles*, by Brent D. Yacobucci.

[26] P.L. 110-343, Division B, §205.

[27] *Detroit News*, "Bill Adds Plug-In Tax Breaks" (October 2, 2008).

[28] P.L. 110-58, §1342.

[29] P.L. 110-343, Division B, §207.

[30] Senator Bingaman, who had been Ranking Member of the Energy and Natural Resources Committee in the earlier Congress, chaired the committee after the change in party control

[31] CRS Report RL3 1792, *Steel: Legislative and Oversight Issues*, by Stephen Cooney, pp. 20-22.

[32] In the interim final rule, DOE will limit the loan amount to "no more than 80 percent of reasonably anticipated total Project Costs."

[33] *Congressional Record* (September 27, 2008), S9958.

[34] *Wall St. Journal*, "The Next Bailout: Detroit" (August 21, 2008), p. A14.

[35] It is not clear what strategy foreign-owned manufacturers will take with regard to the § 136 direct loans. Honda CEO Takeo Fukui has said, in support of the program, "I think it's only natural that the U.S. government tries to provide some support to U.S. manufacturers," but that his company would not apply for the loans; *Automotive News*, "Honda's Fukui Favors Fed Loans, Confirms V-8" (October 20, 2008), p. 4. Auto manufacturers in Europe, in response to the U.S. direct loan program and proposed stringent new European emissions standards, have called for the European Union and national governments to support an even larger program there; *Detroit News*, "Euro Carmakers Seek $54.5B in Aid" (October 8, 2008).

[36] Letter from Sens. Debbie Stabenow, Carl Levin, and Sherrod Brown to Majority Leader Harry Reid and Appropriations Committee Chair Robert C. Byrd (July 15, 2008); *Detroit Free Press*, "Low-Interest Loan Plan for Carmakers Sparks Petition in U.S. House" (July 25, 2008).

[37] *Detroit News*, "Veteran Will Head Auto Loan Program" (October 24, 2008).

[38] Letter from Secretary of Energy Bodman to Chairman Dingell (September 24, 2008), p. 2.

[39] Codified at 5 U.S.C. §§801-808; see CRS Report RL301 16, *Congressional Review of Agency Rulemaking*, by Morton Rosenberg, esp. pp. 2-4.

[40] Codified at 42 U.S.C. §§4321 *et seq*. For a review, see CRS Report RS20621, *Overview of National Environmental Policy Act (NEPA) Requirements*, by Kristina Alexander.

[41] *Ibid*.

[42] *Detroit News*, "Government May Delay Auto Money" (September 26, 2008).

[43] *Detroit Free Press*, "Auto Industry Loans May Take Up to 18 Months" (September 26, 2008); *Detroit News*, "Big 3 Aid May Take Time" (September 27, 2008).

[44] *Ibid*. "Levin to Seek $25B More for Auto Industry" (October 17, 2008).

[45] DOE quote from *Bloomberg.com*, "GM Said to Seek Treasury Aid in Chrysler Merger Talks" (Oct 27, 2008). On federal assistance to the industry and the ongoing GM-Chrysler merger issue, see *Detroit News*, "Levin: Fed Could Aid a Merger" (October 21, 2008); "Treasury Urged to Help Big 3" (October 23, 2008); and, "Feds Fast-Track Loan Plan for GM" (October 29, 2008); *Detroit Free Press*, "Free Up Auto Credit, Lawmakers Say" (October 23, 2008); *Wall St. Journal*, "Bankruptcy Fears Rise as Chrysler, GM Seek Federal Aid" (October 27, 2008), p. A1; and, "U.S. Working on Billions in GM Loans" (October 28, 2008), p. B1; *New York Times*, "White House Explores Aid for Auto Deal" (October 28, 2008), p. A1.

[46] Recent press reports indicate that this merger may be less likely than originally thought. *The New York Times*, "G.M. Suspends Merger Talks With Chrysler" (November 7, 2008).

[47] A review of some of the issues raised by this legislation is CRS Report RS22963, *Financial Market Intervention*, by Edward V. Murphy and Baird Webel.

[48] In addition to the sources quoted above, see *Washington Post*, "Hurdles Emerge for GM, Chrysler" (October 30, 2008), p. D1.

[49] "Dingell-DOE Spat Points To Setbacks For Auto Loan Implementation," *Energy Washington Week* (October 1, 2008).

[50] U.S. Department of Energy, Office of Public Affairs, *Fact Sheet: Advanced Technology Vehicles Manufacturing Loan Program* (November 6, 2008).

[51] U.S. Department of Energy, *Advanced Technology Vehicles Manufacturing Incentive Program: Interim Final Rule; Request for Comment* (November 5, 2008), p. 34.

[52] Ibid. p. 24.

[53] Ibid. pp. 54-55.

[54] P.L. 110-58, Section 136(d)(3)(A).

[55] DOE, op. cit. p. 15.

In: The U.S. Auto Industry and the Role of Federal Assistance   ISBN: 978-1-60741-322-6
Editor: James R. Elliot   © 2010 Nova Science Publishers, Inc.

Chapter 3

MOTOR VEHICLE MANUFACTURING EMPLOYMENT: NATIONAL AND STATE TRENDS AND ISSUES

Stephen Cooney

SUMMARY

The U.S. motor vehicle manufacturing industry employs about 1 million workers, or about 7.5% of the entire U.S. manufacturing workforce, including those who work in manufacturing parts and bodies, as well as those who assemble motor vehicles. Since 2000, the industry has eliminated about 300,000 manufacturing jobs, but the employment level is still almost as high as in 1990. By comparison, manufacturing in general has suffered a much higher rate of job loss.

The Detroit-based U.S.-owned manufacturers (General Motors, Ford, and Chrysler, collectively known as the "Big Three"), all of which are organized by the United Auto Workers union (UAW), have cut back domestic production by 3 million units since 2000, accounting for all the net employment losses. The shift in consumer preferences from trucks and SUVs to smaller vehicles has accelerated a loss of market share by the Big Three producers and gains for foreign-owned domestic manufacturers and imports. Big Three employment losses were partially offset by new investments by foreign-owned manufacturers in the United States. Today, companies owned by foreign investors produce 28% of all U.S.-made light motor vehicles, up from 11% in 1990.

The patterns of job loss and creation have not been evenly distributed around the country. Forty-four percent of all persons in the industry work in a "heartland auto belt" of three states, Michigan, Ohio, and Indiana, each of which has more than 100,000 persons in the industry. Michigan alone has accounted for more than a third of the net job loss in the industry since 2000. Losses in Ohio and Indiana have been less severe, offset somewhat by foreign investment. Alabama has been the big recent job gainer, adding 15,000 jobs since 2000. Tennessee and Kentucky, now the fourth and fifth largest producing states, have added the most jobs since 1990, and South Carolina has also seen a big net gain. These jobs, mostly non-union, have stretched the "auto belt" more to the South.

New fuel economy standards for automobiles and light trucks, as approved by Congress and signed into law (P.L. 110-140), may encourage greater development of small, fuel efficient cars, but the number of such U.S. plants, even for foreign- owned companies, has declined in recent years. S. 2191, approved at committee level in the Senate in December 2007, would use funds from the auction of emission allowances to support domestic manufacture of fuel-efficient vehicles and components. Congress may also consider the proposed Korea-U.S. Free Trade Agreement, which addresses the current imbalance in automotive trade. The Employee Free Choice Act (H.R. 800), approved by the House, but on which a cloture vote failed in the Senate, could help the UAW organize foreign-owned companies.

In seeking to improve the competitiveness of Big Three assembly operations against both non-union domestic producers and imports, the UAW and the Big Three in 2007 negotiated new contract bargaining agreements. The deals addressed health care costs, wage levels, and other issues.

INTRODUCTION[1]

The 110th Congress is addressing many issues that could have a major impact on the U.S. motor vehicle manufacturing industry. This includes adopting new fuel economy standards for automobiles and light trucks (P.L. 110-140), plus consideration of legislation that may be used to help promote the manufacturing of future generations of fuel-efficient vehicles (S. 2191). Also, it includes the proposed Korea-U.S. Free Trade Agreement, because Korea is a major supplier of cars and trucks to the U.S. market. In the field of industrial relations, the Employee Free Choice Act (H.R. 800), approved by the House, but on which a cloture vote failed in the Senate, could be significant in an industry in which all assembly plants owned by U.S. domestic corporations are union-organized, while virtually none operated by foreign-owned companies are.[2]

Any legislative action by Congress that affects U.S. motor vehicle production and sales will have a major impact on U.S. manufacturing employment. The share of U.S. manufacturing employment directly employed in manufacturing motor vehicles and parts in 2006 was 7.5%, or about 1 million workers.[3] There are also many industries whose output is sold in large measure to the automotive industry. For example, 14% of the output of the U.S. steel industry in 2006 was shipped to the motor vehicle industry, which is the second-largest sectoral user.[4]

Within Congress and throughout the country, there have been many concerns expressed about lost jobs in the automotive industry. Indeed, according to the U.S. Labor Department's Quarterly Census of Employment and Wages, automotive manufacturing employment declined by about a quarter between 2000 and 2006. However, over the longer term, automotive manufacturing employment has held up much better than overall manufacturing employment. While the United States has seen overall manufacturing employment decline by about 3.5 million jobs since 1990, employment in the auto industry declined only marginally over this longer period. But the Detroit-based "Big Three" U.S. auto manufacturers (General Motors, Ford, and Chrysler) are still in the middle of restructuring efforts, which could imply further employment reductions in the near future, and the total level of employment could decline further.

By contrast, employment has increased at foreign-owned motor vehicle assembly and parts plants. This change has offset at least partially the decline in employment at the Detroit Big Three and their suppliers. As foreign-owned manufacturers have increased U.S. motor vehicle sales, market share, production, and employment, the perception has grown that contract agreements that bind the domestically owned companies have been impediments to their competitiveness. In the autumn of 2007, the United Auto Workers[5] (UAW) union negotiated new collective bargaining agreements with each of the Detroit Big Three. These new agreements seek to reduce or remove the perceived structural issues in union contracts.

This leads to a further major aspect of the issue, which will be explored in this chapter. Changes in automotive employment have not been geographically balanced. The decline overall has had the strongest impact by far on Michigan, and to a lesser extent on Ohio and Indiana, the other two leading Midwest auto manufacturing states. Other states outside this region, such as New York, New Jersey, Maryland, Georgia, Virginia, and Oklahoma, have lost their Big Three assembly plants since 1990, but are generally less reliant on auto manufacturing employment. Meanwhile, foreign-owned nameplate manufacturers (original equipment manufacturers, or "OEMs" in the industry) have established new plants largely, though not exclusively, in the South during this period. As assembly plants tend to draw parts supply plants in their direction, there is evidence that what *Automotive News* labels the "new American manufacturers" have extended the traditional Midwest "Auto Belt" more into a corridor that includes the mid- South.[6]

This chapter looks at four sets of issues that have received attention in Congress or among the public more widely, with respect to employment in the U.S. motor manufacturing industry:

- *National employment trends.* Is there an employment crisis in the U.S. automotive manufacturing industry?

- *State and regional developments.* What is the impact of automotive manufacturing trends on states and regions? As Michigan has apparently borne the brunt of automotive employment cutbacks and by 2007 was suffering from the nation's highest unemployment rate, is this a "one-state recession," as some have said, or is the impact broader?

- *Fuel economy and small vehicle manufacturing.* In view of the congressional debate over fuel economy rules, where are smaller, fuel-efficient vehicles made in the United States, and who makes them?

- *New UAW labor contracts with the Detroit Big Three.* How do these new agreements address some of the competitiveness issues raised by the domestically owned industry?

- *Impact of federal legislative proposals.* Finally, and in conclusion, the report will briefly review the status of legislative issues that may have a major impact on U.S. automotive employment.

MOTOR VEHICLE MANUFACTURING JOBS: A NATIONAL CRISIS?

Is the national auto manufacturing base in a crisis? One answer might be in perceptions, but perceptions, especially in this case, shape reality. The reality is that many Americans identify American industrial competitiveness with the competitiveness in the marketplace and on the factory floor of the traditional Detroit- based Big Three.[7]

The economic health of the Big Three is not good. The public perception of this circumstance is influenced by a confluence of recent major developments:

- First, there were widely publicized bankruptcies and financial distress in the auto supplier sector associated with the Big Three. Notably, this included the largest industrial bankruptcy of all time, the declaration of Chapter 11 by Delphi Corporation, formerly the parts manufacturing arm of General Motors, in October 2005.

- Since 2005, the Big Three, including Chrysler, which for most of this period was a subsidiary of German-owned DaimlerChrysler AG, each have reported losses cumulating in the billions of dollars.

- Moreover, there have been widely reported "buyouts" by the Big Three of unionized production employees to get their contracts off the company books, and mid-contract "givebacks" on health care coverage requested by each of the Big Three (and negotiated by the UAW with Ford and GM, but denied to Chrysler).

- As oil has climbed near the $100-per-barrel level, as gasoline prices increased by 50% in an unstable global security environment, and as policy concerns with climate change issues increased, sales of pickup trucks and SUVs, the Big Three's most popular and profitable vehicles, stagnated or declined in 2006-2007. Congress approved in 2007, and the President signed into law, new fuel economy rules as part of P.L. 110-140, an energy legislation package, notwithstanding some concerns by the Big Three and the UAW that their employment levels could be hurt.[8] Although Toyota, for example, publicly sided with the Big Three position, the success of its Prius hybrid vehicle reinforced a public impression that the Japanese companies are the leaders in fuel economy.[9]

- Compounding the impression of Japanese technological leadership in fuel economy, Toyota is pressing GM for the overall global leadership in motor vehicle sales and production. It has also overtaken Ford, another U.S. industrial icon, for second place in domestic market share.[10]

On top of these adverse developments from the Big Three's perspective, the overall market, in terms of U.S. and North American sales, declined significantly in 2006 and 2007. Figures 1 and 2 illustrate how both sales and production have declined, affecting especially production at Big Three UAW-organized assembly plants.

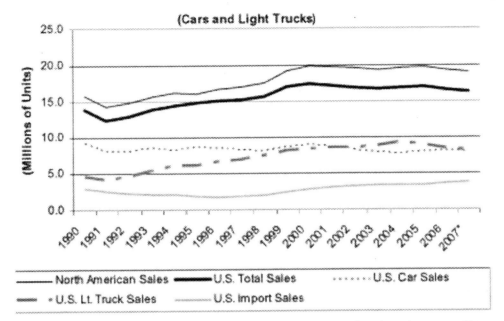

Sources: *Automotive News Market Data Books,* supplemented by 2007 *data from Automotive News and Ward's Motor Vehicle Facts & Figures* (2007) for U.S. imports.
*Annual rate (U.S., Canada - Jan. Oct.; Mexico - Jan.-Sept.).

Figure 1. Motor Vehicle Sales

Sales and Production Trends in the U.S. Market

U.S. Demand for Domestically Made Vehicles Declines — Trucks Worst Affected

Figure 1 illustrates sales of cars and light trucks in the North American and U.S. markets. It shows total North American sales, because the market has been fully integrated since NAFTA entered into effect since 1994, with both the domestic Big Three and their major foreign competitors having assembly operations in the United States, Canada, and Mexico. However, as U.S. sales alone have accounted for 85%-90% of sales throughout the period and because the U.S. UAW organizes only plants in the United States, both this figure and the one following focus primarily on U.S. sales and production, as the main North American trend driver.[11]

U.S. and North American sales generally follow the U.S. business cycle. Thus, U.S. sales fell from about 14 million cars and light trucks after the 1990 peak, to just over 12 million during the 1991 recession. They recovered slowly in the early 1 990s, reaching 15 million units in 1996 — then escalated to over 17 million units annually in 1999-2001. After the recession of that year, and fed by concerns about the economic impact of the "9/11" terror incidents, the Big Three led a wave of discounting and other sales measures to keep production levels up (such as GM's "Keep America Rolling" 0% interest sales campaign). Through 2005, domestic sales continued to average almost 17 million units per year. But with higher gasoline prices in 2006 and the housing slump of 2007, sales slipped to 16.6 million in the former year, and an annual rate closer to 16.0 million in 2007. Many forecasters question whether 2008 domestic U.S. sales will even reach that level.[12]

Perhaps more significant than total sales volume is the composition of sales. As shown in Figure 1, "light truck" sales were less than half car sales in the U.S. market in 1990 (4.6 million versus 9.3 million). But then the "minivan" (introduced by Chrysler in the mid-1980s) and the "sports utility vehicle" (SUV), pioneered by AMC 's Jeep, and popularized by the Ford Explorer, revolutionized the market in the 1990s. U.S. car sales have never regained the 1990 level, while light trucks overtook cars in sales volume in 2002, and by 2004 had opened a margin of 1.5 million units. (9.2 million to 7.7 million, for 54% of the market).

The importance for employment of this market shift is that while foreign-based competitors had even become dominant in some classes in the domestic car market, the Big Three, with their UAW-organized assembly plants, remained dominant in the light truck market. For example, an earlier CRS report showed that by 2003, about 75% of the light trucks sold were Big Three products, but less than half of all cars.[13] Truck-based vehicles had become the redoubt of the unionized, domestically owned motor industry.[14]

Thus, Big Three employment and production would be disproportionately and negatively affected not only by the total fall in sales (less than a million units between the 17 million total of 2005 and the annual rate of 16.3 million through October, 2007), but by the decline of trucks as a share of the total. From its peak of 9.2 million in 2004, truck sales declined by almost a million to 8.4 million units in 2006 and less in 2007. Car sales did not increase to make up for the loss, but they did increase somewhat — and cars remain the strongest suit of the foreign-based manufacturers.

Another trend illustrated in Figure 1 that has an adverse effect on Big Three employment is the recovery of imports. With the arrival of Japanese so-called "transplant" manufacturers in the 1980s, sales of vehicles imported from overseas declined from 3 million in 1990 to less than 2 million annually in 1995-1997.[15] Even as German and Korean manufacturers also established assembly plants in the United States, and the Japanese companies opened new plants, imports subsequently began to increase again. By 2001, the import level was again higher than 3 million units. By 2006, it reached 3.7 million, and the annual rate for 2007 was higher.[16] In 1996, 1.7 million imports represented just 11% of the U.S. domestic vehicle market of 15.1 million. Ten years later, the market was 1.5 million vehicles larger, but the import share was 3.7 million, or 23%. The U.S. market in 2006 for North American-produced vehicles was actually smaller than in 1996.

Big Three UAW Plants Suffer Largest Production Cuts

Figure 2 illustrates the impact of the market changes on U.S. Big Three and foreign OEM manufacturers' output totals. Total U.S. motor vehicle production (excluding other North American production, regardless of ownership) stood at less than 10 million units at the beginning of the 1990s.[17] However, of this output in 1990, 89% was produced by the Detroit Big Three — 8.1 million units directly, and another half- million in three joint venture plants operated by Japanese-owned firms in association with the Big Three, and also organized by the UAW.[18] About 1 million units in that year were produced by foreign OEMs in the United States. All were Japanese- owned, Volkswagen having closed its plant in Pennsylvania, and Hyundai's North American plant at that time located in Quebec.

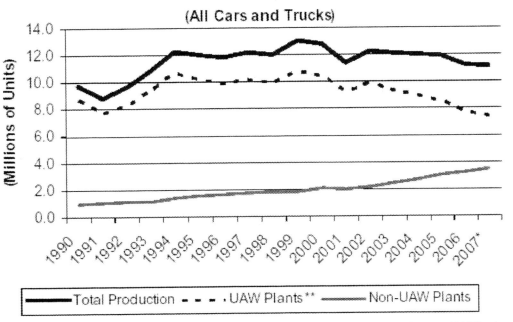

(All Cars and Trucks)

— Total Production   - - - · UAW Plants**   ——— Non-UAW Plants

Sources: Total U.S. production, 1990-2006 from *Ward's Motor Vehicle Facts & Figures* (2007);other
data through 2006 from *Ward's Automotive Yearbooks.*
* Annual rate (U.S., Canada — January-October; Mexico — January-September).
** UAW total includes all assembly plants operated by the Detroit Big Three, and UAW-organized
plants currently or originally operated as joint ventures between the Big Three and other
companies.

Figure 2. U.S. Motor Vehicle Production

U.S. production surpassed 12 million units by mid-decade, and reached a peak of 13
million by 1999. Of that figure, more than 10 million were directly built by the Big Three;
adding in 700,000 vehicles built by their joint-venture affiliates, UAW- built vehicles
accounted for 83% of U.S. production. With expansion by the Japanese OEMs and new plants
opened in South Carolina and Alabama by BMW and Mercedes Benz, respectively, the non-
UAW total units of production had doubled to about 2 million by the end of the decade.

Since then, total U.S. output has declined by 2 million units. Domestic Big Three output
has fallen by a third, while foreign OEMs have continued to increase output. The annual rate
of U.S. Big Three production in 2006 and 2007 was less than 7 million units. Their joint-
venture affiliates maintained their contribution, primarily because the Toyota Corolla, a
popular compact, is built at a joint-venture plant with GM in California, and the Ford
Mustang is built at the Ford-Mazda plant in Michigan. Adding all the UAW plants together,
as in Figure 2, yields a total 2007 annual-rate production of 7.4 million units. Meanwhile,
foreign OEMs have built new plants in new locations (Honda and Hyundai in Alabama,
Nissan in Mississippi, and a new Toyota pickup truck plant in Texas) as well as expanding
existing plants. Their annual-rate 2007 U.S. output is up to 3.4 million units, or on a
combined basis, more than 50% of the output from just the Big Three UAW-organized plants.
The total output of foreign-owned non-UAW OEM plants in the United States in 2007 has
reached 28% of total U.S. motor vehicle production. Moreover, foreign OEMs have

announced the building of more assembly plants in 2006-2007: Toyota in Mississippi, Honda in Indiana, and Kia in Georgia.

The economics consulting firm Global Insight predicts a continued declining share of North American production from the Detroit Big Three. From a forecast 2007 production base of just under 15 million light vehicles in 2007, they estimate that 2008 output will decline to 14.4 million vehicles. They then forecast a slow recovery in both car and light truck production, not exceeding the 2006 level until 2011 or 2012. However, they further predict that "Transplants [will] represent all the growth in North American production." Big Three North American output, which they estimate at 9.5 million units in 2007, would fall to 8.8 million units in 2008 in their forecast, and possibly not reach 9 million units again before 2012. Foreign OEM output, after stagnating around 5.5 million units in 2008, could resume its upward climb thereafter, to about 6.5 million units by 2012.[19]

The Impact of Sales and Production Trends on Employment

National Motor Vehicle Manufacturing Employment Data

Figures 3 and 4 illustrate how these trends have impacted overall employment in the U.S. motor vehicle manufacturing industry. Figure 3 presents the total level of such employment since 1990, as well as employment levels in each of the three subsectors that constitute this manufacturing sector. Under the new North American Industry Classification System (NAICS), these major components are motor vehicle assembly (NAICS 3361), motor vehicle bodies and trailers (NAICS 3362), and automotive parts (NAICS 3363).[20] One advantage of using NAICS categorizations is that all automotive equipment is clearly shown as associated with the motor vehicle industry and not other product groups. NAICS 3362 does include such products as truck trailers, recreational vehicles and motor homes, but using all three NAICS categories insures comprehensive coverage of the motor industry, and more than 90% of employment in the three classes is associated with the manufacture of cars and light trucks. Another advantage of using the NAICS-basis data is that it is indifferent to ownership, so that we can measure employment, for example, at the same parts manufacturing plant, whether it was owned by GM, spun off by GM to Delphi, or owned by a third-party supplier, at any time between 1990 and the present. It still counts as a parts plant and not a motor vehicle assembly plant.

Figure 3 illustrates that total U.S. employment in automotive manufacturing rose from about 1 million persons in 1990, to a peak of 1.3 million in 1999-2000, before falling back to about the 1 million level in 2006-2007. If one disaggregates the total number for the three subcategories, one can see that the overwhelming number of jobs, as well as gains and losses, in the industry have been in the parts sector — about 840,000 at the industry's 1999-2000 peak. By 2007, that number had fallen to near the 600,000 level, which was actually 50,000 below the 1990 level. The workforce in motor vehicle assembly operations (NAICS 3361) has varied by a much smaller amount — growing from 271,000 in 1990 to 291,000 at the 1999-2000 peak, then falling to 222,000 by 2007. The decline, however, in this category has been steeper than the rise, reflecting a number of trends and cross-pressures that will be discussed further below. The third, and smallest, subcategory, bodies, trailers, etc. (NAICS 3362), has been less sensitive to the rise and decline of demand for cars and light vehicles. Employment has fallen a little from the 2000 high of about 180,000, but is still much higher than the level of 130,000 recorded in 1990.

Many commentators have emphasized the loss of jobs in this sector since 2000: for example, a front-page caption in the trade news paper *Automotive News* highlighted the fact that, "The U.S. auto industry employs nearly 25% fewer factory workers today than it did in 2000."[21] However, that is typical of "peak-to-trough" accounting. In a cyclical industry such as motor vehicle manufacturing, there is no reason to believe that employment (hours worked) will not move up and down with the business cycle.

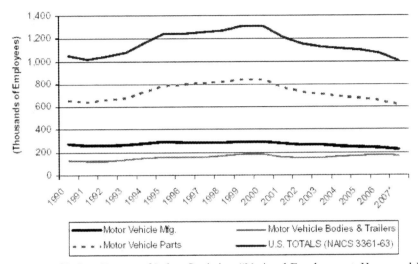

Source: U.S. Dept. of Labor. Bureau of Labor Statistics. "National Employment, Hours and Earnings" (November 13, 2007).
* Annual rate.

Figure 3. U.S. Motor Vehicle Industry Manufacturing Employment

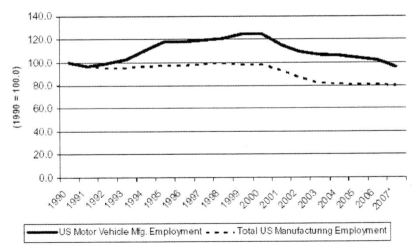

Source: As for Figure 3.
* Annual rate.

Figure 4. Employment Trends, Motor Vehicle and General Manufacturing

Motor Vehicle Manufacturing Holds Up Better Than Other Manufacturing Employment

When employment in automotive manufacturing is compared to manufacturing employment in general (as in Figure 4), one can see that motor vehicle manufacturing has actually sustained its employment numbers over time much better than U.S. manufacturing in general. If one normalizes 1990 as the base employment level, motor vehicle manufacturing increased employment by 25% through 2000, while, despite an economic boom for most of the decade, total manufacturing employment did not actually ever regain the 1990 level. Since motor vehicle manufacturing is a significant share of total manufacturing, one can calculate that, for all other types of manufacturing, employment fell by more than 1 million jobs between 1990 and 2000. Motor vehicle manufacturing employment has, statistically speaking, returned to its 1990 base level, while manufacturing employment in general has declined by 3.7 million jobs since then.

Past Performance and Future Outlook for Motor Vehicle Manufacturing Employment

There are a number of reasons why auto manufacturing employment patterns may have differed from those of industry in general.

- *Foreign OEMs have been steadily expanding or establishing new plants in the United States throughout the period since 1990.* In an earlier CRS report calculations were presented that indicated the total number of persons employed by foreign-owned motor vehicle manufacturers, including parts suppliers, had reached nearly 300,000 by the early 2000s, or about a quarter of the total employment in the industry. This calculation excluded employees of Chrysler, then a subsidiary of a German company.[22] This number has continued to grow, despite the overall automotive employment decline since 2000.

- *Strong Detroit Big Three sales in the 1990s supported employment growth throughout the motor vehicle manufacturing sector independent of foreign companies' U.S. expansion.* Then, as demand for Big Three U.S.-built vehicles declined since 2000, the Big Three and their suppliers have been reducing employment to reflect reduced production and market share levels. *"For every job created by the International [companies] in the U.S., the Big 3 have shed 6.1 jobs ..."*[23]

- *Current and future Big Three restructuring implies further job losses in the industry.* Job declines are directly related to production cuts by the Big Three, and consequent reduction in orders for parts from their suppliers. However, a large share of the employment reduction is also due to improving productivity. Adjustments in union contracts with the industry allow more flexibility in determining employment levels, including through negotiated "buyout" arrangements accepted by labor. For example, GM since 2002 has reduced the average hours needed to assemble a vehicle by 15%, but has reduced its U.S. workforce by 40%. One industry analyst has commented, "In the past, job losses have been cyclical ... But the decline since 2000 is permanent because it's structural. Those jobs are not coming back, and all auto-dependent areas *are sharing the loss."*[24] *While the overall decline in manufacturing employment has slowed since 2003, the decline in Big Three employment, and that of their suppliers, may continue at the current pace, or accelerate.*

To answer the question at the beginning of this section, there is not a general jobs crisis in U.S. automotive manufacturing sector, but there is a crisis in a major part of that sector: unionized Big Three plants, and supplier companies that rely on Big Three production for major shares of their output. This crisis may be viewed as the belated response of the traditional, Detroit-based automotive manufacturing model to international competition, including foreign manufacturers setting up shop in the United States. The rest of U.S. industry has already been undergoing this "downsizing" or "rightsizing" (depending on the observer's perspective), through both the growth period of the 1990s, and the manufacturing recession that occurred after 2001. But only since this latter date have the UAW and the Big Three been able to reach agreements, culminating in the 2007 collective bargaining agreements, that allow this sector of the motor industry to implement labor cost savings and to take fuller advantage of productivity improvements.

The UAW in the 1980s had negotiated agreements with the Big Three to allow more rapid introduction of technology and greater employment flexibility, but founded on the principle that there should be no effort to increase profits by reducing the union-organized employment base. In the industry conditions prevailing since 2000, as production levels stagnated then fell, and profits turned into losses in the billions of dollars, labor has accepted buyouts and other early retirement offers by the Big Three, which has cut or will eliminate the number of jobs in the United States (plus Canada) by a total of 150,000 between 2005 and 2009. "With buyouts or early retirement offers expected at all three Detroit automakers in the wake of [new] UAW contracts that allow new hires to get less in pay or benefits, the number is sure to grow soon."[25]

The new contract agreements will be summarized in the last part of this chapter. But, first, the report will review the latest data on auto industry employment by state. The impact of restructuring to date has been far from even across the country. While it may be ongoing, there has already been a measurable impact on the location of the U.S. motor vehicle industry.

MOTOR VEHICLE MANUFACTURING PERFORMANCE BY STATE

As described in the earlier CRS report on the U.S. motor industry, the domestic Big Three manufacturers have followed a strategy of "reconcentrating" automotive assembly operations in the traditional midwestern heartland of the industry. This strategy has been driven by a number of factors, not only including declining production and loss of market shares on their part, but also a new tendency to proliferate models under different corporate badges off the same underlying vehicle platform. The earlier strategy of locating assembly operations nearer customers to minimize shipping costs has essentially been discarded. Virtually all the Big Three assembly plants on the East Coast have been or are being closed, as well as in disparate locations such as Atlanta (both Ford and GM), Maryland, Virginia, Oklahoma, and California. The new Big Three model consists of centralized locations, each producing one family of cross-badged vehicles, which can be conveniently supplied by parts makers, and from which product can be shipped to customers nationwide.[26] Sean McAlinden of the Center for Automotive Research has described this as "the retreat to the core ... Michigan as the Alamo!"[27]

At the same time, the "new American manufacturers" have extended the traditional U.S. "auto belt" farther to the South, bringing with them an increasing number of auto parts suppliers. This has created more of an "auto corridor" focused on the I-65/I-75 interstate highways. Not all foreign-owned OEMs have invested exclusively in southern plants and the Detroit Big Three produce some vehicles in the South. Despite the now-shuttered plants in Georgia, GM continues to build product in Texas, Louisiana, Tennessee and Kentucky, and Ford also builds trucks in Louisville. But the three largest Japanese manufacturers, plus BMW, Mercedes Benz, and Hyundai have all built plants south and west of the traditional Midwest auto belt, and more new plants (and expansions) are being built by these companies. This upsurge in southern investment continues to bring with it a substantial number of new automotive supplier plants.[28]

The map in Figure 5 illustrates the geographic distribution of employment in the U.S. motor vehicle industry, defined here as 2006 employment reported by the Labor Department's Bureau of Labor Statistics (BLS) in NAICS 3361-62-63.[29] The core of the industry remained in three midwestern states each with employment greater than 100,000: Michigan (about 200,000), Ohio, and Indiana. They are labeled in this chapter as the "Heartland Auto Belt." Then there is a group of seven states filling out what are labeled as seven other leading states in terms of automotive employment. These states have at least one light vehicle assembly plant (in most cases more) and at least 30,000 automotive industry workers. They include some traditional midwestern auto manufacturing states (Illinois and Missouri). They also include some states with both Big Three and foreign OEM assembly plants (California and Texas), but which mainly make the list because of large supplier industries. Three other leading states have mainly risen through heavy investments by foreign-owned companies in the past 20 years (Tennessee, Kentucky, and Alabama).

The remaining states in the national map are classed according to the number of employees in the automotive manufacturing sector. Some of them still have major light motor vehicle assembly plants, some formerly had such plants but now are primarily equipment suppliers (such as New York), and others (like North Carolina) have never had a light vehicle manufacturing plant, but are important suppliers to the industry. In Table 1, the report provides some further details on the "Heartland Auto Belt," the other leading states, and all other states that either have a large number of persons working in the industry or at least one light motor vehicle assembly plant. Excluded from the table are those states, such as Iowa, Pennsylvania, and Oregon, whose industry is primarily dominated by the medium and heavy truck building, or bodies and trailers.

The Heartland Auto Belt

A "One-State Recession" in Michigan

Michigan remains unambiguously the state most highly dependent on automotive manufacturing. While two other midwestern states also employ more than 100,000 persons in the industry, a third of all manufacturing jobs in Michigan in 2006 were in motor vehicle manufacturing, compared to 22% in Indiana and 16% in Ohio. In terms of its "intensity quotient" shown in Table 1, the percentage of employment in the motor industry compared to the national average, Michigan ranked 4.4 times more reliant on the industry than the national average, while Indiana was about three times above the national average, and Ohio about twice that level.

But unlike the other two heartland auto states, Michigan has experienced no investment in motor vehicle assembly operations by foreign companies in the past 20 years (excluding the Daimler acquisition of the entire Chrysler group), meaning that, essentially, the relative decline of the Detroit Big Three's role in U.S. motor vehicle manufacturing during this period has been an unalloyed negative development for Michigan.[30] Between 2000 and 2006, Michigan lost 351,000 jobs overall — 241,000 of this net job loss was in manufacturing, and the net loss in motor manufacturing was 116,000 jobs, about half of the total, according to BLS data. That meant a loss of 35% of all motor industry jobs. While there had been some gain in motor vehicle manufacturing employment there in the 1990s, the net gains have all been wiped out since then in all three of the industry's subsectors. More than a quarter of all jobs in U.S. motor vehicle manufacturing in 1990 were in Michigan; by 2006, the share was down to one-fifth. About 40% of the net national decline in motor industry manufacturing jobs in 2000-2006 was accounted for by the net loss of jobs in Michigan.[31]

As a consequence partly of this decline, Michigan by 2007 had the worst unemployment rate in the nation. According to seasonally adjusted Labor Department data, Michigan's unemployment level as of October 2007 was 7.7%, more than 1.5 points above the level in the next two most affected states (Mississippi and Alaska). Thus, on a Labor Department map, Michigan was the only state with unemployment higher than 7% of the workforce, and was three points higher than the national average of 4.7%.[32]

Mixed Results in Ohio and Indiana

By comparison with Michigan, **Ohio**, the second-leading motor vehicle manufacturing state, has seen a much more moderate decline in employment, as shown in Table 1. Since 2000, it has lost 37,000 motor manufacturing jobs (22%) — 11,000 of them in motor vehicle assembly, and 21,000 in parts, which in 2006 employed about three times as many people in the state. Manufacturing overall saw a net decline of 228,000 jobs in Ohio in 2000-2006, so unlike Michigan, the motor vehicle industry directly accounted for only about 16% of the net loss. Ohio's unemployment rate, at 5.8 % is higher than the national average, but is thus not primarily due to auto industry job losses. Note that, unlike Michigan, Ohio has seen major investment in foreign-owned assembly plants in the state, with two Honda facilities.

In Indiana, the state has actually gained motor vehicle assembly and body and trailer-building jobs over both 1990 and 2006 (NAICS 3362 accounts for a much higher share of motor vehicle employment in Indiana than in either Michigan or Ohio). However, the state has lost about 23,000 parts manufacturing jobs since 2000, many of them in plants owned by the Big Three or their major suppliers. This led to an overall net decline of 15,000 in motor industry jobs in the state. As in Ohio, this was only a fraction of the state's overall net manufacturing job loss (15%). Moreover, as of 2006, Indiana actually had recorded a small increase in automotive employment over 1990, and its overall unemployment rate in October 2007 was about equal to the national average. Future job losses owing to Big Three downsizing may be offset to some degree by a new Honda assembly plant announced in 2007.

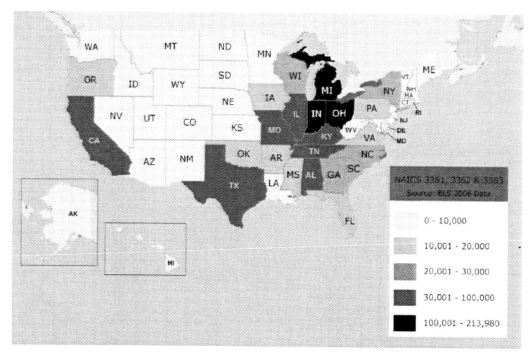

Figure 5. U.S. Motor Vehicle Manufacturing Employment by State

Table 1. Motor Vehicle Manufacturing States

	Employment (2006)	Change from 2000	Change from 1990	% of U.S. Total	% of State Mfg.	Rel. to U.S. Avg. (=1.0)
		(Thousands)				
Heartland Auto Belt						
Michigan	214	-116	-83	20.1	32.9	4.4
Ohio	127	-37	-22	11.9	16.0	2.1
Indiana	124	-15	7	11.7	21.9	2.9
Other Leading Auto Manufacturing States						
Tennessee	54	-5	18	5.1	13.5	1.8
Kentucky	53	-2	25	5.0	20.3	2.7
Illinois	39	-9	-2	3.7	5.8	0.8
California	39	-7	-6	3.7	2.6	0.3
Texas	35	0	9	3.3	3.8	0.5
Alabama	35	15	19	3.3	11.6	1.5
Missouri	32	-6	0	3.0	10.6	1.4
Other Auto Manufacturing States[a]						
N. Carolina	28	-5	4	2.6	5.1	0.7
S. Carolina	25	1	12	2.4	9.9	1.3
New York	24	-11	-18	2.3	4.2	0.6
Wisconsin	22	-9	-9	2.0	4.3	0.6
Georgia	21	-4	1	2.0	4.7	0.6

Table 1. (Continued)

	Employment (2006)	Change from 2000	Change from 1990	% of U.S. Total	% of State Mfg.	Rel. to U.S. Avg. (=1.0)
	(Thousands)					
Mississippi	13	1	0	1.2	7.4	1.0
Virginia	13	-1	3	1.2	4.4	0.6
Kansas	9	-1	-2	0.8	4.7	0.6
Minnesota	7	-3	-1	0.6	2.0	0.3
Louisiana	5	0	1	0.4	3.1	0.4
Delaware	3	-2	-1	0.3	10.1	1.3
U.S. TOTAL	1,064	-251	-54	100.0	7.5	1.0

Sources: Department of Labor. Bureau of Labor Statistics. "Quarterly Census of Employment and Wages" for state data; U.S. totals from "National Employment, Hours and Earnings."
a. More than 20,000 motor vehicle manufacturing jobs, or at least one assembly plant in 2006.

The overall statistics for loss of auto industry jobs since 2000 in the "heartland auto belt" do not necessarily suggest that the motor vehicle industry is dying in this region. Almost half of the nation's employees in motor vehicle manufacturing (44%) still work there. Both the Big Three and foreign investors have been aggressive in developing new facilities in these states. Each of the Detroit Big Three has made major investments in rebuilding or renovating assembly plants in Michigan. Chrysler has created a new "modularized" campus for building Jeeps in Ohio. Besides expanding its assembly plant in Princeton, Indiana, Toyota has added a new assembly line in a former Isuzu plant in the same state. And Honda, as mentioned above, has announced a new assembly plant, also to be built in Indiana.

Employment Mostly Stable in Other Leading States

Table 1 identifies seven other states as being leading motor vehicle manufacturing states. These states all have one or more motor vehicle assembly plants, as well as major parts supply industries, with auto industry employment greater than 30,000 persons in 2006. Each state ranges between three and five percent of total U.S. motor vehicle manufacturing employment. The states have had diverse experiences in recent decades in auto manufacturing.

Alabama is the star of the group. With no motor vehicle manufacturing assembly plant as of 1990, Alabama successfully recruited Mercedes Benz' U.S. assembly plant in the 1990s, and plants built by Honda and Hyundai since 2000. Toyota has an engine manufacturing plant there, leading a large group of parts suppliers establishing themselves in the state. Since 2000, while the United States as a whole was losing 250,000 motor vehicle manufacturing jobs, Alabama was adding 15,000 — the only gain of this magnitude in the country. Of these jobs, 10,000 were in vehicle assembly, with another net 4,000 in parts manufacturing. With Kia announcing a new plant to be opened just across the river in West Point, Georgia, parts manufacturing jobs in the state may continue to increase. Despite these gains, motor vehicle manufacturing employment in 2006 was still only 11.6% of Alabama's manufacturing workforce, significantly less than in the heartland auto belt states, and its intensity quotient, at 1.5 times the national average, is also lower.

Two other southern states in the I-65/I-75 auto corridor, Tennessee and Kentucky, succeeded in the 1980s in attracting auto manufacturing plants from foreign OEMs, as well as GM's Saturn plant in Spring Hill, Tennessee. Both states in 2006 had more than 50,000 persons employed in motor vehicle manufacturing, and had higher shares of their workforce so employed than Alabama. With 20.3% of the workforce in the motor industry in 2006, Kentucky actually recorded a higher level than Ohio's 16%, and a higher intensity quotient as well. Both states have shown dramatic employment gains in the industry since 1990 (Tennessee, up 18,000 — Kentucky, up 25,000). However, both states have also lost other auto industry jobs, from a Big Three assembly plant in Kentucky and NAICS 3 362-63 plants in Tennessee since 2000, and have recorded small net losses in the current decade.

Texas has recorded a gain in assembly operations, mostly from a large new Toyota truck plant that began operating in San Antonio in 2006, but a net loss in parts manufacturing jobs left the auto employment level in the state flat since 2000. Illinois, Missouri, and California, all of which have been major auto manufacturing states for decades, failed to attract any new foreign or domestically owned assembly plants since 1990, and were the major net job losers since 2000 among this group of states. Except in Missouri, by 2006 the auto industry shares of these states' manufacturing workforces were less than 10% and below the average intensity quotient.

Other Motor Vehicle Manufacturing States

Table 1 includes also all the remaining states with at least one light motor vehicle assembly plant, including those in which closures of the plants had been announced by 2006. The table also includes states that have a major role in the industry only through leading roles as parts suppliers, notably North Carolina, New York (whose last assembly plant, in Tarrytown, was closed in the 1990s), and Virginia (where Ford's truck plant in Norfolk was closed in 2007). But while motor vehicle industry-related employment has been relatively stable in North Carolina and Virginia, it has declined by 18,000 jobs or 42% in New York since 1990, a higher rate of loss over that time even than in Michigan.

The only state in this group showing a major overall gain in automotive employment since 1990 is South Carolina. BMW's North American plant was established there in the 1 990s and further expansion of that facility was announced in 2007. South Carolina has recorded a net gain of 12,000 auto industry jobs since 1990, and the sector in 2006 accounted for almost 10% of the state's manufacturing workforce. Delaware, a small state but one with two assembly plants, is the only other state in this group where auto manufacturing employment accounts for 10% of the manufacturing workforce, and where the intensity is greater than the national average. However, one of the state's two plants, the Chrysler plant in Newark, is now slated for closure. Despite establishment of the big Nissan assembly plant in Canton, Mississippi has recorded little net overall gain, but this may change once the Toyota plant announced for the state is in operation.

In other states in this group, two assembly plants in Georgia, both in the Atlanta area — one owned by Ford, the other by GM, are in the process of closing. Ford has also announced closure of the only assembly plant in Minnesota. Chrysler closed its large assembly plant in Kenosha, Wisconsin (a former AMC plant), two decades ago, but still maintains an engine plant there, and GM assembles trucks in Janesville. GM also builds trucks in Kansas and Louisiana. In none of these states is the auto industry share of manufacturing employment greater than 5%.

U.S. MANUFACTURING OF SMALL MOTOR VEHICLES

During recent debates on energy legislation and automotive fuel economy standards in both houses of Congress, the issue was raised as to whether proposed bills would damage, or even cause the disappearance of, the manufacturing of small, fuel-efficient motor vehicles in the United States. It was stated by the UAW, for example, that there are in the United States 67,000 workers "who assemble or make parts for these vehicles."[33] Therefore, it was argued that a statutory "anti-backsliding" provision was required to prevent companies from meeting new fuel economy rules by importing more vehicles from abroad, to the detriment of their continued manufacture at domestic plants.[34]

If it is difficult to produce smaller vehicles at a profit in the domestic market, as is sometimes alleged, it was feared that these jobs would be in danger of being outsourced overseas, if stringent new fuel economy rules were adopted. A CRS report, cited earlier, illustrates how a surge in imports of motor vehicles from Japan in 2006 was linked to increase in sales of small cars, owing to sharp increases in gasoline prices.[35] Data for 2007 indicate that subcompact vehicles, all imported to the United States, are the fastest-growing segment of the U.S. car market. Through November 2007, sales of such vehicles were up about 22% over the previous year. They may have taken sales away from the next larger class, compact cars, whose sales were down 3.3% during the same period. While all of the Detroit Big Three manufacture compacts domestically (see Table 4 below), no subcompacts are produced in the United States, and in the auto industry, it is widely believed that it cannot be profitable to do so.[36]

Table 2 illustrates the development over time of plants in the United States, which manufacture motor vehicles defined by CRS as small motor vehicles using data from *Ward's Automotive Yearbook* and Environmental Protection Agency fuel economy guides. It shows these plants as shares of total numbers of plants operated by each U.S. nameplate manufacturer, as they have been opened, closed, or altered product mix since 1975. The list excludes two-seat sports cars and CUVs that may be measured as small in capacity, but do not achieve low fuel economy ratings. Table 3 lists those vehicles that are included under the small car definition. Table 4 provides details on the location of each assembly plant that was still producing small cars as of mid-2007, or for which plans exist to produce small cars there in the future.

For both domestic and foreign OEMs, assembly plants producing small, fuel- efficient vehicles in the United States have declined in number and as a share of total plants operated since the 1985-1990 time period. Table 2 divides the numbers of plants by UAW-organized and non-UAW plants, as the union has been particularly concerned about the potential loss of U.S. small-car manufacturing capacity.

Table 2. Four Decades of U.S. Small Car Manufacturing (numbers of plants)

	1975		1985		1990		1995		2000		2005		2007	
	A	B	A	B	A	B	A	B	A	B	A	B	A	B
UAW-Organized:														
• General Motors	31	1	29	4	27	2	22	3	23	2	24	2	23	1
• Ford	22	2	15	2	15	2	16	1	15	1	18	1	14	1
• Chrysler[a]	11	1	9	1	7	0	11	1	9	1	11	1	11	1
• Foreign-owned[b]			3	2	4	1	4	1	4	1	5	1	5	1
Total UAW[c]	**66**	**4**	**56**	**9**	**53**	**5**	**53**	**6**	**51**	**5**	**58**	**5**	**53**	**4**
Non-UAW[d]	**0**	**0**	**3**	**1**	**8**	**4**	**9**	**3**	**11**	**2**	**17**	**2**	**18**	**2**

A. Total Light Vehicle Assembly Plants.

B. Small Car Plants

Source: Operating plants from *Automotive News Market Data Book*, various years. Small cars are defined as cars in the subcompact or compact classes by *Ward's Automotive Yearbook*, and/or the Environmental Protection Agency (EPA).

Notes: Light vehicles include passenger cars and light trucks, the latter including pickups, minivans and SUVs. Small cars are as listed in Table 2. Small cars may be the sole product of an assembly plant or one of several lines of light vehicles produced in an assembly plant. For the purposes of this table, any plant that has an assembly line devoted solely to small cars is defined as one plant. If a plant produces small cars as well as other light vehicles, the small car assembly line is counted as one plant and all other light vehicle lines are counted as another plant. For example, New United Motor Manufacturing Inc. (NUMMI) of Fremont, CA, a UAW-organized joint venture between GM and Toyota operated by Toyota, produces small cars (Toyota Corolla/Pontiac Vibe) on one assembly line and a light truck (Toyota Tacoma pickup truck) on the other. In this table, NUMMI is counted as two plants.

a. Chrysler includes statistics for American Motors which Chrysler acquired in 1987.

b. Volkswagen, NUMMI, Diamond-Star (Chrysler-Mitsubishi), Auto Alliance (Ford-Mazda).

c. Includes Checker Motors (closed 1982) and International Harvester (light trucks and SUVs; closed 1980). Neither company produced small cars.

d. Honda, Nissan, Toyota, BMW, Subaru-Isuzu, Mercedes-Benz, Hyundai, Kia.

- UAW-organized assembly plants producing small cars peaked in 1985 at nine out of 56 operating at the time (16%). Seven of the nine were operated directly by the Big Three (including in this count an American Motors plant acquired by Chrysler two years later). The other two UAW plants were the Volkswagen plant in Pennsylvania, and the GM-Toyota NUMMI joint venture in California. By 2007, just four of 53 UAW-organized assembly plants still produced small cars (7.5%) — one for each of the domestic Big Three and NUMMI, which produces the Toyota Corolla and the Pontiac Vibe.

- The share of non-UAW plants (all foreign-owned) producing small cars peaked at half the total (four out of eight) in 1990. By 2007, the share was 11% (two out of 18).

One may infer from this that, although foreign-owned manufacturers, especially from Japan and Korea, have a perceived comparative advantage in designing and producing small fuel-efficient vehicles, the most efficient use of their resources in the United States is to expand the production of vehicles aimed more at the evolving "sweet spots" of the U.S.

market — midsize sedans, minivans, SUVs, trucks, and, lately, CUVs. Foreign or domestic, manufacturers in the United States appear to be still following the 1 970s dictum of Henry Ford II, "minicar, miniprofit."[37]

CHANGING DETROIT: THE 2007 COLLECTIVE BARGAINING AGREEMENTS

The 2007 Contract Negotiation Process

Earlier CRS reports detailed UAW labor contract agreements with the Detroit Big Three that many observers contended were making the union-organized sector of the motor manufacturing industry uncompetitive with foreign owned-OEMs that manufactured both in the United States and abroad. Some of these issues included:

Table 3. Identification of Small Cars by Manufacturer (as defined for Table 2)

UAW-Organized Plants:	Non-UAW Plants:
General Motors Chevrolet Cobalt/Pontiac G5[a] Chevrolet Vega Chevrolet Chevette Chevrolet Cavalier Saturn SC, SL, and SW Saturn Ion	**Honda** Civic[a]
Ford Ford Focus[a] Pinto Escort	**Nissan** Sentra (production moved from United States to Mexico in 1999)
Chrysler Dodge Caliber[a] AMC Gremlin (acquired from American Motors) Dodge Omni/Plymouth Horizon Dodge Neon	**Subaru** Legacy[a]
Volkswagen (1978-1988) Rabbit/Golf	
NUMMI (Toyota/GM) Toyota Corolla[a] Pontiac Vibe[a] Chevrolet Nova Geo Prizm Chevrolet Prizm Toyota Voltz (export only)	

Source: As for Table 2.

Note: Many vehicles were sold in multiple versions under different nameplates (e.g., Chevy Cavalier, Pontiac Sunbird, Cadillac Cimarron). This table lists only the most widely sold version.

a. Vehicle still in production in United States.

Table 4. U.S. Small Car Manufacturing Assembly Operations (as of September 2007)

	Location	2007 Assembly Operation	Announced Plan or Commitment
UAW-Organized Plants			
General Motors	Lordstown, Ohio	Chevrolet Cobalt Pontiac G5	Alpha vehicle, 2011 (compact rear-wheel drive)
Ford	Wayne Assembly Wayne, Michigan	Ford Focus	Continue production
Chrysler	Belvidere, Illinois	Dodge Caliber	Continue production
NUMMI	Fremont, California	Toyota Corolla Pontiac Vibe	Continue production
Non-UAW Plants			
Honda	East Liberty, Ohio	Honda Civic	Continue production
	Greensburg, Indiana	(under construction)	Begin Civic production 2010
Subaru	Lafayette, Indiana	Subaru Legacy	Continue production

Sources: *Automotive News*, various dates; Global Insight. *North American Light Vehicle Industry Forecast Report*, various dates. GM data also from *UAW GM Report* on GM plant investment commitments from Sept. 2007 contract agreement, not publicly confirmed by General Motors.

- Nearly free lifetime health care coverage for employees, retirees and dependents — a cost that was estimated by 2005 to cost the companies as much as $1,500 per vehicle produced. Foreign OEMs do not pay such costs to any similar degree because of a younger workforce and few retirees in the United States, as well as different health care systems in their home markets;
- A defined-benefit pension plan, to which employees and their spouses were entitled after 30 years on the job;
- In effect a guaranteed salary — even if a plant closed or was downsized, companies were required to keep hourly employees on the payroll through a "jobs bank," until another suitable position could be found;
- Consequent loss of flexibility in managing production to meet actual demand — production had to be maintained so that employees were generating revenue, even if vehicles were sold at a loss through fleet sales or the use of high-cost incentives (practices that reduced residual values and therefore attractiveness to customers in retail sales).[38]

There had been interim adjustments to the 2003 national contract necessitated by multibillion dollar losses reported by each of the Big Three companies. The 2007 contract negotiations saw a substantial effort by both management and labor at the UAW-represented companies to establish a comprehensive new labor agreement cognizant of the Big Three's competitive problems. As has been traditional in previous UAW-industry contracts, the collective bargaining agreement was reached through a process of "pattern bargaining." The union selected one of the Big Three OEMs with which to bargain, and, in keeping with the UAW's general policy of not allowing domestic producers to seek competitive advantages through differences in labor contracts, to impose that pattern on the other companies once an agreement was reached. However, owing to some major differences in both the financial conditions and organizational structures among the Big Three, significant differences emerged among the collective bargaining agreements that were reached with the three companies in the autumn of 2007.

Negotiation of the 2007 collective bargaining agreements with the Detroit Big Three manufacturers proceeded according to the following chronology:

- **July 20-23:** Official commencement of contract renewal talks between the UAW and each of the Detroit Big Three. (In July, control of the U.S. Chrysler Group of DaimlerChrysler AG of Germany is formally transferred to "the new Chrysler," an independent company owned by Cerberus Capital Limited Partnership, a private equity firm.

- **"Mid-August:"** Big Three officially ask UAW to take over administration of health care benefits for current and retired employees, and their families.

- **September 13:** President Ron Gettelfinger announces to UAW members that GM will be the lead company (strike target) in the contract negotiations. Ford and Chrysler receive contract extensions.

- **September 14:** UAW contract with GM expires — UAW extends on an hour-by-hour basis.

- **September 24:** Negotiators fail to reach agreement and UAW calls first nationwide strike against GM in 40 years.

- **September 26:** GM and UAW settle on a "pattern-setting deal for the U.S. auto industry," and strike ends after two days. The new agreement shifts retiree health care obligations to the UAW, with a large initial contribution from GM. The UAW also agrees to lower pay and a different benefit structure for new hires in "non-core" jobs. In exchange, GM makes new product commitments at existing U.S. factories.

- **October 7:** UAW establishes Chrysler as the next bargaining target. Chrysler is warned of a possible strike by October 10.

- **October 10:** The "one-shift" national strike against Chrysler. UAW walks out, because its bargaining committee cannot agree on terms in view of Chrysler commitments to continued production at U.S. facilities more limited than those provided by GM. UAW tentative agreement announced later that afternoon, including a transfer of retiree health care to UAW, and strike ends. Meanwhile, UAW members at GM complete ratification of their contract by a 65% positive vote.

- **October 27:** After aggressive campaign by UAW leadership (and a split in the negotiating committee), Chrysler workers ratify agreement — supported by only 56% of production workers and 51% of skilled trades.

- **November 1:** Chrysler announces plans to end shifts at five assembly plans, terminate production of selected products, and to eliminate 12,000 jobs in addition to cuts announced earlier in 2007.

- **November 3:** UAW and Ford reach an agreement. Ford will make significantly lower contributions than GM when retiree health care transferred to union. Ford also gets right to pay lower-tier wages to all new hires, up to 20% of the total hourly workforce. In exchange, Ford announces that it will keep open five plants it had planned to close.

- **November 14:** UAW contract with Ford ratified by an 81% positive vote, completing the negotiation process.[39]

The UAW first negotiated all elements of the issues with GM, to establish a "pattern" with the company that was then considered financially the strongest of the three, and the farthest along in terms of restructuring. Having established this pattern, the UAW then moved on to Chrysler, a company whose management was in transition, with respect to both structure and personnel.[40] The agreement negotiated with Chrysler was the most controversial, both among the UAW negotiating committee and its membership, as revealed in the relatively close margin of ratification. Further uncertainty was added by the Chrysler job cuts announced immediately after ratification. But when Ford agreed in its negotiation with the UAW to rescind five planned factory closings, the result was the highest level of ratification approval of any of the agreements. This was despite Ford's smaller contribution to the new union-run retirement health care plan than GM, and Ford's greater leeway than the other two Big Three OEMs in replacing hourly workers under the current contract with new employees under a lower-tier wage structure and a different benefits format. Part of the rationale for this differentiation of treatment was the perception by the UAW that Ford may be the financially weakest of the Big Three, and that maintaining current production facilities insofar as possible was the key union goal.[41]

Summary of New Contract Bargaining Agreements

The following analysis summarizes the changes in the UAW contract reached in these collective bargaining agreements.[42]

Transfer of Retiree Health Care to UAW

A leading objective of the UAW in the negotiations was the protection of retiree benefits already guaranteed by previous contracts. Given the real possibility that one or more of the Big Three could face bankruptcy at some time in the future, the UAW was amenable to consideration of transferring an open-ended commitment to retiree health care to an independent entity managed by the UAW (a "Voluntary Employees' Beneficiary Association," or VEBA).[43] The cost of this to each of the Big Three varies. GM will contribute $31.8 billion, including $4.4 billion in a note convertible to GM stock and a pledge to back up the VEBA for up to $2 billion, if inflation is higher than expected.[44] Ford and

Chrysler had fewer retirees affected. The upfront contributions for Ford and Chrysler to the VEBAs were $13.2 billion and $8.8 billion respectively. Because of legal and organizational issues, the VEBAs will not be set up until 2010, but the automakers might be able financially to recognize savings earlier. The major benefit of this change for the Big Three is that, for a defined, upfront contribution, they largely eliminate the uncertainties of future retiree health care costs and the legal obligation to provide health care to retirees.

Two-Tier Pay and Benefits

The UAW broke with a longstanding tradition in a national contract negotiation by agreeing to allow the Big Three OEMs to provide pay and benefits on a differential structure to workers in the same plants. As opposed to more than $28 in base wages for current production workers, the new hourly starting wage for new hires will be about $14, rising to $1 5-$ 16 after an initial period. In the first agreement, with GM, the lower tier wages for new hires was limited to hourly pay for "non-core" activities, such as machinists, line workers on drivetrain parts and sub-assemblies, inspectors, stampings, material handlers, and drivers. The definition was so broadly defined that it could include as many as 23,000 positions, covering almost a third of GM's current UAW-represented employees. A similar definition was used in the Chrysler contract, again covering nearly a third of present positions, or 13,000 employees. "Non-core" would receive seniority when vacancies arose in core production jobs, and they could move into those positions at the full, "first-tier" contract rate of pay.

With Ford, the distinction between "core" and "non-core," which preserves the principle that all UAW-covered workers receive the same rate of pay for the same job, was eliminated. Ford received the right to hire any new workers, including line production jobs, up to a level of 20% of the total hourly workforce. The percentage cap excludes new hires at facilities Ford had agreed to close or at plants Ford had taken back from its former parts-making affiliate, Visteon. In addition, while GM agreed to move production workers currently employed on a temporary basis into permanent positions, neither Ford nor Chrysler accepted this obligation.

The new "two-tier" structure also applies to employee benefits. Current hourly employees covered by the "first-tier," traditional union contract will receive the full pension for which they remain eligible on retirement. They will also receive full retiree health care benefits, though these will be provided after 2010 by the UAW- administered VEBA, not by the companies. Thus, the UAW will be responsible for any adjustments in coverage necessitated by any future shortfalls in VEBA resources.

"Second-tier" employees (new hires, however defined at each company) will never be eligible for a traditional pension or the current retiree health care coverage. As active employees, they participate in a health plan with $300 to $600 in annual deductibles, plus they receive a flexible health care spending account, from which to purchase customized coverage. With respect to retirement, they will accumulate a cash balance pension, while the company contributes to a 401(k) account that the employee can use for health care expenses after retirement. CAR analyst Sean McAlinden also defines a third class of employees, which he defines as "Tier 1.5" or "the new traditionals." These are permanent workers who move from a "Tier 2, non-core" job, into a job included at the "Tier 1" pay level. These workers "will not have retiree health benefits *ever*. They will not receive defined pension benefit."[45]

Jobs Bank Changes

The burden of the "jobs banks" maintained by the Big Three companies was to a great extent alleviated by the buyouts put into place starting in 2006. The union continued to maintain the principle that currently employed UAW workers cannot be terminated unconditionally through corporate downsizing. However, going forward, the rules for staying in the jobs bank indefinitely were significantly tightened. At all three companies, participation in the jobs bank is now basically limited to a period of two years, with limits placed on the number of refusals an employee can make when offered a new position either within or outside their area of residence.

Detroit Big Three Cost Benefits

The new agreements may promise major labor cost savings for the Big Three. Much of the discrepancy in hourly cost levels (pay and benefits) estimated at $30,000 per year against non-union producers in the U.S. market may be eliminated. With respect to new hires, the Big Three may be paying even less than the competition. McAlinden reports that the total cost per hour of UAW labor currently under "Tier 1" contracts at $78 per hour today at GM. The "Tier 2" labor cost would drop to $25.65 per hour, and even the "Tier 1.5 new traditionals" would only cost a total of $38.47 per hour. Nor are these numbers purely hypothetical — the average hourly GM employee is nearly 49 years old, with 22.5 years of service, and 63.5% are eligible to retire in five years. For Ford and Chrysler average age and service levels are lower, but about 30% can retire in five years (under the traditional UAW "30 and out" guarantee). McAlinden further estimates for GM total labor cost savings of $3.3 billion by 2011, and retiree health care cost savings of $2.8 billion. Based on estimated North American production of about 500,000 vehicles per year in North American in the later year, he projects a savings of $981 per car in labor costs, and $676 in retiree health cost savings.[46]

Labor Gains in Job Security

Besides maintaining the retirement security for current UAW workers in "Tier 1" positions, the UAW won guarantees of continued production, and in some cases, promises of new product, at most existing Big Three plants. UAW active membership has declined from a high of 1.5 million to less than 500,000 in 2007. Each of the Big Three is continuing aggressive buyout campaigns aimed at current employees, and one source states, "The union's auto company membership is expected to drop to 150,000" by 2010.[47] Thus, it was important for the UAW as an organization, as well as its current workforce, to secure such guarantees going forward.[48]

- GM made the most extensive new product guarantees. It laid out plans for continued production and replacement models for all of its assembly plants, at least through 2011 and beyond. The only exception is Doraville, Georgia (Atlanta), still scheduled to close in 2008, plus three parts operations. Some products do remain "business-case dependent" on the list, or, as with the Chevrolet Volt "plug-in hybrid" planned for the Detroit Hamtramck plant, may be technologically speculative.[49] Global Insight predicts two additional GM plant closings that have not been announced. The plant in Moraine, Ohio, that produces the Chevy Trail Blazer/GMC Envoy, is not listed in UAW's report. The Wilmington, Delaware, plant is listed as continuing to produce two-seat sports cars through 2012, but is assigned no new products. Global Insight believes that GM must take out 400,000 units of capacity by the end of the decade to achieve a 90% capacity utilization rate, and suggests these are the two plants most likely to be shut.[50]

- UAW opponents of the Chrysler agreement "complained that the deal lacked the specific future product guarantees found in the GM deal ... The UAW argued that Chrysler had promised to keep operating all but a few facilities and has identified more than $15 billion in potential investments."[51] The listing released by the UAW mostly includes commitments to continue production "through the current product life cycle," with two assembly plants, Newark, Delaware and a small Detroit-area plant, slated for closure after that.[52] In a more favorable analysis, McAlinden states Chrysler promised to "continue and/or expand production at 6 assembly, 4 stamping and 8 powertrain plants," and "reversed 4 closures."[53]

- With Ford, the big news for the UAW was the reprieve of five plants from the list of planned closures, including Avon Lake, Ohio, and two other assembly plants (Chicago and a Detroit-area truck plant) for which closure plans had not yet been publicly announced. The UAW also highlighted new investment and modernization plans at Ford plants. The previously announced closure at Twin Cities (St. Paul) was confirmed, though a year later than originally announced along with the closure of a casting plant and a transmission plant.[54]

In addition to these commitments to keep plants operating, McAlinden notes commitments to "insource" jobs and allow UAW-organized operations to bid on jobs previously committed to outside suppliers (a total of more than 5,000 jobs at the three companies). The Big Three also committed to moratoria on future outsourcing.[55]

Reducing Detroit's Commitment to Canada?

As discussed earlier in the CRS baseline report on the motor vehicle industry, the Detroit Big Three have a longstanding commitment to building motor vehicles in Canada in a two-way sectoral free trade system that goes back to 1965. This deal has ensured Canada's role as the largest U.S. export market for motor vehicles and parts, the largest two-way trade partner, and a virtually permanent large Canadian automotive trade surplus.[56] Under this agreement, Ontario has overtaken Michigan as the largest auto-producing state or provincial jurisdiction in North America.

But one reason the Big Three have made significant investments in Canada has been savings derived from the Canadian health care system, as opposed to expensive, company-provided health care in the United States. Another advantage has been the currency exchange rate, with the Canadian dollar falling as low as 65¢U.S. in the past decade. The Canadian Auto Workers have reportedly used these cost differentials to leverage contract gains not enjoyed by their UAW counterparts in recent years. But with Canada's dollar reaching parity with the American dollar in 2007, and with the Big Three offloading retiree health care costs and making other health care gains in the new UAW contracts, Canadian production is less attractive now to the Big Three. One source forecasts that Ontario production capacity will decline by 600,000 units by 2012, while Michigan will gain 100,000 units.[57] In the near future, Ford is predicted to close one of its two Canadian assembly plants, in St. Thomas, Ontario, where it builds large, rear-wheel-drive sedans on an aging platform.[58]

Conclusion: A Competitive Detroit Big Three?

Outlook for U.S. Motor Vehicle Manufacturing Employment

As to whether the new UAW labor contracts will renew the competitiveness of the Big Three and stop their erosion of U.S. market share, labor relations specialist Harley Shaiken summed up the view of many analysts: "The contract allows the three automakers to be more competitive, but it doesn't remotely ensure success — that requires the right models and the right strategic vision."[59] It is clear that the UAW has accepted that a different labor model is required, or the union will end up with the reputation of organizing only losers among the OEMs. The deal may be viewed as a model of how the union-organized segment of the industry can respond to competitive challenges.

At the national level, the prospects for employment growth in the industry as a whole are not strong during the remaining years of this decade. Foreign-owned manufacturers continue to invest in the United States. However, insofar as the new labor deals allow UAW-organized manufacturers to operate more flexibly, predictions of a continued slowdown in U.S. motor vehicle sales may mean that employment created by these new investments is more than offset by Big Three efforts to reduce labor overhead through increased production efficiencies. This will be especially true if their output is downscaled to demand.

From the state perspective, Big Three cutbacks and plant closures have been widespread, but the negative effects have been felt disproportionately by one state, Michigan. It has suffered about 40% of the total net job loss in automotive manufacturing between 2000 and 2006. Although buyouts will continue, most Michigan Big Three plants will apparently survive, using the new UAW "Tier 2" labor contracts. But as the older class of highly compensated workers retires, the new contract means a clear cut in the pay rate for the new hires who join the industry.

Other states have not been so negatively affected in the 2000s. Within the "heartland auto belt," Ohio and Indiana have lost jobs on a net basis. Unlike Michigan, however, their Big Three losses have been somewhat offset by foreign OEMs. New York, a major parts manufacturing state, has perhaps suffered a job loss in the industry that is proportionally as large as Michigan's, but the automotive sector is relatively small there as a share of total manufacturing employment.

Southern states have not seen the large overall gains that one might expect to have seen, except for Alabama, which has gained 15,000 net new jobs since 2000 — the largest increase of any state. If one goes back to the period since 1990, Alabama is joined by three other southern states — Tennessee, Kentucky, and South Carolina — as the biggest net gainers of auto manufacturing jobs, especially through foreign investment.

Legislative Initiatives May Affect Automotive Manufacturing Employment Outlook

The future of U.S. automotive manufacturing has been a major concern of many Members of Congress. The outlook for future employment in the industry may be affected by federal legislation in the present Congress.

The "Employee Free Choice Act" (H.R. 800/S. 1041)

This bill was approved by the House 241-185 on March 1, 2007. This union-endorsed measure might assist organizing efforts in non-union plants by making it easier to use a "card check" process that supporters believe is a more effective and efficient means of determining support for union representation. On June 26, 2007, the Senate refused to close debate on its equivalent bill (S. 1041) on a vote of 51 yeas to 48 nays.

Fuel Economy Legislation (Title I of P.L. 110-140)

Federal fuel economy standards for all light motor vehicles have been made more stringent in energy legislation approved in the 110th Congress.[60] A version approved by the House on December 6, 2007, by a vote of 235-181 adopted with some changes an earlier Senate-approved bill, which mandated a general fuel economy standard of 35 miles-per-gallon by 2020. The Senate twice failed to close debate on the bill, but then on December 13, 2007, approved by 86-8 a different version with an identical section on automotive fuel economy.[61] To assure passage, the Senate removed most of the tax provisions. However, the Senate did leave in sufficient tax provisions to offset the federal revenue that would be lost from the auto fuel economy measures.[62] The House on December 18, 2007, then approved the version of the bill as amended by a vote of 314-100. President Bush signed the bill into law on December 19, 2007.

Fuel economy mandates can have a major impact on the automotive market, with different effects on different manufacturers. The new law contains provisions designed to offset any negative impacts on U.S. motor vehicle manufacturing. Section 112 establishes that 50% of the civil fines collected from OEMs who fail to meet the new CAFE requirements shall be transferred to a Department of Transportation program for grants in support of the domestic manufacture of advanced technology vehicles and components. Under the "improved vehicle technology" subtitle, the Department of Energy is authorized to make grants for converting and retooling plants for the production of advanced technology fuel-efficient vehicles, and to issue loan guarantees for parts and battery manufacturers for such vehicles.[63]

Funding Advanced Vehicle Manufacturing in Greenhouse Gas Reduction Legislation (S. 2191)

This bill includes the use of proposed auctions of greenhouse gas (GHG) emission credits to fund the development and manufacture of clean, advanced technology vehicles. Eight bills were introduced in the first session of the 110th Congress with the goal of reducing GHG (including carbon dioxide, CO_2) through a market-oriented program along the lines of the trading provisions of the current U.S. acid rain reduction program. One of them, S. 2191, co-sponsored by Senators Joseph Lieberman and John Warner, was ordered to be reported by the Senate Environment and Public Works Committee in an 11-8 vote on December 5, 2007.[64]

S. 2191 would allocate limits on emissions to utilities and industries, under a general cap, aimed at reducing total GHG emissions over time. Trading in emissions credits would be monitored and additional emissions credits would be auctioned by a "Climate Change Credit Corporation" established under the bill. By Section 4401 of the bill, up to 20% of the proceeds of these auctions could be used to carry out an advanced technology vehicles manufacturing program. In Section 4405, "advanced technology vehicles" are defined as "hybrid or advanced diesel light duty motor vehicles" meeting prescribed emissions and fuel economy standards. Funding would be available to "automobile manufacturers and component suppliers" to cover the "engineering integration" of advanced technology components into vehicles and up to 30% of the cost of "reequipping or expanding an existing manufacturing facility to produce" vehicles and components.

According to one analysis, compared to relatively modest amounts that would be provided from fines and loan guarantees under P.L. 110-140, "the cap-and-trade bill would mean real money." It is calculated to generate "as much as $40 billion from the sale of emissions permits."[65]

The Proposed U.S.-Korea Free Trade Agreement

Another major issue for the automotive industry that may be faced by Congress in the second session of the 110th Congress is whether to approve the proposed U.S.-Korea Free Trade Agreement. Many in the U.S. automotive sector are concerned that agreement as negotiated is unbalanced. It would enhance access to the U.S. market for Korean- based OEMs (Hyundai-Kia), which already in 2006 sold 750,000 vehicles in the United States (4.6% of the domestic market, more than 500,000 imported), by eliminating all tariffs on products brought in from Korea, while U.S. OEMs have only been able to export a few thousand units to Korea. Ford and Chrysler explicitly oppose congressional approval of the deal.[66] GM, with a substantial stake in Korean manufacturer Daewoo, has remained neutral.[67] The UAW is strongly opposed to the agreement. In testimony before the House Ways and Means Committee's Trade Subcommittee, UAW Legislative Director Alan Reuther stated that the agreement as contemplated "would exacerbate the totally one-sided auto trade imbalance between Korea and the U.S. and jeopardize the jobs of tens of thousands of American workers."[68]

End Notes

[1] John Williamson of the CRS Knowledge Services Group assisted in the preparation of the data for this chapter, especially for Tables 2-4.

[2] On this divergence in industrial relations organization, see CRS Report RL32883, *U.S. Automotive Industry: Policy Overview and Recent History*, by Stephen Cooney and Brent D. Yacobucci, pp. 37-43.

[3] This ratio is based on annual data for 2006 reported by the U.S. Dept. of Labor, Bureau of Labor Statistics, in "National Employment, Hours and Earnings," drawn from the *Current Employment Statistics* survey. It includes all employees at manufacturing establishments, and, for motor vehicles, all employees included in North American Industry Classification System categories 3361, 3362, and 3363 (these categories will be described below in this chapter). Unless otherwise defined, this categorization is the basis for statements in this chapter regarding motor vehicle manufacturing employment.

[4] However, this does not include steel shipments to metals service centers, some of which also may supply auto parts manufacturers; see "Steel Markets" in American Iron and Steel Institute, *Annual Statistical Report* (2006).

[5] Formally, the United Automobile, Aerospace and Agricultural Implement Workers of America.

[6] For a detailed analysis of this phenomenon, see Thomas H. Klier and Daniel P. McMillen, "The Geographic Evolution of the U.S. Auto Industry," in Federal Reserve Bank of Chicago, *Economic Perspectives* (2nd qtr., 2006), pp. 2-13.

[7] This perspective may have been reinforced by a seminal and critical work on Big Three auto production methods authored by the MIT International Motor Vehicle Project in *The Machine That Changed the World* (New York: Rawson Associates, 1990).

[8] A discussion of this legislation is in CRS Report RL33982, *Corporate Average Fuel Economy (CAFE): A Comparison of Selected Legislation in the 110th Congress*, by Brent D. Yacobucci and Robert Bamberger.

[9] A voter survey taken by the Pew Campaign for Fuel Efficiency and the National Environmental Trust indicated that 69% said they supported the across-the-board 35 mpg light-vehicle standard by 2020 that would be required in the original Senate-passed measure. Only 19% said they supported a moderate alternative (H.R. 2927) proposed in the House and supported by auto manufacturers and the UAW. "When read several of the arguments made by automakers in lobbying ads against the [Senate] plan, including predictions of job cuts and more expensive vehicles, none garnered more than 25% support from those polled." *Detroit Free Press*, "Give Us More M.P.G., Voters Say" (November 10, 2007).

[10] By the accounting in the 2007 *Automotive News Global Market Data Book* (p. 5), Toyota actually outpaced GM in the number of vehicles sold worldwide in 2006, 8.808 million to 8.679 million. According to *Automotive News'* 10-month data for 2007, Toyota had sold 2.199 million cars and light trucks in the U.S. market, compared to 2.166 million vehicles for Ford.

[11] The UAW formerly organized plants in Canada as well, but the separate Canadian Auto Workers union split from the UAW in 1985. The issue of how recent U.S. developments may affect motor vehicle production in Canada is addressed in a later section.

[12] Global Insight. *U.S. Automotive Outlook Webcast* (December 13, 2007), p. 28; and, "Motor Vehicles: News and Views — Forecast Highlights" (December 10, 2007). This source forecast final 2007 U.S. demand at 16.07 million units, with 2008 demand at 15.5 million units. General Motors officials "expect a flat market" in 2008, while Nissan CEO Carlos Ghosn "said the market would be flat at best, ranging between 15.5 and 16 million vehicles;" *Detroit News* (detnews.com), "Slow Auto Sales Forecast for 2008" (November 23, 2007); *Wall St. Journal.online*, "GM Finance Chief Expects Lower Industry Sales" (November 30, 2007).

[13] CRS Report RL32883, Table 3.

[14] It should be noted that by the early 2000s, the market had also seen the evolution of a new product, the "crossover utility vehicle" (CUVs, nicknamed dismissively by off-road purists as "cute utes"). Generally, SUVs are based on a heavy, pickup-truck-type body-on-frame platform. CUVs are lighter, smaller vehicles built to a car-based unibody design, but are still classed as "trucks" within the industry. The Toyota RAV-4 and the Honda CRV, along with Ford's Escape/Mercury Mariner, are the best-known models.

[15] In keeping with conventional automotive terminology, U.S. "imports" do not include vehicles assembled at plants in Canada or Mexico — all the Big Three, as well as all the major foreign OEMs, have assembly plants in one or both countries. CRS Report RL32883, especially Appendix 1, measures the rising trend of vehicles manufactured in such plants.

[16] CRS has examined the increase from Japan in 2006, and concluded that the primary cause was an increase in compact and subcompact vehicles sold in the U.S. market in the face of rising gasoline prices; CRS Report RS22620, *The 2006 Increase in U.S. Motor Vehicle Imports from Japan*.

[17] Totals for Figure 2 include medium and heavy trucks, but these are less than a half-million units annually, and do not alter the trends in the figure, which essentially reflect light vehicle output.

[18] The three plants were GM-Toyota (Fremont, CA), known by the acronym of NUMMI (New United Motor Manufacturing Inc.); the Ford-Mazda "AutoAlliance" plant in Flat Rock, MI; and, the Chrysler-Mitsubishi "DiamondStar" plant in Normal, IL. All are still operating, although Chrysler has dropped out of its j .v. with Mitsubishi.

[19] Global Insight. *Auto Webcast*, pp. 33, 40-41.

[20] Data organized under the NAICS system has been recalculated to cover the entire period.

[21] *Automotive News*, "Endangered Species: Factory Jobs" (November 26, 2007), p. 1.

[22] CRS Report RL32883, pp. 31-33 presents this calculation, based on U.S. Commerce Dept. foreign investment data.

[23] Center for Automotive Research (CAR). *The Big Leave: The Future of Michigan's Automotive Industry*, presentation by Sean McAlinden to RSQE Economic Outlook Conference (November 15, 2007), p. 23. A specialist in the supplier industry forecasts that "half of the estimated 5,200 suppliers in the United States are expected to disappear over the next five years ... About one-third will likely find new buyers, and the rest will go out of business." *Detroit Free Press*, "Component Crisis: Suppliers Dwindling" (November 28, 2007).

[24] Prof. James Rubenstein, quoted in *Automotive News*, "Endangered Species ... ," p. 34.

[25] *Detroit Free Press*, "150,000 Cuts Enough?" (November 5, 2007).

[26] CRS Report RL32883, pp. 33-37, largely based on the work of Thomas Klier and colleagues for the Federal Reserve Bank of Chicago.

[27] McAlinden, *The Big Leave*, pp. 29-30.

[28] This development in discussed in more detail in CRS Report RL32883, pp. 35-36.

[29] In Figure 4 above, and Figure 5 and Table 1 below, it was not possible to include state employment in auto assembly plants (NAICS 3361) for all states, because of federal data disclosure rules. Totals for states that had one or two light vehicle assembly plants were completed by information supplied to CRS by the OEMs themselves.

[30] Toyota and Hyundai have established technical centers in Michigan, and Volkswagen has had its U.S. headquarters in the state, which it announced will be moved to Virginia. Also, foreign-owned auto parts suppliers have numerous operations in the state.

[31] These data are from the same source as the data in Table 1.

[32] Department of Labor, BLS. "Unemployment Rates by State," map and table (December 5, 2007).

[33] U.S. House. Committee on Energy and Commerce, Subcommittee on Energy and Air Quality. *Hearing on Alternative Fuels, Infrastructure, and Vehicles* (June 7, 2007). Testimony of Alan Reuther, Legislative Director — UAW, p. 2. More frequently cited is the UAW count of "17,000 small car production jobs in the United States." See, for example, *Detroit News* (*detnews. com*), "Auto Industry Backs CAFE Deal" (December 2, 2007). Table 2 below provides data on employment at individual assembly plants.

[34] See, for example, comments of House Energy and Commerce Committee Chair John Dingell, quoted in *New York Times*, "Lawmakers Set Deal on Raising Fuel Economy" (December 1, 2007). As Chairman Dingell noted in that article, a provision in present law, requiring that manufacturers meet specified fuel economy standards for both their imported vehicle fleet and their vehicle fleet manufactured in North America, was retained in P.L. 110-140. See 49 U.S.C. §32904(b) for this provision.

[35] CRS Report RS22620.

[36] *Detroit News* (*detnews.com*), "Subcompact Sales Boom" (December 10, 2007).

[37] Quoted in Douglas Brinkley, *Wheels for the World* (New York: Penguin Books, 2003), p. 666. On the same page a Chrysler executive from the same era is quoted as saying, "Even if we don't believe in small cars, we have to build them. There's a law."

[38] These issues are discussed in CRS Report RL32883, pp. 43-46; and CRS Report RL33 169, *Comparing Automotive and Steel Industry Legacy Cost Issues*, pp. 1-6. Sean McAlinden of CAR summarizes the impact on company management in *The Big Leave*, p. 9.

[39] Based on *Detroit News* (*detnews. com*), "Timeline: The Road to Ratification" (November 16, 2007); also, ibid., "New Era Begins for Big 3" (November 15, 2007).

[40] Failure of DaimlerChrysler management to gain similar health care "givebacks" from the UAW (contract modifications) to those agreed with Ford and GM in 2006 is said to have been one of the motivating factors in the decision to sell the Chrysler Group. *Automotive News*, "DCX Board Chief Aims to Undo Schrempp Legacy" (April 2, 2007), p. 3.

[41] See the section on Ford in a *Detroit News* "special report" (*detnews.com*), "Historic UAW Contracts Forged from Angry Words, Picket Lines, Harsh Reality" (November 16, 2007).

[42] While there are many press sources and accounts of these negotiations and agreements, the best summary of the final deals are in McAlinden, *The Big Leave*, pp. 15-20, 47-49. Complete summaries are provided in the following documents: *UAW GM Report* (September 2007); *UAW Chrysler Newsgram* (October 2007); *UAW Ford Report* (November 2007).

[43] For details on the legislative background of VEBAs, see CRS Report RL33505, *Tax Benefits for Health Insurance and Expenses: Overview of Current Law and Legislation*, by Bob Lyke and Julie M. Whittaker.

[44] As summarized in *Financial Times* (*FT.com*), "UAW Could Hold Top GM Stake" (October 1, 2007).

[45] Quoted from McAlinden, *The Big Leave*, p. 17.

[46] Pay and service estimates are from ibid., pp. 18-19. Another account comparing GM with Toyota estimates that total average hourly cost savings would bring GM down to about $50 per hour, compared to Toyota's cost of $47 per hour; *Detroit Free Press*, "How Deal Can Pull GM Even with Toyota" (October 2, 2007).

[47] *Business Week*, "Labor's New Roll of the Dice" (December 24, 2007), p. 37.

[48] The following summary is based on press reports, including commentary on based on publicly circulated UAW documents.

[49] The full list is at *UAW GM Report*, p. 11. See, among many other analyses, *Detroit Free Press*, "UAW Contract: Nuts and Bolts" (September 29, 2007).

[50] Global Insight. *Auto Webcast*, p. 44.

[51] *Detroit Free Press*, "Tough UAW Vote" (October 28, 2007).

[52] *UAW Chrysler Newsgram*, p. 14.

[53] McAlinden, *The Big Leave*, p. 49.

[54] Ibid., and *UAW Ford Report*, pp. 3-5.

[55] McAlinden, *The Big Leave*, p. 49

[56] See CRS Report RL32883, especially pp. 18-23 and Appendix 5.

[57] *Detroit News* (*detnews.com*), "Canada Loses Luster for Big 3" (December 10, 2007).

[58] Ibid., "Ford Will Close Ontario Plant" (December 10, 2007); Global Insight, *Auto Webcast*, p. 44. The latter source also noted on p. 43, however, that Toyota is adding capacity to build 150,000 RAV4 CUVs at Woodstock, ON, in 2008.

[59] Quoted in *Detroit News*, "New Era Begins for Big 3."

[60] On the history of automotive fuel economy legislation, including in the 110th Congress, see CRS Report RL33413, *Automobile and Light Truck Fuel Economy: The CAFE Standards*, by Brent D. Yacobucci and Robert Bamberger.

[61] On House passage, *Washington Post*, "Broad Energy Bill Passed by House" (December 7, 2007), p. A1. On the Senate's actions, *Daily Report for Executives* (*DER*), "Senate Rejects Motion to Limit Debate on Energy Bill

with $21 Billion Tax Package" (December 10, 2007), p. G-5; "Democrats Go Back to Drawing Board on Energy Bill after Senate Roadblock" (December 10, 2007), p. A16; and, "Senate Passes Revised Energy Measure Boosting Fuel Economy, Renewable Fuels" (December 14, 2007), p. A-38.

[62] Ibid., "Senate Passes Energy Legislation after Nixing $21.8 Billion Tax Title" (December 14, 2007), p. G10. Because of anticipated reduction in fuel consumption, tax revenue for the Highway Trust Fund is expected to decline.

[63] P.L. 110-140 §132-135.

[64] These bills are discussed in CRS Report RL33 846, *Greenhouse Gas Reduction: Cap-and-Trade Bills in the 110th Congress*, by Larry Parker and Brent D. Yacobucci. All the bills from both houses are summarized in Appendix A. On approval by the Senate committee, see *DER*, "Senate Committee Approves Legislation to Place Cap on Greenhouse Gas Emissions" (December 6, 2007), p. A-44.

[65] *Automotive News*, "Climate Bill Dangles $40 Billion for Auto Industry" (December 17, 2007), pp. 4 and 45.

[66] Executive Office of the President. Office of the U.S. Trade Representative. *Report of Industry Trade Advisory Committee on Automotive and Capital Goods (ITAC 2)* (April 27, 2007), pp.1-2; and "Ford Motor Company Assessment of the Automotive Provisions of the US-Korea FTA," appended to that report.

[67] "General Motors Corporation Assessment of the Automotive Provisions of the US-Korea FTA," appended to ibid.

[68] U.S. House of Representatives. Committee on Ways and Means. Subcommittee on Trade. Testimony of Alan Reuther (March 20, 2007); and, letter of Alan Reuther to all Members of the House (April 18, 2007), p. 2. A similar letter was sent to all Members of the Senate.

In: The U.S. Auto Industry and the Role of Federal Assistance   ISBN: 978-1-60741-322-6
Editor: James R. Elliot   © 2010 Nova Science Publishers, Inc.

Chapter 4

CHRYSLER CORPORATION LOAN GUARANTEE ACT OF 1979: BACKGROUND, PROVISIONS, AND COST

James M. Bickley

SUMMARY

The American automobile industry has serious financial problems. Corporate executives from the Big Three (General Motors, Ford, and Chrysler) have testified before Congress about their need for federal credit (direct loans and guaranteed loans). This chapter examines the Chrysler loan guarantee program for possible insights that could assist Members of Congress in evaluating proposals to provide federal credit assistance.

In 1979, Chrysler applied for federal loan guarantees. In 1979 and 1980, the economy was in recession and the price of oil had unexpectedly increased dramatically. However, at that time there was no financial liquidity crisis, as is the case today. Most of the arguments for and against the proposed Chrysler loan guarantee program are relevant to current proposals for credit assistance to the Big Three. For example, in the 1979 debate, proponents argued that the Chrysler loan guarantee would save many jobs. But opponents contended that the financial capital obtained for Chrysler by the proposed loan guarantee would have been used by other firms to expand their productive facilities, output, and employment. Thus, any Chrysler job losses could be offset by gains at other firms.

Provisions in the Chrysler Loan Guarantee Act of 1979 included the establishment of a Chrysler Loan Guarantee Board, extensive federal oversight of Chrysler's operations, detailed reporting requirements by Chrysler's management, shared sacrifice of parties benefiting from the loan guarantee, and protection of the federal government's interest.

Chrysler used federal loan guarantees to borrow $1.2 billion of the $1.5 billion available and redeemed its guaranteed loans in 1982. Some critics argued that Chrysler was only able to return to profitability because of the imposition by the U.S. government of "voluntary" import quotas on Japanese vehicles. In 1980, the Chrysler loan guarantee was treated as a contingent liability with no initial cost at the time the guarantee was provided. Because Chrysler repaid all of its guaranteed loans, the U.S. government incurred no budgetary cost. Furthermore, the

U.S. government received warrants to buy Chrysler stock, which it subsequently sold at auction to Chrysler for $311 million. Thus, it can be argued that the U.S. government made a profit from the loan guarantee program.

Currently, the Federal Credit Reform Act requires that the reported budgetary cost of a credit program equal the estimated subsidy costs to the taxpayer at the time the credit is provided. For proposed legislation establishing a new credit program, the Congressional Budget Office is responsible for making the initial estimate of the subsidy cost. Once legislation has been enacted, the Office of Management and Budget estimates the subsidy cost on the credit program. An appropriation for the annual subsidy cost of each credit program is made into a budget account called a "credit program" account. Thus, under today's budgetary rule, legislation providing direct loans or loan guarantees to assist the automobile industry would require the inclusion of the estimated subsidy cost, which would require an appropriation of budget authority.

The American automobile industry has serious financial problems. Corporate executives from the Big Three (General Motors, Ford, and Chrysler) have testified before Congress about their need for federal credit (direct loans and guaranteed loans). This chapter examines the Chrysler Corporation Loan Guarantee Act of 1979 for possible insights that could assist Congress in evaluating proposals to provide federal credit assistance.

BACKGROUND

In the 1960s and 1970s, the Chrysler Corporation had a history of financial instability. During recessionary periods it had incurred large losses, but during periods of prosperity the corporation had usually earned high profits. Yet between 1967 and 1980, the company's domestic market share had declined from 16% to 8.6%, arguably due to managerial errors, foreign competition, regulatory controls, and the energy shortage at that time.

Chrysler failed to introduce a small car in the late 1960s, even though Ford produced the Pinto and General Motors began manufacturing its Vega. Chrysler refused to manufacture a new small automobile until it introduced its Plymouth Horizon and Dodge Omni models in 1977. The rising cost of gasoline, changing consumer tastes, and Environmental Protection Agency's (EPA's) fuel- efficiency standards contributed to Chrysler's troubles, because it had not shifted its production to smaller vehicles. Some corporate financial experts assert that Chrysler should have reduced its dividends in the early 1970s and used the funds to modernize its plant and equipment. Also, Chrysler made a belated attempt to compete overseas with Ford and General Motors, which was unsuccessful.

In 1979, huge losses compelled Chrysler to sell off some of its subsidiaries, close plants, and reduce its employment. In July 1979, Chrysler requested and subsequently received federal loan guarantees to avoid bankruptcy. Losses continued throughout 1979, and Chrysler's total loss for the year was $ 1.126 billion.[1]

Ford and General Motors were in better financial condition than Chrysler, but also experienced large losses in 1979 and 1980 because of the sharp rise in the price of gasoline and the worst economic downturn since the Great Depression. "In 1980, the Big Three [General Motors, Ford, and Chrysler] lost a record $4.2 billion as their sales in that year plummeted 30% below 1978 sales, reaching their lowest level since 1961."[2] As will be discussed in a subsequent section of this chapter, in 1981, the Big Three advocated and received the imposition by the federal government of "voluntary" import quotas on Japanese vehicles. These "voluntary" import quotas contributed to the return to profitability of General Motors and Ford, as well as Chrysler.

ARGUMENTS FOR AND AGAINST THE GUARANTEE

Advocates of the loan guarantees advanced four primary arguments. First, if Chrysler defaulted there would be an enormous loss in employment. Many of these job losses would occur in firms supplying parts and materials to Chrysler. Data Resources Inc. conducted a simulation of the Chrysler collapse and concluded that there would be a 500,000 near-term loss in employment and a longer-term additional employment loss of between 200,000 and 300,000. Second, some of Chrysler's difficulties were beyond its control, particularly large price increases in oil obtained by the Organization of Petroleum Exporting Countries. Third, federal safety, environmental, and fuel efficiency standards had been disproportionately costly for Chrysler compared to General Motors and Ford, because the larger corporations had longer production runs and thus could spread out their regulatory costs over more units. Consequently, Chrysler "deserved" federal compensation for its costs incurred in meeting federal regulations. Fourth, Chrysler manufactured the main battle tank for the U.S. Army; hence, if Chrysler went bankrupt national defense would be weakened.

Opponents of the loan guarantee to Chrysler buttressed their case with five basic arguments. First, they contended that the analysis made by Data Resources Inc. was misleading. The financial capital which Chrysler would obtain with the loan guarantee could be used instead by other firms to expand their productive facilities, output, and employment. In addition, part of Chrysler's lost sales would be picked up by General Motors and Ford. Second, the entire economy was experiencing high energy costs; thus a single firm such as Chrysler did not warrant preferential treatment due to the energy problem. Third, most of the regulatory costs incurred by Chrysler were due to fuel-efficiency standards. Yet Chrysler would have been compelled to improve the average mileage of its automobiles anyway, because of the rising cost of energy. Fourth, if Chrysler went bankrupt it would go into receivership under existing bankruptcy legislation. Profitable operations, such as its tank production division, would continue as a subsidiary of another corporation or as a new corporation. Fifth, the Chrysler loan guarantee might encourage other large corporations to obtain federal financial assistance. This would lead to a greater federal role in the economy and a reduction in the efficiency of private capital markets in allocating credit.

MAJOR PROVISIONS OF THE LOAN GUARANTEE ACT

In January 1980, Chrysler Corporation Loan Guarantee Act of 1979 (the Act) was signed into law as P.L. 96-185. The Act included numerous provisions, which are summarized as follows:[3]

- The Act established the Chrysler Corporation Loan Guarantee Board (the Board), which was composed of the Secretary of the Treasury (chairperson of the Board), the

Chairman of the Board of Governors of the Federal Reserve System, and the Comptroller General of the United States. The Secretary of Labor and the Secretary of Transportation served as ex officio nonvoting members of the Board.

- The Board was responsible for determining the terms and conditions under which it would make commitments to guarantee the payment of principal and interest on loans to Chrysler if the Board determined that (1) Chrysler had an energy- saving plan satisfactory to the Board, (2) the loan guarantee was necessary to prevent serious negative effects of the economy, (3) Chrysler had submitted a satisfactory operating plan, and (4) Chrysler had submitted to the Board a satisfactory financing plan to meet the financing needs of the operating plan and which included an aggregate amount of nonfederally guaranteed assistance of at least $1.43 billion from Chrysler, banks, financial institutions, other creditors, suppliers, dealers, stockholders, labor unions, employees, management, state and local and governments, and others directly deriving benefit from the production, distribution, or sale of the products of Chrysler.

- A loan guarantee could be issued only if the Board determined that (1) credit was not otherwise available to Chrysler under reasonable terms or conditions, (2) Chrysler's prospective earning power and the value of the security pledged had to furnish reasonable assurance of the repayment of the guaranteed loan, (3) the loan to be guaranteed had an interest rate determined by the Board to be reasonable, (4) Chrysler's operating and financing plans continued to meet Board requirements, (5) Chrysler was in compliance with its operating and financing plans, (6) the Board had received assurances that Chrysler's operating and financing plans are realistic and feasible, (7) Chrysler agreed to reporting requirements of a revised operating and financial plan covering the period of the loan guarantee; and within 120 days following the close of each fiscal year, an analysis reconciling the corporation's actual performance with the operating and financial plan was submitted, (8) there was no substantial likelihood that Chrysler would be absorbed by or merged with any foreign entity, and (9) Chrysler was in compliance with the terms and conditions of the commitment to issue the guarantees required by the Board. Any determination by the Board that the conditions established by the Act had been met would be conclusive. The Board would prescribe and collect a guarantee fee sufficient to compensate the federal government for all administrative expenses related to the guarantee but in no case could such fee be less than one-half of 1% per annum of the outstanding principal amount of loans guaranteed. The Board was to ensure that the federal government is compensated for the risk assumed in making guarantees. Thus, the Board was authorized to collect an additional fee above the fee to cover administrative costs, to enter into contracts allowing the federal government to participate in gains from the financial success of Chrysler, or use instruments deeded appropriate by the Board. All amounts collected by the Board would be deposited in the Treasury as miscellaneous receipts.

- The Act described the proportionate share to be contributed by employees in order for Chrysler to receive the loan guarantees.

- The Act required Chrysler to establish an employee stock ownership plan (ESOP).

- The amount of loan guarantees could not at any time exceed $1.5 billion in aggregate principal amount outstanding.

- Loans guaranteed under the Act would be payable in full not later than December 31, 1990.
- The Board was authorized to inspect and copy all accounts, books, records, memoranda, correspondence, and other documents and transactions of Chrysler.
- In order to protect the federal government's interest, the Board was granted extensive oversight authority including approval of the sale of any asset with a value in excess of $5 million and a labor contract having an aggregate value of future wages and benefits of $10 million or more. Debts owed the federal government would have priority, but the Board could wave such priority.
- The Secretary of Transportation would submit to the Board and to Congress a planning study providing an assessment of the long-term viability of Chrysler's involvement in the automobile industry.
- The Board would submit reports to Congress semiannually for 1980 and 1981 and annually for later years.
- The authority of the Board to issue loan guarantees was to expire on December 31, 1983.
- The administrator of the Small Business Administration would investigate whether or not small-business automobile dealers should receive federal loans and loan guarantees.
- The Act included amendments to the Electric and Hybrid Vehicle Research, Development, and Demonstration Act of 1976.

RESULTS OF LOAN GUARANTEE

Chrysler used $1.2 billion of the $1.5 billion in loan guarantees. The corporation downsized its operations and returned to profitability. "The restructuring took place fairly quickly with less interruption of the firm's operations than would have occurred in a bankruptcy."[4] In 1982, Chrysler was profitable and redeemed its government guaranteed notes in June and August of that year.[5]

"Voluntary" Import Quotas

Some critics argue that Chrysler was able to return to profitability because of the imposition by the U.S. government of "voluntary" import quotas on Japanese automobiles, which were negotiated by the Reagan Administration and announced by the Japanese government on May 1, 1981. The Big Three and the United Automobile Workers advocated for restrictions on Japanese automobile imports. Supporters of quotas in the Reagan Administration argued that the American automobile industry needed temporary restraints on imports in order to permit "breathing room" for the Big Three to retool their factories for the production of more fuel efficient vehicles.[6] The "voluntary" import quotas provided financial benefits to the Big Three and American workers in the automobile industry. But, major Japanese manufacturers realized "windfall" profits and American consumers paid higher prices for vehicles.[7]

Budgetary Cost of Guarantee

Before FY1992, federal loan guarantees were treated as a contingent liability of the U.S. government. Thus, at the time a loan guarantee was granted, there was no budgetary cost. Because Chrysler repaid all of its guaranteed loans, no budgetary cost was incurred by the U.S. government. In addition, in return for the loan guarantee, the U.S. government had received from Chrysler 14.4 million warrants to purchase Chrysler stock at $13 per share until 1990. On September 12, 1983, the U.S. government auctioned these warrants, and Chrysler purchased them for $311 million.[8] Thus, it can be argued that, from a budgetary standpoint, the Chrysler loan guarantee program made money for the U.S. government.

CURRENT BUDGETARY COST OF FEDERAL CREDIT

The Omnibus Budget Reconciliation Act of 1990 (P.L. 101-508) added Title V to the Congressional Budget Act.[9] Title V, also called the Federal Credit Reform Act of 1990 (FCRA), changed how the unified budget reports the cost of federal credit activities (i.e., federal direct loans and loan guarantees).[10] Before FY1992, for a given fiscal year, the budgetary cost of a new direct loan or loan guarantee was the net cash flow for that fiscal year. This cash flow measure did not accurately reflect the true cost of a loan or loan guarantee, which is its subsidy cost over the entire life of the loan or loan guarantee.

Beginning with FY1992, federal credit reform legislation required that the reported budgetary cost of a credit program equal the estimated subsidy costs at the time the credit is provided. The FCRA defines the subsidy cost as "the estimated long-term cost to the government of a direct loan or a loan guarantee, calculated on a net present value basis, excluding administrative costs." This places the cost of federal credit programs on a budgetary basis equivalent to other federal outlays. This change means, because the subsidy costs of discretionary credit programs are now provided through appropriations acts, the discretionary credit programs must then compete with other discretionary programs on an equal basis. Funding for most mandatory credit programs (generally entitlement programs) is provided by permanent appropriations. For a proposed credit program, the Congressional Budget Office is required to estimate the subsidy cost. If legislation is passed that includes this credit program, the Director of the Office of Management and Budget (OMB) is responsible for coordinating the estimation of subsidy costs.

An appropriation for the annual subsidy cost of each credit program is made into a budget account called a *credit program account*. Funding for the subsidy costs of discretionary credit programs is provided in appropriation acts and must compete with other discretionary programs for funding available under the constraints of the budget resolution. Most mandatory credit programs receive automatic funding for the amount of credit needed to meet the estimated demand by beneficiaries. Mandatory programs are generally entitlement programs for which the amount of funding depends on eligibility and benefits rules contained in substantive law. The subsidy cost of federal credit is scored as an outlay in the fiscal year in which the credit is disbursed by either the federal government or a private lender [Section 504d]. For mandatory credit programs, any additional cost from reestimates of subsidies for a credit program is covered by permanent indefinite budget authority. This additional cost is displayed in a subaccount in the credit program account.

Also, beginning with FY1992, each credit program has a nonbudget *financing account*. Each of these nonbudget financing accounts receives payments from its associated credit program account equal to the subsidy cost at the time a new loan or loan guarantee is provided. They also acquire the value of the unsubsidized portion of the loans (actual disbursements by the government minus the subsidy cost). These amounts are borrowed from the Treasury through the loan program.[11] Furthermore, the financing accounts contain all other cash flows between the public and the government associated with each credit program [Section 502(5E6-7)]. These flows include "the disbursement and repayment of loans, the payment of default losses on guarantees, and the collection of interest and fees."[12] Because they are nonbudget, the cash flows into and out of these accounts are not reflected in total outlays, receipts, or surplus/deficit. The budget authority of a credit program provides the means for the credit program account to pay to the financing account an amount equal to that program's estimated subsidy costs. The off budget borrowing from the Treasury for the unsubsidized portion of a credit program is included in the national debt.

CONCLUSIONS

This chapter examined the Chrysler Corporation Loan Guarantee Act of 1979 for possible insights that would assist Congress in evaluating proposals to provide federal credit assistance to the Big Three. In 1979-80, the economy was in recession and the price of oil had unexpectedly increased dramatically. However, there was no financial liquidity crisis, which currently exists. Most of the arguments for and against the proposed Chrysler loan guarantee program are relevant to current proposals for credit assistance. Provisions in the Chrysler Loan Guarantee Act of 1979 included the establishment of a Chrysler Loan Guarantee Board, extensive oversight of Chrysler's operations, detailed reporting requirements by Chrysler's management, shared sacrifice of parties benefiting from the guarantee, and protection of the government's interest. Chrysler borrowed $1.2 billion of $1.5 billion available and redeemed its guaranteed loans in 1982. Some critics argued that Chrysler was only able to return to profitability because of the imposition by the U.S. government of "voluntary" import quotas on Japanese vehicles. In 1980, the Chrysler loan guarantee was treated as a contingent liability with no initial cost at the time the guarantee was provided. Currently, the FCRA requires that the reported budgetary cost of a credit program equal the estimated subsidy costs at the time the credit is provided. For proposed legislation establishing a new credit program, CBO is responsible for making the initial estimate of the subsidy cost. For example,

> The Advance Technology Vehicles Manufacturing Loan Program (ATVMLP) was authorized under Section 136 of the Energy Independence and Security Act of 2007 (P.L. 110-140). Congress provided the necessary funding for the loans in a continuing resolution for federal appropriations (P.L. 110-329), approved Sept. 30. The continuing resolution contained provisions to enable automakers to access $25 billion in government loans to retool assembly lines to make more fuel-efficient vehicles. The resolution, enacted to fund the federal government through March 2009, included $7.5 billion to cover the cost of the loan program as estimated by the Congressional Budget Office.[13]

Once legislation has been enacted, OMB estimates the subsidy cost on the credit program.

This chapter's examination of the Chrysler loan guarantee program raises some concerns relevant to today's debate about credit assistance to the Big Three. First, current economic conditions differ for the automobile industry. In 1979, the downturn in automobile sales for the Big Three appeared temporary. Today, the downturn in automobile sales for the Big Three may be protracted and sales may not recover if brands are eliminated and plants permanently closed. Second, in 1979, the budgetary treatment of loan guarantees and direct loans was on a cash flow basis. A loan guarantee was initially treated as cost free because it was a contingent liability of the U.S. government. Thus, possible future costs of a default were not considered. A direct loan was treated as a direct outlay, which did not consider the repayment of principal and interest. Today the cost of a credit program is the estimated subsidy cost to the taxpayer at the time the credit is provided. Third, in 1979 and 1980, if Chrysler ended automobile manufacturing, part of this decline in employment would have been offset by increased employment by General Motors and Ford. But, today this would not occur because all of the Big Three are in financial trouble and are requesting federal credit assistance.

End Notes

[1] U.S. General Accounting Office, *Guidelines for Rescuing Large Failing Firms and Municipalities*, GAO Report GGD-84-34, March 29, 1984, p. 15.

[2] Stephen D. Cohen, *The Route to Japan's Voluntary Export Restraints on Automobiles*, Working Paper No. 20, School of International Service, American University, p. 2. Available at http://www.gwu.edu/~nsarchiv/japan/scohenwp.htm, visited Dec. 1, 2008.

[3] The provisions described in this section of this chapter are from the following source: U.S. Congress, House, *Chrysler Corporation Loan Guarantee Act of 1979*, Conference report no. 96-730 (to accompany H.R. 5860), Washington, Dec. 20, 1979, 19 p.

[4] U.S. General Accounting Office, Guidelines for Rescuing Large Failing Firms and Municipalities, p. 18.

[5] Ibid., p. 17.

[6] Stephen D. Cohen, p. 6.

[7] Robert W. Crandall, "Import Quotas and the Automobile Industry: The Costs of Protectionism," *The Brookings Review*, vol. 2, no. 4, summer 1984, pp. 8-16.

[8] Gary Putka, Chrysler to Pay U.S. $311 Million for Its Warrants, *Wall Street Journal*, Sept. 13, 1983, p. 3.

[9] For a comprehensive analysis of the current budgetary treatment of federal credit, see CRS Report RL30346, *Federal Credit Reform: Implementation of the Changed Budgetary Treatment of Direct Loans and Loan Guarantees*, by James M. Bickley.

[10] Currently, the budgetary cost of federal credit does not include market risk. A Congressional Budget Office (CBO) report examined two ways of including the market price for risk: risk-adjusted discount rates and option-pricing methods. CBO made estimates for the cost of the Chrysler loan guarantee using these two methods, which are available in the following report: Congressional Budget Office, *Estimation the Value of Subsidies for Federal Loans and Loan Guarantees*, Aug. 2004, 27 p.

[11] These transfers within the government represent transfers of budgetary resources rather than actual financial resources.

[12] U.S. Executive Office of the President, Office of Management and Budget, *Analytical Perspectives, Budget of the United States Government, Fiscal Year 2009*, p. 359.

[13] Bureau of National Affairs, *Daily Report for Executives*, no. 216, Nov. 7, 2008, p. A4.

In: The U.S. Auto Industry and the Role of Federal Assistance   ISBN: 978-1-60741-322-6
Editor: James R. Elliot   © 2010 Nova Science Publishers, Inc.

Chapter 5

AUTO INDUSTRY: A FRAMEWORK FOR CONSIDERING FEDERAL FINANCIAL ASSISTANCE

Gene L. Dodaro

WHY GAO PREPARED THIS STATEMENT

The current economic downturn has brought significant financial stress to the auto manufacturing industry. Recent deteriorating financial, real estate, and labor markets have reduced consumer confidence and available credit, and automobile purchases have declined. While auto manufacturers broadly have experienced declining sales in 2008 as the economy has worsened, sales of the "Big 3" (General Motors, Chrysler, and Ford) have also declined relative to those of some other auto manufacturers in recent years because higher gasoline prices have particularly hurt sales of sport utility vehicles.

In addition to causing potential job losses at auto manufacturers, failure of the domestic auto industry would likely adversely affect other sectors. Officials from the Big 3 have requested, and Congress is considering, immediate federal financial assistance.

This testimony discusses principles that can serve as a framework for considering the desirability, nature, scope, and conditions of federal financial assistance. Should Congress decide to provide financial assistance, we also discuss how these principles could be applied in these circumstances. The testimony is based on GAO's extensive body of work on previous federal rescue efforts that dates back to the 1970s.

WHAT GAO FOUND

From our previous work on federal financial assistance to large firms and municipalities, we have identified three fundamental principles that can serve as a framework for considering future assistance. These principles are (1) identifying and defining the problem, (2) determining the national interests and setting clear goals and objectives that address the problem, and (3) protecting the government's interests. First, problems confronting the industry must be clearly defined—separating out those that require an immediate response from those structural challenges that will take more time to resolve. Second, Congress should determine whether the national interest will be best served through a legislative solution, or whether market forces and established legal procedures, such as bankruptcy, should be allowed to take their course. Should Congress decide that federal financial assistance is warranted, it is important that Congress establish clear objectives and goals for this assistance. Third, given the significant financial risk the federal government may assume, the structure Congress sets up to administer any assistance should provide for appropriate mechanisms, such as concessions by all parties, controls over management, compensation for risk, and a strong independent board, to protect taxpayers from excessive or unnecessary risks.

These principles could help the Congress in deciding whether to offer financial assistance to the domestic auto manufacturers. If Congress determines that a legislative solution is in the national interest, a two-pronged approach could be appropriate in these circumstances. Specifically, Congress could 1) authorize immediate, but temporary, financial assistance to the auto manufacturing industry and 2) concurrently establish a board to approve, disburse, and oversee the use of these initial funds and provide any additional federal funds and continued oversight. This board could also oversee any structural reforms of the companies. Among other responsibilities, Congress could give the board authority to establish and implement eligibility criteria for potential borrowers and to implement procedures and controls in order to protect the government's interests.

Chairman Frank, Ranking Member Bachus, and Members of the Committee:

We appreciate the opportunity to testify on possible federal assistance to the domestic auto industry. The current economic downturn has added to the significant financial stress facing that industry. Deteriorating financial, real estate, and labor markets have reduced consumer confidence and available credit, and automobile purchases have declined. After reaching a recent high of about 1.8 million in July 2005, the number of vehicles sold in the United States dropped to about 800,000 in October 2008, approximately a 54 percent decline. While most auto manufacturers have experienced declining sales in 2008, recent economic conditions have particularly hurt sales of the "Big 3" domestic auto manufacturers (General Motors, Ford, and Chrysler), in part because these companies have historically derived most of their sales from vehicles such as sport utility vehicles, which are less fuel efficient, but more profitable than small cars. Higher gasoline prices over the past several years, which rose to over $4 per gallon in the summer of 2008 before falling steeply this fall, have contributed to a sharp decline in consumer demand for these vehicles. The tightening of the credit markets has also affected the Big 3 and their suppliers, which together employ about 730,000 people. In addition to potential job losses at auto manufacturers, the collapse or partial collapse of the domestic auto industry would adversely affect auto dealers, suppliers, and other sectors.

Officials from the Big 3 have requested immediate federal financial assistance, reporting that their companies are experiencing significant financial stress.[1] Less than three days ago, the Big 3 submitted business plans to Congress that describe their requests for federal assistance and restructuring plans. Congress has asked us to review these plans. In deciding whether to provide financial assistance, Congress must consider and balance the perceived need for expedience with the need to put a structure in place to ensure that the interests of taxpayers are safeguarded and the specific problems that have put the industry in its current financial crisis are addressed.

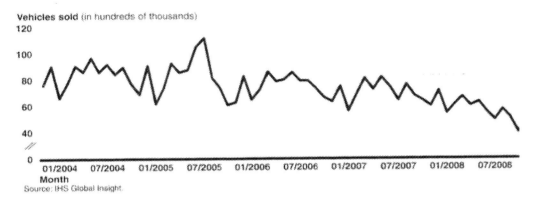

Number of Vehicles Sold By the Big 3, 2004 to 2008

In my statement today, I will discuss principles that could serve as a framework for considering the desirability, nature, scope, and conditions of possible federal financial assistance and, should Congress decide to provide financial assistance, how these principles could be applied in these circumstances. My remarks are based on our extensive body of work on previous federal financial assistance efforts that dates back to the 1970s, including those efforts directed to individual large corporations, such as the Chrysler Corporation and Lockheed Aircraft Corporation, as well as municipalities and commercial aviation.[2]

SUMMARY

From our previous work on federal financial assistance to large firms and municipalities, we have identified three fundamental principles that can serve as a framework for considering future assistance. First, the problems confronting the industry need to be clearly defined—distinguishing between those that require an immediate financial response from those that are likely to require more time to resolve. Second, Congress must determine whether the national interest will be served best through a legislative solution, or whether market forces and established legal procedures, such as bankruptcy reorganization, should be allowed to take their course. Should Congress decide that federal financial assistance is warranted, it is important that Congress establish clear objectives and goals for this assistance. Third, given the significant financial risk the federal government may assume on behalf of taxpayers, the structure Congress sets up to administer any assistance should provide for appropriate mechanisms, such as concessions by all parties, controls over management, compensation for risk, and a strong independent board, to protect taxpayers from excessive or unnecessary risks.

Congress could apply these principles when deciding whether to offer any financial assistance to the domestic auto manufacturers. If Congress determines that a legislative solution is in the national interest, a two-pronged approach in applying the principles could be appropriate in these circumstances. Specifically, Congress could 1) authorize immediate, but temporary, financial assistance to the auto manufacturing industry and 2) concurrently establish a board to approve, disburse, and oversee the use of these initial funds and provide any additional federal funds and continued oversight. This board could also oversee any structural reforms of the companies. Among other responsibilities, Congress could give the board authority to establish and implement eligibility criteria for potential borrowers and to implement procedures and controls in order to protect the government's interests.

PRINCIPLES FOR LARGE-SCALE FEDERAL FINANCIAL ASSISTANCE EFFORTS COULD GUIDE CONGRESSIONAL CONSIDERATION OF AUTO MANUFACTURERS' REQUESTS

We have identified three fundamental principles that can serve as a framework for considering large-scale federal assistance efforts. These principles are (1) identifying and defining the problem, (2) determining the national interests and setting clear goals and objectives that address the problem, and (3) protecting the government's interests.

- **Identify and define the problem:** The government should clearly identify and define the specific problems confronting the industry— separating out those that require an immediate response from those structural challenges that will take more time to resolve. According to the auto manufacturers, the most immediate threat to the industry comes from inadequate cash reserves and negative projected cash flows combined with a tightening or denial of credit by commercial lending institutions. General Motors and Ford have not been profitable since at least 2006, and sales have decreased substantially for the Big 3 in 2008.[3] In this regard, deteriorating financial and real estate markets, weakening labor markets, and high fuel prices have contributed to reductions in consumers' demand for new vehicles, particularly less fuel-efficient vehicles. In addition, tightening consumer credit has made it difficult for some consumers to obtain auto loans. The industry, however, also faces structural challenges that will need to be dealt with, including higher labor and pension costs than competitors, dealership relationships and structure, and fleet characteristics— especially in the area of fuel efficiency.

- **Determine national interests and set clear goals and objectives that address the problem:** After defining the problem, Congress must determine whether a legislative solution best serves the national interest. If Congress determines that the benefits of federal intervention exceed those of bankruptcy reorganization for one or more of the domestic manufacturers, Congress could draft legislation to guide the availability and use of federal assistance. It is important that the legislation include a clear and concise statement of the objectives and goals of the assistance program. A statement of the objectives and goals of the program would help Congress and program administrators determine which financial tools are needed and most appropriate for the industry and for company- specific circumstances; provide criteria for program decisions; and serve as a basis for monitoring progress. Finally, although Congress may decide that there is a compelling national interest in providing financial assistance to help ensure the long-term viability of the Big 3, companies receiving assistance should not remain under federal protection indefinitely. Identifying the conditions that will signal an end to that protection would serve as congressional guidance on when the industry should emerge from the assistance program.

- **Protecting the government's interest:** Because these assistance programs pose significant financial risk to the federal government, appropriate mechanisms should be included to protect taxpayers from excessive or unnecessary risks. Mechanisms, structures, and protections should be implemented to ensure prudent use of taxpayer resources and manage the government's risk consistent with a good faith attempt to achieve the congressional goals and objectives of any federal financial assistance program.[4] This can be achieved through the following four actions—all of which have been used in the past.[5]

    1. *Concessions from others:* Congress should require concessions from others with a stake in the outcome—including management, labor, suppliers, dealers, and creditors. The concessions are not meant to extract penalties for past actions, but to ensure cooperation and flexibility in securing a successful future outcome.

    2. *Controls over management:* The government must have the authority to approve an aid recipient's financial and operating plans and new major contracts. The authority is meant to ensure a restructuring plan with realistic objectives and to hold management accountable for achieving results.

    3. *Collateral:* To the extent feasible, the government should require that the recipient provide adequate collateral, and that the government be in a first lien position.

    4. *Compensation for risk:* The government should receive compensation through fees and/or equity participation in return for providing federal aid. The government's participation in any upside gains is particularly important if the program succeeds in restoring the recipient's financial operational health.[6]

USING THE PRINCIPLES AS A FRAMEWORK FOR CONSIDERING FINANCIAL ASSISTANCE FOR THE AUTO MANUFACTURING INDUSTRY

Congress could apply these principles if it decides to offer financial assistance to the domestic auto manufacturers. If Congress determines that the systemic, economic consequences of risking the immediate failure of any or all of these companies are too great, a two-pronged approach in applying the principles could be appropriate. Specifically, Congress could 1) authorize immediate, but temporary, financial assistance to the auto manufacturing industry and 2) concurrently establish a board to approve, disburse, and oversee the use of these initial funds and provide any additional federal funds and continued oversight. This board could also oversee any structural reforms of the companies. Among other responsibilities, Congress could give the board authority to establish and implement eligibility criteria for potential borrowers and to implement procedures and controls in order to protect the government's interests.

The federal government has a range of tools it could use to provide such bridge assistance, including loans and loan guarantees.[7] Historically, the federal government has used loans and loan guarantees in its financial assistance to specific companies. In providing such credit assistance, the government has assumed that the federal role is to help the industry overcome a cyclical or event-specific crisis by gaining access to cash in the short term that it otherwise cannot obtain through the markets. Credit assistance assumes that the aided companies will eventually return to financial health and have the capacity to pay back the loans. The government has offered such assistance in return for companies providing various forms of collateral and/or equity to protect taxpayer interests, as well as for various concessions by interested parties to share the risk and promote shared responsibility. For example, any federal assistance to an auto manufacturer might seek to ensure that all parties, including labor and management, share responsibility for bringing the company back to profitability, and that no party makes excessive concessions relative to the other parties. Finally, accountability should be built in so that Congress and the public can have confidence that the assistance was prudent and consistent with the identified objectives. For example, as a condition for receiving federal assistance, the auto manufacturers should be required to provide program administrators and appropriate oversight bodies with access to their financial records and submit detailed operating and financial plans indicating how the funds and other sources of financing will be used to successfully return the companies to profitability. Such information would allow program administrators to oversee the use of funds and to hold the companies accountable for results.

Congress should concurrently establish a board to approve, disburse, and oversee the use of these initial funds and provide any additional federal funds and continued oversight. This board could also oversee any structural reforms of the companies. The federal government has established boards to implement past financial assistance efforts, including when providing assistance to Lockheed in 1971 and Chrysler in 1980. More recently, in the aftermath of the 2001 terrorist attacks on the United States, Congress created the Air Transportation Stabilization Board (ATSB) to provide loan guarantees to the airline industry. The voting members of ATSB included a member of the Board of Governors of the Federal Reserve System and representatives from the Departments of the Treasury and Transportation. While the exact membership of a board to provide financial assistance to the Big 3 auto manufacturers could differ, past federal financial assistance efforts suggest that it would be prudent to include representatives from agencies knowledgeable about the auto manufacturing industry as well as from those agencies skilled in financial and economic analysis and assistance. In creating such a board, it will be crucial for Congress to ensure that the board, similar to boards created to implement past federal financial assistance efforts, has access to all financial or operational records for any recipients of federal assistance so that informed judgments and reviews can occur.[8] It would also be important to ensure that the board has the authority and resources to hire or contract for necessary legal, financial, and other expertise.[9] For example, ATSB hired an executive director, financial analyst, and legal counsel to help the board carry out its duties.

Beyond access to records and expertise, however, to succeed in achieving the goal of a restructured industry, the board is likely to need the authority to implement procedures and controls to protect the government's interests. This would include bringing the parties with a stake in a successful outcome to the table. Our review of past large-scale financial assistance efforts leads us to conclude that all of these parties must make concessions—not as penalties for past actions but rather to ensure cooperation in securing a successful future. The board would also need authority to approve the borrower's operating and financial plans and major new contracts to ensure the plans are realistic and to assess management's efforts in achieving results. In addition, the federal government should be the first creditor to be repaid in the event of a bankruptcy or when the company returns to profitability. In 1980, when providing assistance to Chrysler, Congress mandated that Chrysler meet additional policy-oriented requirements such as achieving certain energy efficiency goals and placed limits on executive compensation. More recently, as a condition of receiving federal assistance in the wake of the September 11 terrorist attacks, the Air Transportation Safety and System Stabilization Act required that airlines limit executive compensation.[10]

In addition, the board, consistent with congressional direction, could require that manufacturers, with the cooperation of labor unions, take steps to help control costs. Such steps could include reducing excess capacity by closing or downsizing manufacturing facilities, reducing work- rule restrictions that limit flexibility in terms of which workers can do what types of jobs, and ending contracts with dealerships that require the manufacturer to pay a large buyout to a dealer if a product line is eliminated. Some of these steps should be specifically addressed in the legislation. It will be important to keep in mind, however, that the affected parties will cooperate only if the assistance program offers a better alternative than bankruptcy. The government should not expect creditors, for example, to make concessions that will cost them more than they would expect to lose in a bankruptcy proceeding.[11] Finally, Congress should provide the board with enough flexibility to balance requirements in each recipient's business plan to achieve and maintain profitability.

The board could be the logical entity to establish and implement clearly defined eligibility criteria for potential borrowers, consistent with statutory direction provided by Congress, and establish other safeguards to help protect the government's interests and limit the government's exposure to loss. The safeguards could vary, depending on the nature of the financial assistance tools used. Examples of safeguards over loans and loan guarantees that have been used in the past include the following:

- Potential borrowers have been required to demonstrate that they meet specific eligibility criteria, consistent with congressional direction as to the problems to be addressed and the objectives and goals of the assistance.
- Potential borrowers have been required to demonstrate that their prospective earning power, together with the character and value of any security pledged, provided reasonable assurance of repayment of the loan in accordance with its terms.
- Potential borrowers have been required to clearly indicate the planned use of the loans so that the board could make appropriate decisions about the borrower's financial plan and terms and conditions, as well as collateral.
- The government has charged fees to help offset the risks it assumed in providing such assistance.
- For loan guarantees, the level of guarantee has been limited to a given percentage of the total amount of the loan outstanding.

To further enhance accountability and promote transparency, the board should monitor the status of federal assistance on a regular basis and require regular reporting from companies receiving assistance. This reporting should, at a minimum, include information on cash flow, financial position, and results of independent audits. In addition, the board should be required to provide periodic reports to Congress. This reporting should include status reports on the amount and types of assistance provided to the auto manufacturing industry, periodic assessments of the effectiveness of the assistance, and status of any repayments of loans that the federal government has provided to the industry.

In addition to providing oversight and accountability of the federal funds, the board could be charged with overseeing efforts of the assisted companies to implement required changes and reform. The board would likely need to consider industry-specific issues in implementing financial assistance and industry reform. Employee compensation would be one of those issues, and a very complex one. Benefits for auto industry workers represent a significant long-term financial commitment of the companies seeking assistance, much of it to retirees and their families. Although success in a company's future will depend in part on sacrifice from all stakeholders, most of the changes in this area will necessarily take effect over the long term. The complexities of these arrangements and their interface with active workers and with existing government programs will make implementing federal assistance particularly challenging. For example, the board would need to consider the impact that a possible bankruptcy filing by an auto manufacturer would have on the Pension Benefit Guaranty Corporation, the federal agency that insures private employers' defined benefit pensions, and whose cumulative balance is already negative.

CONCLUDING OBSERVATIONS

In conclusion, Congress is faced with a complex and consequential decision regarding the auto manufacturers' request for financial assistance. The collapse or partial collapse of the domestic auto manufacturing industry would have a significant ripple effect throughout other sectors of the economy and serve as a drag on an already weakened economy. However, providing federal financial assistance to the auto manufacturing industry raises concerns about protecting the government's interests and the precedent such assistance could set for other industries seeking relief from the current economic downturn.

My remarks today have focused on principles Congress may wish to consider as it contemplates possible financial assistance for the auto manufacturing industry. These principles are drawn directly from GAO's support of congressional efforts over several decades to assist segments of industries, firms, the savings and loan industry, and municipalities. Although the principles do not provide operational rules outlining exactly what should be done, they do provide a framework for considering federal financial assistance. By defining the problem, determining whether a legislative solution to that problem best serves the national interest, and— assuming that such a solution is appropriate—establishing an appropriate governance structure, Congress might better assure itself and the American people that the federal assistance will achieve its intended purpose.

Thank you Mr. Chairman, Ranking Member Bachus, and members of the committee for having me here today. We at GAO, of course, stand ready to assist you and your colleagues as you tackle these important challenges.

End Notes

[1] For example, as of September 30, 2008 General Motors reported total liabilities of over $169.4 billion with total assets of about $110.4 billion, resulting in negative equity of nearly $59 billion. General Motors has requested total financial assistance of $18 billion. As of September 30, 2008 Ford reported total liabilities of debt of about $242.6 billion with total assets of about $242.1 billion, resulting in negative equity of approximately $0.5 billion. Officials from Ford have requested a "stand-by" line of credit up to $9 billion, to be used if conditions worsen. Because Chrysler is privately owned, data on its financial condition is not currently available to the public. Nevertheless, officials from Chrysler have stated that without immediate assistance, its liquidity could fall below the level necessary to sustain operations. Chrysler has requested $7 billion of financial assistance.

[2] GAO, *Troubled Financial Institutions: Solutions to the Thrift Industry Problem* (GAO/GGD-89-47, Feb. 21, 1989), *Resolving the Savings and Loan Crisis* (GAO/T-GGD-89-3, Jan. 26, 1989), *Guidelines for Rescuing Large Failing Firms and Municipalities* (GAO/GGD-84-34, Mar. 29, 1984), and *Commercial Aviation: A Framework for Considering Federal Financial Assistance* (GAO-01-1163T, Sept. 20, 2001).

[3] Chrysler is a private company and does not report its profits or losses publicly.

[4] GAO-01-1163T.

[5] GAO/GGD-84-34.

[6] In a previous financial assistance package for Chrysler, the government obtained equity participation in the form of warrants that allow the government to purchase shares of a recipient's stock at a specified price. A decision on whether equity participation should be included as well as its form and amount should be made on a case-by-case basis.

[7] Loan guarantees help borrowers obtain access to credit with more favorable terms than they may otherwise obtain in private lending markets because the federal government guarantees to pay lenders if the borrowers default, which makes extending credit more attractive to lenders. Loan guarantees have the advantage of encouraging private-sector participation and potential expertise, with higher levels of federal guarantees likely generating the most participation. The Office of Management and Budget's Circular A-129, *Policies for Federal Credit Programs and Non-Tax Receivables* prescribes policies and procedures for justifying, designing, and managing federal credit programs. This guidance states that lenders should have a substantial stake in full repayment, generally 20 percent. Limiting the federal guarantee to 80 percent ensures that lenders share in the risks associated with the loan. However, given the current problems in the credit sector, lenders may be unable to provide large loans and unwilling to accept such risks.

[8] In addition, prior federal assistance programs for failing firms and municipalities gave GAO the authority to audit the accounts of the recipients and the right of access to the records needed to do so. This authority enabled GAO to support congressional oversight of the assistance program.

[9] Staff could also be detailed from federal agencies represented on the board to support the board's review and oversight function.

[10] P.L. No. 107-42.

[11] GAO/GGD-84-34.

In: The U.S. Auto Industry and the Role of Federal Assistance   ISBN: 978-1-60741-322-6
Editor: James R. Elliot   © 2010 Nova Science Publishers, Inc.

Chapter 6

STATEMENT OF THE MOTOR AND EQUIPMENT MANUFACTURER'S ASSOCIATION

James McElya

The Motor & Equipment Manufacturers Association (MEMA) represents almost 700 companies that manufacture motor vehicle parts for use in the light vehicle and heavy duty original equipment and aftermarket industries. MEMA represents its members through three market segment associations: Automotive Aftermarket Suppliers Association (AASA), Heavy Duty Manufacturers Association (HDMA), and Original Equipment Suppliers Association (OESA).

Today's auto industry is interdependent such that it is economically impossible to separate the economic success of the suppliers from their manufacturer customers. Congress must include suppliers in any auto industry financial assistance package or the country will be faced with massive job losses and the eventual breakdown of this vital sector of our economy.

A recent study by the Center for Automotive Research (CAR) shows that the collapse of any single vehicle manufacturer will cause over 2 million jobs lost and will have an impact over $100 billion on the nation's economy.[1] When faced with those facts, Congress may be tempted to deal only with the challenges of the vehicle manufacturers. However, the automotive industry is so interdependent that we must address the needs of the automobile manufacturers *and* suppliers to forestall an immediate crisis and future shut-downs of the entire auto industry. A potential bankruptcy by a major vehicle manufacturer will cause serious disruptions and will directly impact the ability of the entire industry to function. At the same time, suppliers must have an infusion of working capital to continue to operate.

MEMA urges Congress to immediately pass legislation providing direct financial assistance to the automotive industry, including suppliers. This could be accomplished through the establishment of a loan program for the auto industry through the Troubled Asset Relief Program (TARP) or other funding. Use of the TARP is appropriate since it was designed and structured to assist the economy and improve both credit and economic measures. It will also provide a back-stop from further employment reductions and future bankruptcies.

Quite simply –

- Motor vehicle suppliers are leaders in innovation in the auto industry.
- Motor vehicle suppliers are the nation's largest manufacturing employer. Our high wage, high skill jobs are critical to the industrial base of the country, and are located throughout the United States. Suppliers are the largest manufacturing sector in seven states: Ohio, Indiana, Kentucky, Michigan, Missouri, South Carolina, and Tennessee.
- Motor vehicle suppliers are restructuring to meet the demands of the 21st century.
- Motor vehicle suppliers account for 40 percent of total automotive investment in research and development.
- Motor vehicle suppliers provide a growing amount of content of all vehicles manufactured in the U.S.
- The current economic challenges, particularly the virtual elimination of banking credit, have developed into a crisis for the entire automotive industry.

INDUSTRY OVERVIEW

The motor vehicle manufacturer and supplier industry are leaders in the development of safety and energy technology critical to creating today's vehicles and those of the next generation. The members of MEMA have long worked with their customers to develop technologies that improve vehicle performance, safety, and fuel economy through a variety of components. A recent study found that suppliers now account for as much as 70 percent of the value-added in the manufacture of motor vehicles[2]. Suppliers account for over 40 percent of total automotive investment in research and development and continue to take on a greater role in the design, testing, and engineering of new vehicle parts and systems – a role that is expected to grow significantly over the next five years. Supplier companies are not only becoming increasingly responsible for producing significant segments of motor vehicles but also are more likely to solely design and engineer those parts.

The employment base of the supplier industry reaches far beyond Michigan across all 50 states. (See *Appendix 1*) In fact, the collective direct employment in the other six states where suppliers are the largest manufacturing sector far exceeds the employment in Michigan: Ohio (97,323); Indiana (86,934); Kentucky (35,102); Missouri (18,888); South Carolina (20,943); and, Tennessee (45,749). Every supplier job contributes an additional 5.7 jobs to the local economy with a total of 4.5 million private industry jobs dependent on the motor vehicle supplier industry.

While supplier employment is contracting, it remains the largest manufacturing sector in the United States. The 2007 CAR study found that suppliers to the automotive industry directly employed 722,600 U.S. workers. As of June 2008, that domestic industry employment fell to 590,000 workers. That is a loss of more than 130,000 good paying American jobs in less than two years. These figures do not take into account recent workforce reductions or impact of job losses in the aftermarket and heavy duty sectors.

Some analysts have indicated that as much as half of the supply base is in distress. The U.S. light vehicles sales dropped 14.6 percent year-to-date by October 2008 with a projection of 13.2 million sales this year, far below the 16.15 million in 2007. North American light vehicle production – including all manufacturers – has fallen 16 percent year-to-date and production schedules remain tenuous through the remainder of the year. These are levels we have not seen since 1980 and the additional pressure of unprecedented frozen consumer and commercial credit exacerbates the financial distress. It is critical to resolve the financial crisis and return credit availability to consumers to turn vehicle sales and production around.

ROLE OF SUPPLIERS IN LIGHT VEHICLE MARKET

Original equipment suppliers to the passenger car market interact directly with motor vehicle manufacturers. Each of the more than 300 different new light vehicle models sold every year in the U.S. has 8,000 to 10,000 components. Original equipment suppliers design and manufacture the parts needed by the automakers to assemble motor vehicles.

Although most vehicle purchasers recognize only the nameplate on a car, in reality the industry is composed of two types of manufacturers: car manufacturers and parts manufacturers. More and more responsibility for new technology innovation and development derives from the parts manufacturers or suppliers. (See *Appendix 2*)

"The supply base of today's carmakers is structured like a pyramid. On top of the pyramid is the carmaker. Below the carmakers are ... Tier 1 suppliers that sell parts directly to carmakers. Tier 1 suppliers in turn purchase materials from Tier 2 suppliers, who purchase from Tier 3 suppliers, and so on down the supply chain." *Who Really Made Your Car at 109.*

Until the last decade, U.S. carmakers generally produced a majority of their own parts. This role has changed dramatically with the responsibility for the manufacture of most parts falling to suppliers. These suppliers, in turn, depend less on any single car manufacturer as a customer. Ford, General Motors, and Chrysler controlled 84 percent of the North American production in 1992 versus an estimated 59 percent in 2008. The suppliers are also completely engaged on the logistics side providing the car manufacturers with just-in-time (JIT) delivery of parts with neither party having a significant stock pile of unused supplier inventory. Less vertical integration and customer concentration, along with greater JIT deliveries, makes the industry completely interdependent.

According to the authors of *Who Really Made Your Car*, "... carmakers are offering large contracts to only a handful of suppliers, which are consolidating into fewer larger firms ..." *Who Really Made Your Car at 19.* The authors go on to note:

> "Productivity improvements and the declining market share of domestic OEMs have led to considerable consolidation among motor vehicle parts suppliers" (Hill, Menk, and Szakaly 2007, p.10). "Since the early 1990s ... the largest 20-30 suppliers in the industry have taken on a much larger role in the areas of design, production, and foreign investment, shifting the balance of power in some small measure away from lead firm towards suppliers" (Sturgeon, Van Biesebroech, and Gereffi 2007, p. 3). As a result, "(w)hile the total number of vehicles produced in North America grew by 40 percent between 1991 and 2005 ... the combined sales of the largest 150 suppliers in North America almost tripled over the same period ..." (Hill, Menk, and Szakaly 2007, p. 24).

The dramatic and sudden contraction of the auto industry will directly impact the supply base but the failure of any single, critical supplier will impact a wide range of car manufacturers. The collapse of a relatively small number of suppliers will directly and negatively impact vehicle production and sales beyond General Motors, Ford, and Chrysler.

Other vehicle manufacturers including Toyota, Honda, and Nissan will likely have to close or limit production for months while waiting for new sources of supply to be developed.

INNOVATION AND CHANGE IN THE INDUSTRY

Suppliers are working daily on a wide variety of fuel efficiency and safety technologies. The new corporate average fuel economy (CAFE) requirements provide both opportunities and challenges for the supplier industry. In March 2006, the National Highway Traffic Safety Administration (NHTSA) announced the Final Rule on Light Truck Average Fuel Economy standards, increasing the miles-per-gallon (mpg) truck target to an average of 24 mpg in model year (MY) 2011. This was the first change to the CAFE program in over two and a half decades. The Energy Independence and Security Act of 2007 (EISA) mandated changing fuel economy standards for all U.S. cars, light trucks and SUVs raising CAFE to an average of 35 mpg – a 40 percent increase over current levels – for MYs 2011 and 2020. By year's end, it is expected that NHTSA will publish the new CAFE Standards Final Rule for MYs 2011-2015.

Many suppliers are ready for these new challenges. The fuel efficiency initiatives give an overview of the scope of tasks undertaken by the supply industry. These include key enablers for hybrids, plug-in hybrids, electric, and fuel cell vehicles and to the development of components required for and compatible with the use of cellulosic and non-carbon fuel sources. The attached technology roadmap (See *Appendix 3*) provides a visual overview of the new technologies on which suppliers are currently working to bring to market on a wide scale.

MEMA supported the passage of EISA and the appropriations of $25 billion in funding for the Advanced Technology Vehicle Manufacturing Incentive (Section 136) loan program. The industry believes this funding will provide a necessary infusion of capital to bring many of the new and important technologies to market. This funding should not be repositioned to address the broader financial needs of the automotive industry.

The industry is reorganizing at a rapid pace while at the same time developing new initiatives to meet the demands of the 21st century. According to Grant Thornton (See *Appendix 4*) a significant amount of restructuring through merger, acquisition, and bankruptcy has taken place in 2008. Grant Thornton cites 20 major mergers and acquisitions in 2008, while AlixPartners (See *Appendix 5*) cites 22 major bankruptcy filings since 2001 equaling sales of almost $75 billion[3]. Despite the stresses of restructuring, this industry continues to reinvent itself and to be innovative.

A CRISIS OF LIQUIDITY

The U.S. auto industry is facing significant issues including –

- Plummeting consumer confidence in the overall economy
- A continued nationwide and systematic lack of credit availability
- Decrease in volume of vehicles built and sold

It is the inability to get credit that has pushed these seemingly unrelated factors into a crisis. According to Fitch Ratings in an October 27, 2008 report on the Liquidity of U.S. Auto Suppliers:

> "The primary risk for the Detroit Three and the auto supply base is the widening effect of the credit crisis further restricts the ability and willingness to extend credit to and within the industry, leading to the withdrawal of trade credit. Trade credit is a critical part of the industry's financial structure and, as is the case in the retail segment, the curtailment of trade credit is typically the catalyst for a bankruptcy filing. The risk of this occurring in the auto sector remains high repercussions." *Fitch at p. 7*

There have been recent and serious repercussions. On November 13, 2008, Standard & Poor's Rating Service took an unprecedented step of placing 15 North American auto suppliers on Credit Watch based on their significant exposure to General Motors, Ford, and Chrysler. The report stated in part, "The suppliers placed on Credit Watch span a wide range of credit quality and have varying degrees of exposure to the Michigan-based automakers. We believe certain companies would be able to withstand the liquidity shock of a sudden bankruptcy filing by one or more of the manufacturers, but they may not be able to do so and remain at current rating levels." (See *Appendix 6*)

The automotive industry requires capital to manufacture the innovative products required by consumers. The U.S. industry is now placed in the position of competing with manufacturers from other countries who have been provided with a wide range of financial support. Support has been provided in countries as far-flung as France and China. In order for our industry to stabilize and to continue to innovate, assistance must be provided within our borders.

CONCLUSION

The future of U.S. economy is directly tied to the success of the automobile industry. According to Dr. David Cole, Chairman of the Center for Automotive Research, success of the industry will require improvements in cost, revenue, agility and innovation. MEMA is not advocating for a blank check against these forces. The proposed $25 billion bridge loan through the TARP will permit the automotive industry sufficient time to right size without further damaging other portions of the industry in current distress but not in crisis.

The country is faced with two interwoven and dire conditions in the auto industry. First, a potential bankruptcy of a major automobile manufacturer will cause a chain reaction of unpaid payables with subsequent additional bankruptcies that will severely and negatively impact the entire sector. Secondly, on a parallel course, is the inability of the automotive supplier industry to get sufficient working capital from its traditional sources to function. Congress must pass legislation that addresses both of these challenges. Due to the indubitable interdependency in the auto industry, any funding made available to the carmakers must also be made available to automotive suppliers.

Addressing these issues with funding is not a bail-out; rather it provides companies the urgently needed access to capital so that they can reinvest in our nation's communities. We are faced with a difficult time, but suppliers will continue to provide good jobs for American families, build cutting-edge technologies for tomorrow's vehicles, and support a strong manufacturing sector. We look forward to working with you on these urgent matters. The health of the U.S. automotive and supplier industry and the jobs they create for millions of Americans depend on the success of our efforts.

APPENDIX 1 . AUTOMOTIVE SUPPLIER INDUSTRY EMPLOYMENT DATA

State	Direct Employment
TOTAL	**783,061**
Michigan	145,818
Ohio	97,323
Indiana	86,934
Tennessee	45,749
Illinois	40,063
Kentucky	35,102
New York	31,017
California	28,596
North Carolina	27,589
Pennsylvania	22,917
Georgia	22,701
Wisconsin	21,502
South Carolina	20,943
Texas	20,175
Missouri	18,888
Alabama	15,965
Mississippi	13,179
Florida	9,273
Arkansas	7,922
Virginia	7,796
Kansas	7,508
Oklahoma	6,986
Iowa	6,680
Minnesota	6,671
Connecticut	4,109
Utah	4,047
Nebraska	4,041
Arizona	3,369
New Jersey	3,356
Maryland	2,413
Washington	1,918
Louisiana	1,868
Oregon	1,783
Colorado	1,756
Massachusetts	1,589
West Virginia	912
Rhode Island	822

Nevada	747
New Hampshire	747
South Dakota	378
Vermont	370
North Dakota	363
Delaware	313
Maine	290
Wyoming	150
Hawaii	125
New Mexico	100
District of Columbia	70
Idaho	68
Montana	50
Alaska	9

Source: Center for Automotive Research (2007 Study)

There are 16 states with direct supplier employment in excess of 15,000 jobs. These states represent 87 percent of the total employment associated with automotive parts manufacturing. While the majority of these direct jobs are concentrates in the upper-Midwest, Alabama, California, Kentucky, North Carolina, South Carolina, and Tennessee are within those 16 top employment states. This geographic dispersion is reversing an industry trend of geographic concentration that occurred through the last 20 to 25 years.

	U.S.	MI	OH	IN	IL	TX	CA	NY	TN	PA
DIRECT	783,061	145,818	97,323	86,934	40,063	20,175	28,596	31,017	45,749	22,917
INTERMEDIATE	1,972,067	192,732	183,988	119,855	123,265	110,443	110,550	93,813	69,854	83,008
EXPENDITURE-INDUCED	1,704,561	185,164	159,231	114,261	104,284	98,524	83,473	80,506	67,075	66,872
TOTAL EMPLOYMENT CONTRIBUTION	4,459,689	523,714	440,542	321,050	267,612	229,143	222,620	205,336	182,677	172,797
National Multiplier	5.7									

	NC	GA	KY	WI	FL	MO	SC	AL	Balance of U.S.
DIRECT	27,589	22,701	35,102	21,502	9,273	18,888	20,943	15,965	92,506
INTERMEDIATE	66,518	64,530	51,113	56,553	56,363	40,802	38,580	40,384	469,714
EXPENDITURE-INDUCED	54,527	54,970	44,933	42,674	43,233	39,593	33,069	32,537	399,635
TOTAL EMPLOYMENT CONTRIBUTION	148,635	142,201	131,148	120,729	108,870	99,283	92,593	88,886	961,856
National Multiplier									

State	State Total Impact	State Total Labor Force April 2005	All Impact as % Labor Force
AL	88,885	2,146.30	4.1%
AK	4,593	337.7	1.4%
AZ	31,976	2,830.50	1.1%
AR	42,955	1,354.10	3.2%
CA	223,412	17,640.30	1.3%
CO	34,967	2,544.60	1.4%
CT	38,486	1,814.20	2.1%
DE	8,265	435.4	1.9%
DC	9,467	297.6	3.2%
FL	108,870	8,611.70	1.3%
GA	142,201	4,561.50	3.1%
HI	5,000	630.1	0.8%
ID	8,376	735.1	1.1%
IL	267,612	6,463.70	4.1%
IN	321,051	3,196.10	10.0%
IA	44,032	1,657.30	2.7%
KS	50,668	1,473.30	3.4%
KY	131,148	1,993.10	6.6%
LA	42,269	2,108.20	2.0%
ME	11,522	708.4	1.6%
MD	45,875	2,920.90	1.6%
MA	58,933	3,362.90	1.8%
MI	523,715	5,105.90	10.3%
MN	69,441	2,962.60	2.3%
MS	49,349	1,348.10	3.7%
MO	99,283	3,021.50	3.3%
MT	5,892	491.1	1.2%
NE	23,499	985.9	2.4%
NV	17,715	1,210.50	1.5%
NH	12,325	730.4	1.7%
NJ	79,029	4,408.70	1.8%
NM	10,102	933.4	1.1%
NY	205,335	9,397.20	2.2%
NC	148,635	4,311.80	3.4%
ND	4,613	357.9	1.3%
OH	440,543	5,892.20	7.5%
OK	41,299	1,735.30	2.4%
OR	21,929	1,857.30	1.2%
PA	172,797	6,295.80	2.7%
RI	8,122	567.5	1.4%
SC	92,592	2,067.40	4.5%
SD	6,176	431.1	1.4%

(Continued)

State	State Total Impact	State Total Labor Force April 2005	All Impact as % Labor Force
TN	182,677	2,912.70	6.3%
TX	229,142	11,176.30	2.1%
UT	26,387	1,261.40	2.1%
VT	6,558	354.1	1.9%
VA	86,391	3,919.90	2.2%
WA	25,850	3,275.50	0.8%
WV	23,189	796.5	2.9%
WI	121,915	3,036.70	4.0%
WY	4,627	282.8	1.6%

JOBS	INDUSTRY DESCRIPTION
783,100	**Motor Vehicle Parts Manufacturing**
649,500	Printing and Related Support Activities
550,500	Plastics Product Manufacturing
461,400	Aerospace Product and Parts Manufacturing
450,800	Semiconductor and Other Electronic Component Manufacturing
433,400	Navigational, Measuring, Electromedical, and Control Instruments Manufacturing
348,800	Other Miscellaneous Manufacturing
344,100	Converted Paper Product Manufacturing
343,900	Machine Shops; Turned Product; and Screw, Nut, and Bolt Manufacturing
313,900	Other Wood Product Manufacturing
309,600	Medical Equipment and Supplies Manufacturing
292,400	Pharmaceutical and Medicine Manufacturing
285,300	Other Fabricated Metal Product Manufacturing
264,700	Other General Purpose Machinery Manufacturing
248,200	Cement and Concrete Product Manufacturing
223,700	Motor Vehicle Manufacturing
211,700	Agriculture, Construction, and Mining Machinery Manufacturing
208,800	Computer and Peripheral Equipment Manufacturing
201,900	Metalworking Machinery Manufacturing
171,000	**Motor Vehicle Body and Trailer Manufacturing**

APPENDIX 2. DIAGRAMS ILLUSTRATING A VEHICLE'S COMPONENT PART FRAMEWORK

Suppliers to the 2008 Ford Taurus

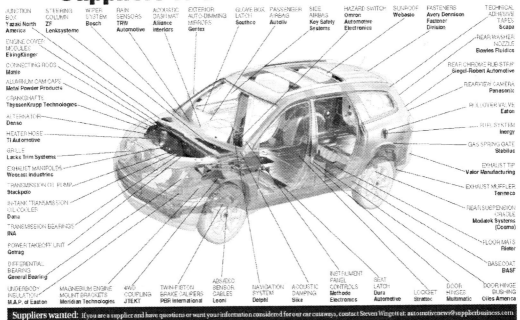

Suppliers to the 2008 Buick Enclave

Suppliers to the 2009 Dodge Ram

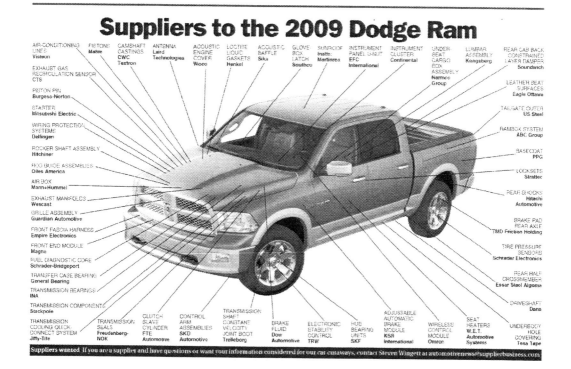

Suppliers to the 2009 Toyota Corolla

Source: Automotive News

APPENDIX 3. VEHICLE TECHNOLOGY ROADMAP

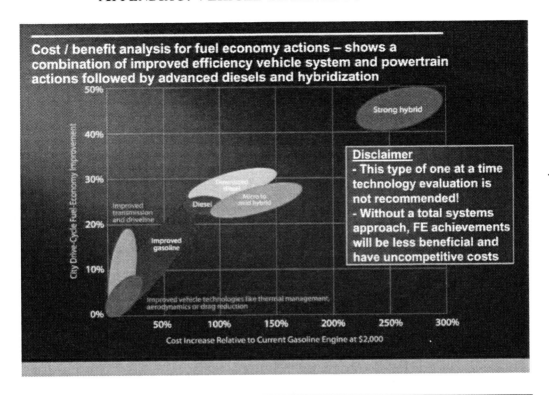

Cost / benefit analysis for fuel economy actions – shows a combination of improved efficiency vehicle system and powertrain actions followed by advanced diesels and hybridization

Disclaimer
- This type of one at a time technology evaluation is not recommended!
- Without a total systems approach, FE achievements will be less beneficial and have uncompetitive costs

Roadmap - Road Transport Powertrains

Powertrains will evolve through downsizing of combustion engine, electrification and use lower carbon liquid fuels

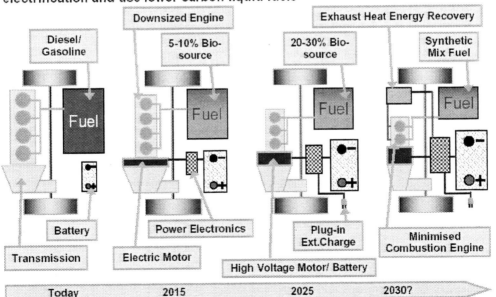

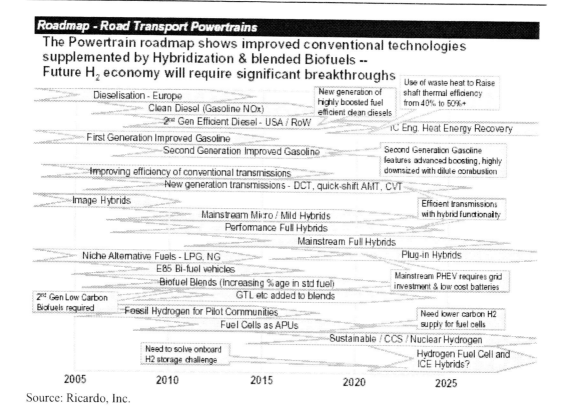

Source: Ricardo, Inc.

APPENDIX 4. "AUTOMOTIVE INDUSTRY REVIEW"

2nd Quarter U.S. Automotive Highlights

OEMs Back Away From Profitability Pledges / Speak Out against BK Concerns

As news of continued poor sales results at GM, Ford and Chrysler spread across the industry, the current restructuring and profitability plans of the "Detroit 3" continued to be called into question. Although sales have recently plummeted, this is not the first time critics have raised concerns about the future of the D3.

Merrill Lynch & Co. analyst John Murphy, announced bankruptcy "is not impossible" if the U.S. auto market worsens. GM's CEO, Rick Wagoner said that GM has "no thoughts whatsoever" of bankruptcy and has "robust" cash reserves with options for raising more money in the future. Chrysler's executive Jim Press, in a letter to dealers, stated that such reports suggesting Chrysler might file for bankruptcy are "without merit" and encouraged dealers to "hang in there and fight for every sale."

As it stands, the D3 have cash to operate (in the near-term), appear to be making steps to get through 2009 until the economy rebounds and will attempt everything in their playbook before resorting to bankruptcy. Two questions remain: How many plays are left in their playbook and how fast can they implement these necessary changes?

Commodity Price Increases Pinching Supply Base Margins

In the first six months of the year, increasing commodity prices continued to afflict upward cost pressure on automakers. Decreasing supply, higher raw material costs, and increasing energy prices have caused the relentless rise in prices. >

CONTENTS

This communication is being provided strictly for informational purposes only and is not intended as a recommendation or an offer or solicitation for the purchase or sale of any security referenced herein.

This material has been prepared by Grant Thornton LLP, employing appropriate expertise, and in the belief that it is fair and not misleading. The information upon which this material is based was obtained from sources believed to be reliable, but has not been independently verified, therefore, we do not guarantee its accuracy. This is not an offer to buy or sell any security or investment. Any opinion or estimates constitute our best judgment as of this date, and are subject to change without notice. Grant Thornton LLP and their affiliates and their respective directors, officers and employees may buy or sell securities mentioned herein as agent or principal for their own account.

About Grant Thornton LLP, Corporate Advisory and Restructuring Services

The combined access of the Grant Thornton International member firms gives a unique insight into supply chain and network distribution issues. Whether you are interested in acquiring underperforming component plants, or considering the creation of a dealer network in Europe or the US, we have the experience to provide advice on the strategic options and assistance with implementing the strategy.

Financial Statistics
Automotive Industry – Public Markets Multiples As of 6/30/2008 (Figures in US$)

Company	Ticker	Stock price			Equity Market Cap	Enterprise Value (EV)	Net Debt/ LTM² EBITDA	EPS		Price earnings		EV/ LTM² EBITDA
		Current	% of 52 week high	Quartile¹				LTM²	NTM³	LTM²	NTM³	
OEM												
Daimler AG	DAI	$61.67	55%	0%	$59,474	$127,168	2.7x	$4.71	$10.06	13.1x	6.1x	6.8x
Ford Motor Co.	F	$4.81	50%	7%	$10,784	$156,190	9.8x	NM	NM	NM	NM	10.7x
General Motors	GM	$11.50	27%	3%	$6,511	$28,702	3.7x	NM	NM	NM	NM	5.1x
Honda Motor Co.	TSE:7267	$34.03	90%	65%	$61,749	$96,708	2.3x	$2.89	$2.73	11.8x	12.5x	2.4x
Nissan Motor Co.	TSE:7201	$8.26	76%	13%	$33,646	$78,764	3.3x	$1.03	$0.83	8.0x	10.0x	3.6x
Toyota Motor Corp.	TSE:7203	$47.00	73%	0%	$148,016	$255,671	2.7x	$4.73	$4.09	9.9x	11.5x	2.9x
Volkswagen AG	DB:VOW	$288.00	100%	99%	$114,226	$182,351	3.4x	$15.33	$19.68	18.8x	14.6x	12.3x
Mean										12.3x	10.9x	6.3x
Median										11.8x	11.5x	5.1x
Supplier												
American Axle	AXL	$7.99	26%	0%	$433	$982	1.7x	NM	NM	NM	NM	3.0x
ArvinMeritor	ARM	$12.48	53%	23%	$921	$1,915	3.4x	NM	$2.07	NM	6.0x	7.1x
Autoliv	ALV	$46.62	72%	12%	$3,387	$4,679	1.4x	$3.86	$5.19	12.1x	9.0x	5.3x
BorgWarner	BWA	$44.38	79%	36%	$5,153	$5,789	0.7x	$2.70	$3.02	16.4x	14.7x	7.9x
Cooper Tire	CTB	$7.84	28%	0%	$462	$714	0.6x	$1.18	$0.07	6.7x	NM	2.7x
Cummins	CMI	$65.52	87%	74%	$13,308	$13,488	(0.1)x	$3.96	$5.23	16.6x	12.5x	10.4x
Dana Holding	DAN	$5.35	40%	3%	$530	$1,581	0.4x	$1.91	$0.65	2.8x	8.2x	3.6x
Delphi	DPHI.Q	$0.07	3%	1%	$41	$5,544	NM	NM	NM	NM	NM	NM
Eaton	ETN	$84.97	82%	49%	$13,986	$17,568	2.0x	$6.47	$7.84	13.1x	10.8x	10.0x
Federal-Mogul	FDML	$16.13	55%	8%	$1,621	$3,889	3.3x	$14.72	$1.32	1.1x	12.2x	5.9x
Gentex	GNTX	$14.44	64%	11%	$2,062	$1,662	(2.2)x	$0.85	$0.90	16.9x	16.1x	9.0x
Goodyear Tire	GT	$17.83	48%	2%	$4,289	$7,236	1.0x	$1.65	$2.50	10.8x	7.1x	3.9x

(Continued)

Company	Ticker	Stock price			Equity Market Cap	Enterprise Value (EV)	Net Debt / LTM EBITDA[2]	EPS		Price earnings		EV/LTM EBITDA[2]
		Current Price	%of 52 week high	Quartile[1]				LTM[2]	NTM[3]	LTM[2]	NTM[3]	
Hayes Lemmerz	HAYZ	$2.84	46%	4%	$287	$898	3.0x	NM	NM	NM	NM	5.1x
Johnson Controls	JCI	$28.68	65%	1%	$17,019	$21,254	1.5x	$2.31	$2.64	12.4x	10.9x	7.8x
Lear	LEA	$14.18	34%	0%	$1,096	$2,871	1.6x	$3.44	$2.78	4.1x	5.1x	2.7x
Linamar	TSX:LNR	$12.24	46%	1%	$822	$1,237	1.1x	$1.55	$1.74	7.9x	7.0x	3.6x
Magna Intl.	TSX:MG.A	$59.40	61%	0%	$6,803	$4,759	(1.1)x	$5.51	$6.48	10.8x	9.2x	2.4x
Navistar Intl.	NAVZ	$65.82	83%	63%	$4,623	$10,798	11.5x	$0.77	$8.00	85.7x	8.2x	20.1x
Tenneco Inc.	TEN	$13.53	36%	0%	$631	$1,952	2.7x	NM	$1.76	NM	7.7x	4.0x
TRW Automotive	TRW	$18.47	47%	1%	$1,866	$4,609	2.1x	$2.60	$2.25	7.1x	8.2x	3.6x
Visteon	VC	$2.63	32%	0%	$344	$1,832	2.4x	NM	NM	NM	NM	3.6x
Mean										15.0 x	9.6x	9.7x
Median										10.8 x	8.6x	5.1x
Dealer												
AutoNation	AN	$10.02	44%	0%	$1,789	$5,653	5.1x	$1.36	$1.34	7.4x	7.5x	7.4x
Asbury Automotive	ABG	$12.85	51%	8%	$410	$1,550	5.5x	$1.92	$1.72	6.7x	7.5x	7.5x
CarMax	KMX	$14.19	52%	0%	$3,103	$3,407	1.0x	$0.66	$0.71	21.4x	20.1x	11.7x
Group 1 Automotive	GPI	$19.87	46%	0%	$461	$2,047	7.2x	$2.91	$3.00	6.8x	6.6x	9.2x
Lithia Motors	LAD	$4.92	19%	0%	$99	$1,042	9.2x	$0.85	$0.62	5.8x	8.0x	10.2x
Penske Automotive	PAG	$14.74	64%	13%	$1,406	$3,931	6.4x	$1.53	$1.64	9.6x	9.0x	9.9x
Sonic Automotive	SAH	$12.89	42%	0%	$521	$2,490	6.1x	$2.51	$1.81	5.1x	7.1x	7.7x
Mean										9.0x	9.4x	9.1x
Median										6.8x	7.5x	9.2x

Company	Ticker	Stock price					LTM¹ Revenues					LTM¹ EBITDA				
		Current	1 month		1 Year%		Current	1 month		1 Year%		Current	1 month		1 Year%	
			Prior	% Δ	Prior	% Δ		Prior	% Δ	Prior	% Δ		Prior	% Δ	Prior	% Δ
OEM																
Daimler AG	DAI	$61.67	$76.03	-19%	$91.95	-33%	$144,574	$138,747	4%	$128,997	12%	$21,802	$22,224	-2%	$25,911	-16%
Ford Motor Co.	F	$4.81	$6.80	-29%	$9.42	-49%	$172,963	$172,455	0%	$162,281	7%	$14,664	$13,841	6%	$10,015	46%
General Motors Corp.	GM	$11.50	$17.10	-33%	$37.80	-70%	$180,405	$181,122	0%	$197,145	-8%	$5,584	$6,320	-12%	$28,205	-80%
Honda Motor Co.	TSE:7267	$34.03	$33.23	2%	$36.29	-6%	$105,021	$102,184	3%	$94,794	11%	$12,875	$12,953	-1%	$10,460	23%
Nissan Motor Co.	TSE:7201	$8.26	$9.40	-12%	$10.72	-23%	$94,709	$97,012	-2%	$89,506	6%	$10,977	$11,022	0%	$10,419	5%
Toyota Motor Corp.	TSE:7203	$47.00	$51.03	-8%	$62.94	-25%	$230,022	$221,190	4%	$204,755	12%	$32,912	$33,583	-2%	$30,962	6%
Volkswagen AG	DB:VOW	$288.00	$279.45	3%	$159.34	81%	$154,923	$149,287	4%	$136,279	14%	$18,074	$17,691	2%	$15,315	18%
Supplier																
American Axle	AXL	$7.99	$18.59	-57%	$29.62	-73%	$3,034	$3,248	-7%	$3,159	-4%	$324	$393	-18%	$257	26%
ArvinMeritor	ARM	$12.48	$14.97	-17%	$22.20	-44%	$6,698	$6,544	2%	$6,517	3%	$271	$251	8%	$269	1%
Autoliv	ALV	$46.62	$54.67	-15%	$56.87	-18%	$6,898	$6,769	2%	$6,319	9%	$883	$877	1%	$823	7%
Borg-Warner	BWA	$44.38	$51.71	-14%	$43.02	3%	$5,550	$5,329	4%	$4,708	18%	$729	$683	7%	$607	20%

(Continued)

Company	Ticker	Stock price					LTM¹ Revenues						LTM¹ EBITDA					
		Current	1 month		1 Year%		Current	1 month		1 Year%			Current	1 month		1 Year%	
			Prior	%Δ	Prior	%Δ		Prior	%Δ	Prior	%Δ			Prior	%Δ	Prior	%Δ
Cooper Tire	CTB	$7.84	$10.98	↓-29%	$27.62	↓-72%	$2,942	$2,933	↑0%	$2,648	↑11%		$261	$280	↓-7%	$175	↑49%
Cummins	CMI	$65.52	$70.42	↓-7%	$50.61	↑29%	$13,705	$13,048	↑5%	$11,501	↑19%		$1,291	$1,221	↑6%	$1,254	↑3%
Dana Holding	DAN	$5.35	$10.60	↓-50%	N/A	-N/A	$8,888	$8,721	↑2%	$8,452	↑5%		$440	$404	↑9%	$220	↑100%
Delphi	DPHI.Q	$0.07	$0.11	↓-30%	$2.37	↓-97%	$21,853	$22,283	↓-2%	$21,446	↑2%		$(157)	$(139)	↑13%	$(658)	↓-76%
Eaton	ETN	$84.97	$96.68	↓-12%	$93.00	↓-9%	$13,416	$13,033	↑3%	$12,389	↑8%		$1,751	$1,710	↑2%	$1,627	↑8%
Federal-Mogul	FDML	$16.13	$19.96	19%	N/A	-N/A	$7,057	$6,914	↑2%	$6,443	↑10%		$660	$710	↓-7%	$630	↑5%
Gentex	GNTX	$14.44	$17.56	↓-18%	$19.69	↓-27%	$675	$654	↑3%	$590	↑14%		$184	$179	↑3%	$161	↑14%
Goodyear Tire	GT	$17.83	$25.41	↓-30%	$34.76	↓-49%	$20,087	$19,644	↑2%	$18,788	↑7%		$1,848	$1,613	↑15%	$1,070	↑73%
Hayes Lemmerz	HAYZ	$2.84	$3.92	↓-28%	$5.35	↓-47%	$2,202	$2,127	↑4%	$1,826	↑21%		$177	$172	↑3%	$159	↑11%
Johnson Controls	JCI	$28.68	$34.06	↓-16%	$38.59	↓-26%	$36,812	$35,898	↑3%	$33,242	↑11%		$2,714	$2,618	↑4%	$2,327	↑17%
Lear	LEA	$14.18	$25.75	↓-45%	$35.61	↓-60%	$15,447	$15,995	↓-3%	$17,567	↓-12%		$1,065	$1,088	↓-2%	$920	↑16%
Linamar	TSX:LNR	$12.24	$17.02	↓-28%	$18.12	↓-32%	$2,276	$2,154	↑6%	$1,983	↑15%		$339	$317	↑7%	$272	↑25%
Magna Intl.	TSX:MG.A	$59.40	$70.50	↓-16%	$91.51	↓-35%	$25,452	$24,271	↑5%	$21,584	↑18%		$1,931	$1,869	↑3%	$1,410	↑37%
Navistar Intl.	NAVZ	$65.82	$75.95	↓-13%	$66.00	↓0%	$13,060	$12,101	↑8%	$12,124	↑8%		$536	$286	↑87%	$544	↓-1%
Tenneco Inc.	TEN	$13.53	$23.98	↓-44%	$35.04	↓-61%	$6,344	$6,184	↑3%	$4,951	↑28%		$484	$486	↓0%	$424	↑14%

Company	Ticker	Stock price					LTM¹ Revenues					LTM¹ EBITDA				
		Current	1 month Prior	1 month %Δ	1 Year Prior	1 Year %Δ	Current	1 month Prior	1 month %Δ	1 Year Prior	1 Year %Δ	Current	1 month Prior	1 month %Δ	1 Year Prior	1 Year %Δ
TRW Automotive	TRW	$18.47	$24.95	↓-26%	$36.83	↓-50%	$15,279	$14,702	↓4%	$13,315	↑15%	$1,266	$1,229	↑3%	$1,136	↑11%
Visteon	VC	$2.63	$4.04	↓-35%	$8.10	↓-68%	$11,238	$11,266	↓0%	$11,230	↓0%	$502	$409	↓23%	$356	↓41%
Dealer																
AutoNation	AN	$10.02	$15.79	↓-37%	$22.44	↓-55%	$17,391	$17,692	↓-2%	$18,377	↓-5%	$761	$797	↓-5%	$859	↓-11%
Asbury Automotive	ABG	$12.85	$16.47	↓-22%	$24.95	↓-48%	$5,598	$5,713	↓-2%	$5,729	↓-2%	$206	$215	↓-4%	$219	↓-6%
CarMax	KMX	$14.19	$19.66	↓-28%	$25.50	↓-44%	$8,320	$8,285	↑0%	$7,865	↑6%	$291	$347	↓-16%	$384	↓-24%
Group 1 Automotive	GPI	$19.87	$26.04	↓-24%	$40.34	↓-51%	$6,400	$6,393	↓0%	$6,189	↑3%	$222	$218	↑2%	$219	↑1%
Lithia Motors	LAD	$4.92	$6.83	↓-28%	$25.34	↓-81%	$3,144	$3,219	↓-2%	$3,120	↑1%	$103	$116	↓-12%	$127	↓-20%
Penske Automotive	PAG	$14.74	$20.89	↓-29%	$21.29	↓-31%	$13,082	$12,958	↑1%	$11,652	↑12%	$396	$394	↑1%	$363	↑9%
Sonic Automotive	SAH	$12.89	$18.65	↓-31%	$28.97	↓-56%	$8,355	$8,337	↑0%	$7,982	↑5%	$322	$326	↓-1%	$295	↑9%

¹ Quartile is calculated as (stock price current minus 52 week low)/(stock price 52 week high minus 52 week low).
² Latest 12 months diluted earnings per share before extraordinary items.
³ Next 12 months estimated diluted earnings per share, based on today's date.
↑Up ↓Down ▪Same
Source: Capital IQ

APPENDIX 5. 2008 ALIXPARTNERS GLOBAL AUTOMOTIVE REVIEW™ – EXCERPT "RECENT NORTH AMERICAN SUPPLIER BANKRUPTCIES"

Chicago Dallas Detroit Düsseldorf London Los Angeles Milan Munich New York Paris San Francisco Shanghai Tokyo

Assets >$100 million

Company – Sales $M (Year)	Year Ch. 11	Current Status
Federal-Mogul - $6,914 (2007)	2001	Emerged from bankruptcy in Dec 2007
ANC Rental - $3,163 (2001)	2001	Alamo and National acquired by Cerberus in October 2003 for $2.4 billion
Hayes Lemmerz -$2,130 (2007)	2001	Emerged in June 2003 with 37% owned by Joseph Littlejohn Levy
Harvard Industries - $330 (2000)	2002	Liquidated in 2002 after four bankruptcies in 25 years
Exide Technologies - $2,939 (2007)	2002	Emerged in May 2004; reduced debt by 70%
Daewoo Motors - $3,500 (2002E)	2002	Majority of global operations acquired by GM
Budget Group - $2,161 (2001)	2002	Acquired by Cendant in November 2002 for over $500 million
Venture Holdings - $1,700 (2002E)	2003	Acquired by creditors and renamed New Venture Holdings
Intermet - $731 (2003)	2004	Emerged from Chapter 11 November 2005, reorganized into five business groups
Oxford Automotive - $1,000 (2004E)	2004	Emerged March 2005 to focus on European operations
Amcast - $424 (2003)	2004	Filed Chapter 11 November 2004, emerged August 2005
Tower Automotive - $2,816 (2003)	2005	Filed Feb 2005, finalized emergence July 2007 by selling assets to affiliate of Cerberus for ~$1B
EaglePicher- $685 (2003)	2005	High commodity prices & insufficient cash – Filed CH 11 on April 11th

(Continued)

Company – Sales $M (Year)	Year Ch. 11	Current Status
Meridian Automotive - $1,000 (2003E)	2005	First day motions approved - Chapter 11 on April 26th
Collins & Aikman - $3,784 (2003)	2005	Filed Chapter 11 May 2005, obtained confirmation of a liquidating chapter 11 plan in July 2007
Delphi – $27,000 (2005E)	2005	Seeking relief from high labor costs + union prohibition on closing/selling plants
Dana – $8,700 (2007)	2006	Filed Chapter 11 March 2006, emerged February 2008
Dura - $2,350 (2005)	2006	Received approval to emerge from Chapter 11 in May 2008
Citation Corp. - $714 (2007E)	2007	2 Filings in 3 years, previously emerged from Chapter 11 May 2005
Remy - $1,129 (2007)	2007	Filed and emerged from Chapter 11 in late 2007
American LaFrance - $166 (2007E)	2008	Filed Chapter 11 January 2008
Plastech - $1,400 (2007E)	2008	Filed Chapter 11 February 2008
Total -$74.7 billion		

APPENDIX 6 STANDARD & POOR'S RATINGS SERVICES NOVEMBER 15, 2008 REPORT: "RATINGS ON 15 NORTH AMERICAN AUTO SUPPLIERS PLACED ON WATCH NEG ON EXPOSURE TO U.S.-BASED AUTOMAKERS; TWO ARE ALSO DOWNGRADED"

Ratings On 15 North American Auto Suppliers Placed on Watch Neg on Exposure To U.S.-Based Automakers; Two Are Also Downgraded

Publication date: 13-Nov-2008
Primary Credit Analysts: Robert Schulz, CFA, New York (1) 212-438-7808; robertschulz@standardandpoors.com
Gregg Lemos Stein, New York (1) 212-438-1730; gregglemos-stein@standardandpoors.com
Nancy C Messer, CFA, New York (1) 212-438-7672; nancymesser@standardandpoors.com
Secondary Credit Analysts: Lawrence Orlowski, CFA, New York (1) 212-438-7800; lawrenceorlowski@standardandpoors.com
Greg Pau, Toronto (1) 416-507-2518; gregpau@standardandpoors.com

Table 1. U.S. Auto Suppliers on CreditWatch with Negative Implications

As of Nov. 13, 2008		
	To	From
Ratings lowered and placed on CreditWatch with negative implications		
Dana Holding Corp.	B+/Watch Neg/--	BB-/Negative/--
Magna International Inc.	A-/Watch Neg/--	A/Negative/--
Ratings placed on CreditWatch with negative implications		
ArvinMeritor Inc.	B+/Watch Neg/--	B+/Negative/--
BorgWarner Inc.	A-/Watch Neg/--	A-/Stable/--
Cooper-Standard Automotive Inc.	B/Watch Neg/--	B/Stable/--
Federal-Mogul Corp.	BB-/Watch Neg/--	BB-/Negative/--
Goodyear Tire & Rubber Co. (The)	BB-/Watch Neg/--	BB-/Stable/--
Hayes Lemmerz International Inc.	B/Watch Neg/--	B/Stable/--
Johnson Controls Inc.*	A-/Watch Neg/A-2	A-/Stable/A-2
Lear Corp.	B/Watch Neg/--	B/Negative/--
MetoKote Corp.	B+/Watch Neg/--	B+/Negative/--
Shiloh Industries Inc.	BB-/Watch Neg/--	BB-/Stable/--
Stoneridge Inc.	B+/Watch Neg/--	B+/Stable/--
Tenneco Inc.	BB-/Watch Neg/--	BB-/Stable/--
Visteon Corp.	B-/Watch Neg/--	B-/Negative/--
Existing ratings on CreditWatch with negative implications		
American Axle & Manufacturing Holdings Inc.	B/Watch Neg/--	--
TRW Automotive Inc.	BB+/Watch Neg/--	--
*The short-term rating is not on CreditWatch.		

On Nov. 13, 2008, Standard & Poor's Ratings Services placed the ratings on 15 North American auto suppliers on CreditWatch with negative implications as a result of their significant exposure to General Motors Corp. (CCC+/Negative/--), Ford Motor Co. (B-/Watch Neg/--), and Chrysler LLC (CCC+/Negative/--). Other auto suppliers were already on CreditWatch, in part because of their exposure to the three automakers. (See table 1 for all affected companies and their ratings.)

At the same time, we also lowered the long-term corporate credit ratings on Dana Holding Corp. (to 'B+' from 'BB-') and Magna International Inc. (to 'A-' from 'A'); these ratings are among the 15 that we placed on CreditWatch negative. (For the complete corporate credit rating rationale, please see the research updates on Dana and Magna International, both published Nov. 13, 2008, on RatingsDirect, the real- time Web-based source for Standard & Poor's credit ratings, research, and risk analysis.)

The CreditWatch listings reflect the increasingly beleaguered state of the Michigan-based automakers and the multiple scenarios—almost all of them negative—that could play out over the next few weeks or months. We expect the result to adversely affect the business and financial risk profiles of the rated North American auto suppliers enough in some cases to result in downgrades.

GM has stated that, in the absence of substantial federal government support, it may run out of cash to operate its business beyond the end of 2008. Chrysler does not report financial results to the public, but we believe its cash balances are well below the $11 billion reported as of June 30, 2008, given that the company relies almost exclusively on the North American auto market. Ford used $7.7 billion in cash in its global automotive operations in the third quarter. Although it has $10.7 billion available under its revolving credit facility, the company could face significant liquidity challenges late in 2009, given its increased cash outflows.

Table 2. U.S. Auto Suppliers' Credit Quality and Exposure to Michigan-Based Automakers In North America

Rating category[*]	--Estimated total sales to GM, Ford, and Chrysler in North America--		
	<15%	15%-30%	>30%
Investment grade	BorgWarner Inc.		Magna International Inc.
	Johnson Controls Inc.		
'BB' category	Goodyear Tire & Rubber Co. (The)	Federal-Mogul Corp.	TRW Automotive Inc.
		Tenneco Inc.	Shiloh Industries Inc.
'B' category	Hayes Lemmerz International Inc.	Dana Holding Corp.	Stoneridge Inc.
	ArvinMeritor Inc.	MetoKote Corp.	Cooper-Standard Automotive Inc.
		Visteon Corp.	Lear Corp.
			American Axle & Manufacturing Holdings Inc.

[*]Credit rating as of Nov. 13, 2008.

The automakers may receive increased or expedited U.S. government assistance, although the form, timing, and magnitude of such assistance are difficult to predict. Financial restructurings or bankruptcy filings are also possible, with or without government aid. Also, given the very weak credit markets and grim economic outlook, we cannot rule out the possibility, however remote, that one or more of the automakers might be forced to cease operations. Even with sufficient financial support to avoid a financial restructuring, some or all of the U.S. automakers are unlikely to avoid further sweeping changes to their product lines, market focus, or possibly their status as independent entities. Accordingly, we are likely to reevaluate the business risk profiles of many rated suppliers, in addition to our financial analysis, in connection with determining a supplier's rating.

The suppliers placed on CreditWatch on Nov. 13 span a wide range of credit quality and have varying degrees of exposure to the Michigan-based automakers (see table 2). We believe certain companies would be able to withstand the liquidity shock of a sudden bankruptcy filing by one or more of the manufacturers, but they may not be able to do so and remain at current rating levels. We have taken numerous rating actions in the supplier sector this year; however, the looming potential for changes in the structure and fundamental composition of the domestic automaker customer base will be more sharply reflected in the resolution of today's CreditWatch actions.

Several other rated companies have not been placed on CreditWatch, including those with a relatively minor percentage of sales to the Michigan-based automakers, and certain aftermarket parts producers, truck suppliers, and auto retailers. Still, we believe many of these companies face business and financial challenges that, although not directly related to the domestic automakers' production schedules, reflect the broader challenges affecting vehicle demand in the U.S. and Europe. Accordingly, their respective ratings could be placed on CreditWatch or lowered as a result of our ongoing surveillance process.

We expect to resolve the CreditWatch listings within the next 90 days. Given the potential for immense structural and near-term changes to the industry, we would likely resolve the CreditWatch listings as we receive more information on potential U.S. government assistance to the automakers, or lack thereof. Our reviews will include assessments of any potential effect on the suppliers' liquidity, including their ability to remain in compliance with financial covenants, and prospects for the viability of their businesses more broadly, including future incremental revenue and profitability declines. We may resolve the reviews for certain less-affected suppliers more quickly than for others.

End Notes

[1] CAR Research Memorandum: *The Impact on the U.S. Economy of a Major Contraction of the Detroit Three Automakers*, by David Cole, Ph.D, *et al.*, Center for Automotive Research. November 2008.
[2] *Who Really Made Your Car? Restructuring and Geographic Change in the Auto Industry* by Thomas Klier and James Rubenstein; Published by W.E. Upjohn Institute for Employment Research, 2008.
[3] Based on reports from Summer 2008.

In: The U.S. Auto Industry and the Role of Federal Assistance   ISBN: 978-1-60741-322-6
Editor: James R. Elliot   © 2010 Nova Science Publishers, Inc.

Chapter 7

Testimony of Alan R. Mulally, Ford Motor Company, House Committee on Financial Services

Thank you Chairman Frank, Ranking Member Bachus, and members of the Committee. I appreciate the opportunity to be here with you today representing Ford Motor Company as you consider issues that are absolutely critical to this venerable American company and to the nation.

In my judgment, there are two fundamental questions on the table today:

- Is there a competitive and sustainable future for our domestic automotive industry?
- Is the provision of government assistance to help bridge the domestic auto industry through these difficult economic times more favorable to our nation than the costs of inaction?

I respectfully submit that the answer to these questions is a resounding yes. The domestic industry is increasingly more competitive and sustainable and is in many respects on par with our foreign competitors. A decision to make government assistance available makes much more sense than taking the tremendous risks to our already-fragile economy that come with inaction.

Ford's Competitive Transformation

As you are well aware, we face serious problems in our economy, and the auto industry has been among the most heavily affected by the turmoil in the financial markets and the impact that turmoil has had on spending for consumer products. As public attention has shifted from the credit and financial institution crisis to larger economic issues, we in the auto industry find ourselves at the center of a national debate on the future of our industry. Much of the commentary I've read in the last few weeks is highly critical of our industry, and a common refrain is that our companies "need a new business model."

I completely agree. What many of the commentators and critics fail to recognize, however, is that we at Ford are on our way to realizing a complete transformation of our company — building a new Ford that has a very bright future.

The reason I came to Ford two years ago after 37 years in the aerospace industry working for Boeing was because of my confidence that the incredible talent and resources of the Ford Motor Company could and should be redirected into an effort to transform Ford so it can be one of the strongest competitors in today's global automotive market. Inspired by the compelling vision outlined by our Executive Chairman Bill Ford, Ford had already begun its transformation from a company focused in this country largely on trucks and SUVs. All of our efforts over the last two years have been directed toward speeding up the transformation of Ford to a global profitable business based on the highest quality, sustainable, fuel-efficient, safe, fun-to-drive and best-value world class vehicles.

With that in mind, I'd like to take a few minutes to tell you about the transformation under way at Ford to give you a vision for the future that we are creating today.

Our plan for the past two years has been consistent.

- We have been aggressively *restructuring* to operate profitably at the current lower demand and changing model mix.
- We have been accelerating development of the safe, fuel-efficient, highest-quality new *products* that customers want and value.
- We have been working to *finance* our plan and improve our balance sheet.
- And we have been *working together* as one team — with our employees, dealers, suppliers and union partners — leveraging our global assets like never before.

Our goal has been and remains to create a viable, highly focused, fully integrated Ford Motor Company — a lean enterprise delivering profitable growth for all over the long term.

Restructuring. Few companies in the history of our country have restructured more aggressively. I can tell you that in my experience, the union under Ron Gettelfinger is working with us as part of the solution.

In a very short period of time, working together, we have reduced excess capacity, closing 17 plants in North America — including more than one-third of our assembly plants — in the past five years. We have also reduced our workforce by 51,000 employees in the past three years, shrinking our hourly workforce from 83,000 to 44,000 and reducing salaried headcount by around 12,000 from a base of 33,000.

We negotiated a new contract with our UAW partners to begin a path toward competitiveness and offset some of the massive legacy costs that come with doing business in America for more than 100 years. Most significantly, that contract established a trust that funded our retiree health care obligation and removed the liability from Ford's balance sheet effective 2010. Ford has fully met the funding requirements associated with that agreement, including setting aside an initial $4 billion contribution in January of this year.

Our agreement with the union also established an entry level wage that reduces future costs and will make us more competitive going forward longer-term. And, for the first time ever, it included no base wage increase during the four-year period covered by the agreement.

We have also been engaged in a broader effort to cut our costs, and in North America alone have reduced our costs by $5 billion compared with year-end 2005. We also plan further cost and cash improvements to offset the increasing weakness in the global automotive industry.

Product. We are not simply on a journey to cut and shrink our way to profitability. Instead, we very much recognize the need for a product-led transformation, and believe we have the products to achieve just that. We have dramatically accelerated the introduction of new vehicles; 43 percent of our vehicles will be new or refreshed in 2009, and 100 percent of the Ford, Lincoln and Mercury lineup will be new or refreshed by the end of 2010 compared with 2006 models.

Keenly aware that the world is changing as we transform our company, we are shifting from an emphasis on large trucks and SUVs to a more balanced portfolio that also emphasizes smaller and more fuel-efficient vehicles here in the U.S. — the same world-class small vehicles that have been so successful for us in other high-fuel-cost markets. By the end of 2010, two-thirds of our spending here will be on cars and crossovers — up from one-half today.

We are delivering the best or among the best fuel economy with every new vehicle we introduce. This is possible through affordable, fuel-saving technologies like EcoBoost engines, which use gasoline turbocharged direct-injection technology for up to 20 percent better fuel economy, up to 15 percent fewer CO_2 emissions and superior driving performance versus larger-displacement engines. We are doubling capacity for four-cylinder engines here to meet the consumer trend toward more efficient powertrains and vehicles. We also are doubling the number of offerings and volume of our hybrids in the next year alone, and we have a plan for delivering new electric vehicles and plug-in vehicles.

Ford is taking advantage of our scale and global product strengths. We are delivering a balanced portfolio of small, medium and large cars, utilities and trucks, with a sharp focus on the Ford Blue Oval brand across the globe. Going forward, this balanced portfolio will provide the flexibility to adapt more easily to changes in our environment and to begin to grow profitably as the global economy rebounds.

Our new products will be assembled in plants featuring lean manufacturing techniques, and, in nearly all facilities, flexible body shops will make them competitive with the best in the business. A number of our powertrains will be built in plants that can flex among the 14, V6, V8 or diesel engines. As we make these changes, we are fixing the fundamentals of the business, including a further significant reduction in structural costs next year. We also will continue the ongoing consolidation of our dealer and supplier network. Our plans call for reducing our supplier network by more than 60 percent and thereby improving supplier capacity utilization and financial viability.

We have continued to improve quality with four consecutive years of marked progress. This is another area where much of the recent commentary has not yet caught up with reality. Most recently, Ford, Lincoln, and Mercury vehicles collectively reduced what we call "things gone wrong" — a metric used to assess quality — by 7.7 percent compared with last year. That puts Ford's quality on par with Honda and Toyota.

We achieved a leading number of top safety picks from the U.S. Insurance Institute of Highway Safety, with the 2009 Ford Flex and the 2009 Lincoln MKS recently earning top honors. This builds on Ford's achievement of having the most U.S. government five-star safety ratings in the automobile industry.

The speed and breadth of our product-led transformation is demonstrated by significant actions taking place just this week.

- Today at the Los Angeles Auto Show, we unveil two all-new hybrids, the Ford Fusion Hybrid and the Mercury Milan Hybrid. Both beat the Toyota Camry Hybrid in fuel efficiency by at least five miles per gallon. The conventional versions of these new vehicles also beat the Camry in fuel economy.
- These vehicles are from the same Fusion family that is being recognized on the cover of one of the nation's most prestigious consumer magazines for outstanding reliability and quality — quality that respected third parties now agree is on par with Honda and Toyota.
- Yesterday, Ford submitted our application to the Department of Energy for direct loans authorized by Congress last year in section 136 of the Energy Independence and Security Act of 2007. We appreciate Congress' support for these loans, as they will provide access to lower-cost capital for retooling plants for more fuel-efficient vehicles. While no company has yet received funding through this program, we believe it will be important in the long term in deploying advanced technologies.
- On Friday, we end large SUV production at our Michigan Truck Plant and begin converting the facility to build fuel-efficient small vehicles. It is one of three large truck plants that we are converting to small vehicle production in the next two years.

Financing our Plan. To fund our transformation, we have taken many steps to protect Ford's liquidity position, including:

- Raising $23 billion of available liquidity through an enterprise-wide secured credit facility, going to the capital markets at the right time in 2006 to secure that financing.
- Selling Aston Martin, Jaguar, and Land Rover, and as announced earlier this week, a partial sale of our Mazda interest so that we could have an absolute laser focus on growing the Ford brand.
- Selling other businesses such as Hertz to aid our liquidity and to focus on our core business.

Similarly, Ford Credit, our captive finance company, has consolidated abroad to preserve capital to support U.S. consumers and our Ford dealers here.

The consolidation efforts alone have not been sufficient to overcome the financial market disruption which has significantly diminished our access to traditional funding sources.

Unsecured financing has declined dramatically during the past 12 months and impaired our ability to fully support dealer and consumer needs, or to achieve our growth objectives. Such funding is either non-existent or available today only at uneconomic terms.

Securitization markets, our primary funding source, have likewise been frozen. The asset-backed commercial paper and public term securitization markets also have declined significantly, greatly impairing the company's ability to support dealer and consumer financing needs. Accordingly, many of our low-volume financing products have been eliminated or curtailed as we wait for the credit and financial markets return to some state of normalcy.

Our Ford Credit team is optimistic that government assistance in the form of a purchase program for future term securitizations will allow us to continue financing consumers and dealers. The CPFF has been successful in this regard for providing liquidity to our asset-backed commercial paper program.

In addition, it is important that the FDIC approve Ford Credit's industrial loan bank application as another way for us to be able to offer automobile financing to credit-strapped consumers. First filed in June 2006 and refiled in February after an 18-month FDIC-imposed moratorium, Ford Credit's application for an industrial loan bank is still pending further review by the FDIC. We believe that the application and business plan meet the statutory requirements for approval in every material respect. During this extended period, Ford Credit has operated and will continue to operate at a significant competitive funding disadvantage to its competitors. Both domestic (GMAC) and foreign competitors (Toyota and BMW) benefit from FDIC-insured industrial banks and access to stable, low cost FDIC-insured deposits.

FINANCIAL RESULTS AND ECONOMIC CLIMATE

The bottom line of all of our efforts is that we are now competitive with the best in the world — and it has shown in our financial results. In each quarter of 2007, we delivered year-over-year improvements, excluding special items, and on the same basis posted a $100 million profit globally in the first quarter of this year. We appeared to be well on our way to returning to sustainable profitability next year.

As this year has progressed, however, our companies, dealers, suppliers and customers have faced an unprecedented economic crisis and a severe credit crunch. I know that the Committee is all too familiar with the circumstances of our economy, but just a few statistics put the situation we face in sharp focus.

While the domestic auto industry has made mistakes in the past, the current problems have been exacerbated by one of the worst economies in nearly three decades. The mix of the housing crisis, credit crunch, wildly fluctuating gas prices and major spikes in commodity prices has lead to an unprecedented reversal in the business environment that is driving not just the U.S. but markets around the world into a synchronized economic downturn.

Spending by consumers fell at an annual rate of more than 3% in the third quarter (as compared to the second quarter). According to the early November 2008 reading of consumer confidence from the University of Michigan Survey of Consumers, this is the first time in the 50-year history of that survey that consumers were unanimous in their view that the economy is in recession. Consumers' assessment of their economic and financial conditions is the worst since the early 1980s, when the U.S. economy encountered two consecutive recessions. The unemployment rate of 6.5% is well above the low point of 4.4% in March 2007 and likely will rise significantly in coming months. Job losses are over 1.1 million in the first 10 months of this year, and further reductions in employment are expected.

The auto sector is highly reliant on well-functioning credit markets — from manufacturers and suppliers to dealers and consumers. Our industry is one of the first to suffer from bad economic conditions — indeed, spending on new vehicles historically represents about 4% of GDP and therefore will predictably be closely tied to those conditions. The early evidence of weak economic growth began to set in during the first half of this year, with consumers facing a weaker job market at the same time that rising food and energy prices were taking up an increasing share of their disposable incomes. As the financial crisis persisted, both credit availability and consumers' weakened confidence contributed to a drastic decline in vehicle sales. There has been a broad-based tightening of origination and underwriting standards for automotive financing, spreading beyond the sub-prime arena to affect many prime borrowers as well. The Federal Reserve Senior Loan Officers' survey shows that banks' willingness to extend consumer installment loans has only been weaker at one time in the past 30 years, and that was in June of 1980. More than 60% of banks have tightened standards for consumer credit in the most recent survey.

During the last six months, light vehicle sales fell at a 45% annualized rate, the worst slide since mid-1980. In October, the annualized sales rate for the US industry was only 10.5 million units — compared to over 16 million units just last year. This means the industry has lost over 5 million vehicle sales — the equivalent of two companies the size of Ford in North America — in a single year.

October was the worst auto sales month the U.S. industry has seen in 25 years, and we expect it will not be the weakest result we see over this economic cycle. Total industry volumes in 2009 are expected to be weaker than in 2008 on a full-year basis, with significant pressure in the first half of next year.

This is not just a case of the domestic auto industry failing to anticipate changing economic conditions. Very few in any industry, of course, predicted the kind of economic headwinds we face today. Certainly our foreign competitors have not been immune from the downdraft. Toyota, Honda, and Nissan each reported a decline in sales of more than 23 percent in October. Importantly for Ford, we have held or slightly increased our market share in the midst of this declining market.

The decline in the overall market has been the result of two problems — economic uncertainty that discourages Americans from making major purchases, and a lack of available credit so even some people who want to buy a car are unable to secure credit. But importantly, despite our best efforts, our industry's ability to weather this storm has been directly affected by the external financing environment.

This unprecedented pressure on our industry, which is the result of a financial crisis that was not of our industry's making, is coming just at the time when our efforts to restructure Ford have finally begun to bear fruit. The real challenge for this nation is to find a way to allow our successful restructuring efforts to continue despite these challenging times. To do otherwise would be a disservice to the millions of employees at our plants, suppliers, dealers, and customers who are depending upon our success as well as to the American public.

As quickly as these changes have been occurring, of course, we at Ford have been taking fast and decisive action to deal with them. We reduced our production levels dramatically in the face of a shrinking industry demand. In the third quarter alone, we reduced North American production by 219,000 units from the 637,000 vehicles we produced in the third quarter of 2007. Our fourth quarter plans call for production decreases in excess of 210,000 units from the fourth quarter of last year, leaving the company with a full year reduction of over 600,000 units in 2008. We are firmly committed to managing production carefully rather than simply producing units we know the market cannot absorb.

We have announced plans to further reduce employment and cut benefits and compensation at all levels. In addition to further salaried personnel reductions, we have already announced the elimination of merit raises and bonuses in 2009. We support including reasonable limits on executive compensation if we borrow from the federal government. However, we hope that you will take into account our need to retain and attract top quality talent to ensure our future competitiveness. As a high-skilled research and development focused company, arbitrary and broad limits on compensation would harm our competitiveness going forward.

Even as we take these steps, however, we continue to protect our investment in the fuel-efficient new vehicles that we believe will secure our future. Operating under our "One Ford" principle, we intend to deliver more vehicles worldwide from fewer core platforms, further reduce costs and allow for the increased use of common parts and systems. The result will be a lineup of highly acclaimed, smaller vehicles in global segments (sub-compact, compact, and mid-size vehicles, and commercial vans) beginning in mid-2009. About 40% of Ford's entries in these segments will be shared between Ford North America, Ford Europe, and Ford Asia Pacific by 2010, with 100% alignment achieved by 2013. And, as I mentioned earlier, we are committed to deliver every new product with the best or among the best fuel economy in its segment, driven by the most extensive powertrain upgrades ever for Ford.

THE BRIDGE TO TRANSFORMATION

What I have outlined so far is the dramatic transformation taking place at Ford and the intense economic headwinds we now face as we attempt to continue and complete that transformation. The question remains whether we as a company and collectively as an industry will have time given the unprecedented short-term economic conditions to complete our transformation for the long term.

Speaking only for Ford, we are hopeful that we have enough liquidity based on current planning assumptions and planned cash improvement actions, but we also know that we live in tumultuous economic times in which rapid and unexpected change seems to be the norm rather than the exception. While we are cautiously confident, we must also be prudent, and prudence at this point requires that we prepare ourselves for the prospect of deteriorating economic conditions in 2009.

We also know that at least one of our competitors has reported that, absent the ability to secure additional funding, its estimated liquidity will fall significantly short of the minimum required to operate its business in the first two quarters of next year unless conditions rapidly improve — which we don't expect.

You have requested that we address the role of government-provided debtor-in-possession financing for a prepackaged Chapter 11 reorganization. The difficulty with this approach, in our view, is that Chapter 11 will not facilitate successful restructuring in our industry but would actually impair it by severely damaging sales in an already weak market. A Chapter 11 reorganization requires lengthy negotiations and potential concessions from suppliers, bondholders, the UAW, and the PBGC among other stakeholders — and the industry would be unlikely to survive, even in Chapter 11, during the time it takes to accomplish all of these steps. In short, Chapter 11, even prepackaged, makes no sense for us or for the industry.

Ours is in some significant ways an industry that is uniquely interdependent — particularly with respect to our supply base, with more than 90 percent commonality among our suppliers. In addition, we share an extensive minority and women-owned business supply base which, at Ford, represents $4 billion of the approximately $40 billion that Ford spends annually with U.S. suppliers. Should one of the other domestic companies declare bankruptcy, the effect on Ford's production operations would be felt within days -- if not hours. Suppliers could not get financing and would stop shipments to customers. Without parts for the just-in-time inventory system, Ford plants would not be able to produce vehicles.

Our dealer networks also have substantial overlap. Approximately 400 of our dealers also have a GM or Chrysler franchise at their dealership, and we estimate that as many as 25% of our top 1500 dealers also own GM or Chrysler franchises. The failure of one of the companies would clearly have a great impact on our dealers with exposure to that company.

In short, a collapse of one of our competitors here would have a ripple effect across all automakers, suppliers, and dealers — a loss of nearly 3 million jobs in the first year, according to an estimate by the Center for Automotive Research.

In the face of incredibly fragile economic conditions and the interdependence of our industry, we believe it is appropriate at this time to join our competitors in asking for your support to protect against an uncertain economic future that threatens all of the progress we have made to accomplish a goal that serves the interests of this nation — creating a strong and viable American automotive industry. I know we can achieve this goal because we at Ford are implementing the transformational changes that are required to achieve it — as long as we can survive the present economic turmoil.

Our request today is to gain access to an industry bridge loan that would provide all of us with an available tool to navigate through this difficult economic and financial crisis. We would suggest that the loans only be drawn as needed so that the exposure to the taxpayer would be limited — and, if used, we would repay with interest.

THE PUBLIC INTEREST

It should come as no surprise that we who are testifying before you today believe the domestic automotive industry should be supported and preserved as it transforms to meet the new challenges of meeting changing consumer demands and environmental imperatives in a difficult economic environment. The question before you, however, is one of the public interest — is the public interest better served by offering aid to the industry at this time or by letting market and regulatory forces work to whatever future they might bring?

I respectfully submit that the public interest is clear — this industry merits your support. I have already detailed at length the ways in which our iconic American Ford Motor Company is transforming itself for the future, and I know my colleagues from General Motors and Chrysler are equally confident of presenting a compelling vision of the future. We all believe that future is worth supporting.

But perhaps the most compelling reason for you to support our industry comes upon consideration of the consequences that would be visited on our already fragile economy if this industry should collapse.

At the end of 2007, Chrysler, Ford and General Motors directly employed about 240,000 American workers and indirectly supported more than 4.5 million other workers in the U.S. The Detroit Three are among the nation's largest purchasers of U.S.-manufactured steel, aluminum, iron, copper, plastics, rubber, electronics and computer chips. Last year, they provided health care to nearly 2 million Americans and paid pension benefits to 775,000 retirees or their survivors.

One recent study estimated that in the event the Detroit Three were to cease operations in 2009, employment loss would be nearly 3.0 million jobs, personal income would be reduced by over $150 billion, and the loss to the government in tax revenue would be more than $60 billion — in the first year alone. Even a 50 percent reduction in our operations would result in devastating losses to the economy, according to this study.

Many more statistics are available. Each would demonstrate that the collapse of the U.S. automotive industry would be a calamity for the entire economy. This is not a claim that any individual company is "too big to fail," although of course that sort of claim seems to have been at work in some recent — and far more costly — actions taken in other sectors in response to the economic crisis. Rather, ours is a claim that a large swath of the industry rises and falls together, and that the industry collectively is too big and too important to fail. The linkages we have through our suppliers, dealers, workers and customers mean that there are very few isolated events in our industry. I would therefore urge you as you consider our request not to think of individual companies but rather of the industry — and the economy — as a whole.

Of course, more than mere economics are at play. It would not be overstating the case to observe that our nation's ability to engage in heavy manufacturing is very much at stake and is a matter of national security. No less an authority than former NATO Commander General Wesley Clark eloquently made that point in a column in last Sunday's *New York Times* that I commend to the Committee:

> More challenges lie ahead for our military, and to meet them we need a strong industrial base. For years the military has sought better sources of electric power in its vehicles — necessary to allow troops to monitor their radios with diesel engines off, to support increasingly high-powered communications technology, and eventually to support electric propulsion and innovative armaments like directed-energy weapons. In sum, this greater use of electricity will increase combat power while reducing our footprint. Much research and development spending has gone into these programs over the years, but nothing on the manufacturing scale we really need.
>
> Now, though, as Detroit moves to plug-in hybrids and electric-drive technology, the scale problem can be remedied. Automakers are developing innovative electric motors, many with permanent magnet technology, that will have immediate military use. And only the auto industry, with its vast purchasing power, is able to establish a domestic advanced battery industry. Likewise, domestic fuel cell production — which will undoubtedly have many critical military applications — depends on a vibrant car industry.

Our industry is proud of the role we have played through the years in meeting our national security needs, and we believe that role will continue to be critical in the years to come.

CONCLUSION

We live in difficult and challenging times, and have discovered in recent weeks and months that both old solutions and new must be re-examined and adjusted to meet rapidly changing conditions.

At Ford Motor Company, we remain committed to constant examination and response as we face new challenges. With each of those challenges, however, I become more convinced than ever that we have the right plan to transform Ford and that our best days are ahead of us. The reality is that Ford already is well on our way to realizing a complete transformation of our company — building a new Ford that has a very bright future.

With your help, we will together ensure that bright future for Ford and the entire American auto industry. With your help, we will create a safeguard to deal with the current unprecedented economic uncertainty, while all of us at Ford continue to deliver on our plan. And, as we continue to be an important part of communities across America, we look forward to working with you to be part of the solution on the road to economic recovery.

Thank you.

In: The U.S. Auto Industry and the Role of Federal Assistance   ISBN: 978-1-60741-322-6
Editor: James R. Elliot   © 2010 Nova Science Publishers, Inc.

Chapter 8

UNITED STATES HOUSE OF REPRESENTATIVES COMMITTEE ON FINANCIAL SERVICES, COMMITTEE HEARING, STABILIZING THE FINANCIAL CONDITION OF THE AMERICAN AUTOMOBILE INDUSTRY

Robert Nardelli

Mr. Chairman, members of the Committee, I appreciate this opportunity to address the current economic and financial crisis, the impact it is having on the automotive industry, and the need for immediate action.

During the 15 months I've been part of Chrysler, and since we've emerged as the first privately held American auto company in 50 years, I've been proud to work with a team of dedicated men and women determined to restore this 83-year old, iconic American brand to its rightful place in the automotive industry.

We are asking for assistance for one reason: to address the devastating automotive industry recession caused by our nations' financial meltdown, and the current lack of consumer credit, which has resulted in the critical lack of liquidity within our industry.

With credit markets frozen, our *customers* – average working Americans – do not have access to competitive financing to purchase or lease vehicles... our *dealers* do not have access to market competitive funding to place wholesale orders for new vehicles... resulting in the constriction of cash inflows to auto manufacturers. At the same time, Chrysler has billions of dollars in cash payment obligations every month to pay wages, to pay suppliers, to fund health care and pensions, all in the range of $4 to $5 billion per month.

This crisis has already driven U.S. sales to a 25-year low. In 2008 alone, our volume domestically has dropped from 17 million units to 11 million – a 38 percent decline. That volume drop is more than the total U.S. sales of Ford and Chrysler combined.

Therefore without immediate bridge financing support, Chrysler's liquidity could fall below the level necessary to sustain operations in the ordinary course. This would put at risk health care coverage for retirees, which is part of Chrysler's nearly $20 billion total health care obligation, $2 billion in annual pension payments to our retirees and surviving spouses, approximately $7 billion in current payables, $35 billion in future annual supplier business, and 56,600 direct Chrysler employees earning $6 billion in wages.

Independent research firms have quantified the fallout of a domestic auto maker bankruptcy to the overall economy, and the impact is devastating: 2.3 – 3 million in lost jobs, $275-$400 billion in lost wages, and $1 00-$150 billion in lost government revenue.

But this is not a good option for Chrysler, and more importantly, for the auto industry or the broader economy – for the following reasons:

1. We believe that retail sales would be impacted materially as a result of declining consumer confidence, and we will be forced to heavily discount existing inventory to move our product.

2. Given our common supplier base - at Chrysler, 96 of our top 100 suppliers are common to Ford and GM - the bankruptcy of any one domestic automaker would place enormous pressure on the supply chain and, consequently, that company's competitors.

3. Our factories would likely be idled for a significant period of time while we renegotiate contracts with each of our thousands of individual suppliers.

4. Restructuring and reorganization costs and expenses will be materially higher in connection with a Chapter 11 process: supplier and dealer support and marketing costs will increase, general economic dislocation will follow and significant fees and expenses will be paid to an army of bankruptcy professionals.

5. The overall amount and cost of financing the restructuring will be significantly higher in a Chapter 11 process than the working capital bridge we are requesting here today.

6. And finally, we cannot be confident that we will able to successfully *emerge* from bankruptcy.

That's why as an industry we are requesting a $25 billion working capital bridge to survive this liquidity crisis. However, both our private equity owner and I believe that while the immediate bridge financing is critical, the long-term solution to the industry's problems and challenges requires industry consolidation and cost rationalization to eliminate excess industry capacity and redundant costs.

I would expect Congress to *insist* that the American taxpayer be protected. We are willing to provide full financial transparency, and welcome the government as a stakeholder – including as an equity holder. We are fully prepared to comply with the current conditions and policies already put in place as mandated by the government, under the recently enacted Emergency Economic Stabilization Act.

Our private equity owner, Cerberus Capital Management, L.P., has made it clear that it will forgo any benefit from the upside that would, in part, be created from any government assistance that Chrysler LLC may obtain. The principal of Cerberus Capital has stated that he will enter into legally binding agreements requiring the contribution to the government of the General Partner's future profits interest related to Chrysler LLC which he might receive if any are ever earned.

Immediately on the separating from Daimler in August 2007, and being new to the automotive industry, I recognized the need to question and sometimes challenge the status quo, and seek significant opportunities to improve performance throughout the business. We began an aggressive restructuring and transformation of our business as an independent American auto company.

During the first 60 days, we approved more than 400 line item design changes, representing an investment of half a billion dollars in improvements to our products' reliability, durability, fit and finish, and consumer appeal. We offered our customers a lifetime powertrain warranty to build their confidence. Due to a focused product quality improvement effort during the past year, we've seen our warranty claim rates drop by 29 percent and the improvement trend continues.

We made tough decisions to reduce operating costs and adjusted production schedules immediately. We prioritized every product investment with a strong emphasis on improving energy security and environmental sustainability by introducing advanced powertrain technologies, while at the same time we discontinued four vehicle models. We also identified over $1 billion in non-earning assets to sell and we're more than 75 percent toward achieving that goal.

Since 2007, Chrysler has reduced 1.2 million units of capacity, which represents over 30 percent of our previous installed capacity, and which resulted in the elimination 12 production shifts. Over the past 10 months alone, we've reduced our fixed costs by $2.2 billion, and unfortunately, by the end of the year, we will have furloughed over 32,000 employees. That is the most gut-wrenching part of this job, to see the effect on the lives of good men and women who lose their jobs through no fault of their own, but because of the actions the Company is forced to take in these difficult times.

We have increased our manufacturing productivity to equal Toyota as America's most productive automaker in terms of hours of assembly per vehicle, and our recently negotiated labor agreement was an important step in making our cost structure more competitive with transplants by 2010.

To further enhance our product portfolio, support growth and improve our cost structure, we continue to aggressively pursue strategic alliances and partnerships with other companies. I believe more restructuring and consolidation is required for the industry to be viable in the long-run. We would welcome the opportunity to have an open discussion with the new Administration and Congress on a collaborative approach to restructuring that would ensure any Government resources invested in the industry are used efficiently and help achieve important national public policy objectives.

It is *equally important* that the lack of liquidity to provide loans and leases to customers and financing to dealers is addressed immediately. It is *imperative* that our affiliated financial companies receive access to competitive liquidity and financing capacity. They *must* in order to provide credit to our customers - average working Americans - and support wholesale orders from our dealers.

Historically, over *90 percent* of all new vehicles were purchased or leased with financing assistance, and the lack of readily available financing has simply frozen sales. A perfect example of this consumer credit crisis is that 20 percent of our revenue disappeared overnight when our finance company was unable to offer leases. These sales literally vanished.

At Chrysler, 75 percent of our dealers rely on Chrysler Financial to finance their business, and 50 percent of all customers finance their vehicle purchases through the Chrysler Financial. Normally, these loans and leases are securitized and sold in the secondary market to generate fresh liquidity and financing capacity.

Today, there *is* virtually no secondary market, and therefore, no way to raise capital. Money is not available for dealers to finance their wholesale orders, invest in their facilities, and hire and train employees. Competitive loans for the average working American – our customers – are virtually nonexistent. This has directly and dramatically depressed vehicle sales, putting at risk not only auto manufacturers but also the widespread network of suppliers, vendors. In Chrysler's case, 3,200 entrepreneurs... small businesses owners called dealers, and the approximately 140,000 people they employ in every state across the country. The National Automobile Dealers Association estimates more than 700 of them will go out of business by year end. If we don't secure a bridge loan, all 13,600 dealers are at risk.

There are 4.5 million people depending on this industry, and without assistance, nearly *three million of them could lose their jobs* in the next 12 months, according to a research memorandum published November 4, 2008, by the Center for Automotive Research. Failing to act now will hurt many American families and undermine our country's economic recovery, far outweighing the costs related to supporting an industry that touches every district in every state of the nation.

The crippling of the industry would have severe and debilitating ramifications for the industrial base of the United States, would undermine our nation's ability to respond to military challenges and would threaten our national security. Chrysler has long contributed to our national defense. Our Jeep® was an indispensable part of our nation's efforts in World War II and Korea.

Immediate financial assistance will serve the country and the economy directly in two key ways. First, the lifeblood of the U.S. economy will continue to flow. The industry will be able to continue to pay at its current levels $22 billion in annual wages to our employees, $13 billion in annual pensions to our retirees and surviving spouses, and meet our current commitment of $102 billion in healthcare costs to employees. We will continue to pay $156 billion annually to our suppliers and work to keep them strong by providing significant additional financial relief for distressed suppliers fighting to stay in business.

Second, America's auto companies are investing in innovation. Capital investment in new technologies, improved operations, and future product will be able to continue, including a combined $12 billion in annual spending for research and development. As an industry, we are moving full speed ahead to make the transition to advanced propulsion vehicles that will help support national energy security and environmental sustainability goals.

Chrysler plans to emerge from the current downturn as a lean, agile company. We are, and will continue to be the quintessential *American* car company. Currently, 73 percent of our sales are in the U.S., 61 percent of our vehicles are produced in the United States, 74 percent of employees work in the U.S., 78 percent of our materials are purchased in the U.S. and 62 percent of our dealers are based in the U.S.

Today, Chrysler has a very strong pipeline, with a product renaissance for 2010. In September we revealed our ENVI electric vehicle program, and announced that we will begin producing one of these electric-drive models for North American consumers in 2010. This underscores our commitment to deliver environmentally friendly, fuel-efficient vehicles to customers, and to meet this social responsibility faster and more broadly than any other manufacturer.

Today we are asking you to help us bridge a chasm created by an unprecedented financial meltdown. We are also asking you to consider investing in a company that will deliver real results for the American taxpayer.

I recognize that this is not an insignificant amount of money. However, we believe this request is the least costly alternative considering the options we face... with less impact on human capital, and would *provide stimulus,* as opposed to further depress the economy.

Thank you very much.

Nardelli, Robert L.
Chairman and Chief Executive Officer, Chrysler LLC
Board of Managers, Chrysler LLC

Robert L. Nardelli joined Chrysler LLC as Chairman and Chief Executive Officer and as a member of the Board of Managers in August 2007.

Prior to joining Chrysler, Nardelli served as Chairman, President and CEO of The Home Depot beginning in 2000. Nardelli began his career at GE in 1971, and advanced through a series of leadership positions in the company's Appliances, Lighting and Transportation Systems business units. In 1988, he left GE to join Case Corporation in Racine, Wis., where he led Case Construction Equipment's global business. He returned to GE in 1992 and was ultimately named President and CEO of GE Power Systems and Senior Vice President of General Electric.

His work and academic background includes:

- Chairman and Chief Executive Officer and member of the Board of Managers, Chrysler LLC, August 2007
- Board of Managers, Cerberus Operating and Advisory Company LLC, 2007
- Chairman, President and Chief Executive Officer, The Home Depot, 2000
- President and CEO, GE Power Systems, Senior Vice President, General Electric, 1995
- President and CEO, GE Transportation Systems, 1992
- Executive Vice President and Chief Executive Officer, Canadian Appliance Manufacturing, (subsidiary of GE), 1991
- Executive Vice President and General Manager, Case Construction Equipment, 1988
- Manufacturing Engineer, various management positions at General Electric Appliances, GE Lighting, and GE Transportation Systems, 1971
- Master of Business Administration, University of Louisville, 1975
- Bachelor of Science, Western Illinois University, 1971

He chairs the Atlanta Board of Visitors of the Savannah College of Art and Design, and has also served on President Bush's Council on Service and Civic Participation. He has received the Distinguished Pennsylvanian Award from Gannon University (1995) and the Distinguished Alumni Award from the College of Business and Technology at Western Illinois University (1997 and 1999). He is an alumni fellow and 2001 Alumnus of the Year of the University of Louisville, and serves on the Board of Advisors, University of Louisville Graduate School of Business, as well as on the College of Business & Technology Advisory Board for Western Illinois University, and is a member of The Business Council.

Nardelli was born on May 17, 1948, in Old Forge, Penn.

In: The U.S. Auto Industry and the Role of Federal Assistance   ISBN: 978-1-60741-322-6
Editor: James R. Elliot   © 2010 Nova Science Publishers, Inc.

Chapter 9

TESTIMONY OF RON GETTELFINGER, INTERNATIONAL UNION, UNITED AUTOMOBILE, AEROSPACE AND AGRICULTURAL IMPLEMENT WORKERS OF AMERICA (UAW) ON THE SUBJECT OF STABILIZING THE FINANCIAL CONDITION OF THE AMERICAN AUTOMOBILE INDUSTRY BEFORE THE COMMITTEE ON FINANCIAL SERVICES, UNITED STATES HOUSE OF REPRESENTATIVES

INTRODUCTION

Mr. Chairman, my name is Ron Gettelfinger. I am President of the International Union, United Automobile, Aerospace & Agricultural Implement Workers of America (UAW). The UAW represents 1 million active and retired workers, most of whom work or receive retirement benefits from the Detroit-based auto companies or auto parts suppliers around the country. We appreciate the opportunity to testify today on the subject of stabilizing the financial condition of the American automobile industry.

The UAW strongly supports legislation to amend the Emergency Economic Stabilization Act (EESA) to clarify that the Treasury Department should use the existing financial rescue program to quickly provide a $25 billion emergency bridge loan to GM, Ford and Chrysler to enable these companies to weather the current credit and economic crises that have had such a devastating impact on our entire country. This bridge loan would be paid from the funds that Congress has already provided under the financial rescue program; there would not be any new federal funds. As with other rescue efforts under this program, the bridge loan to the automakers would be conditioned on stringent limits relating to executive compensation, as well as provisions granting the federal government an equity stake in the auto companies in order to protect the investment by taxpayers.

The UAW believes that the Treasury Department already has the authority under existing law to make the bridge loan to the auto companies. But because there is disagreement on this point, we believe Congress should act quickly to approve legislation to make it clear that the Treasury Department should act now to provide this urgently needed relief.

The Detroit-based Auto Companies Are Facing a Crisis

The situation now facing GM, Ford and Chrysler is extremely dire. Because of the credit and financial crises that have engulfed our nation, overall vehicle sales have plummeted to the lowest level in 25 years. In October, sales were at an annualized level of 10.8 million vehicles, far below the normal level of 16-18 million vehicles.

There is no great mystery as to why this enormous decline in sales has occurred. Buying a vehicle is the second biggest purchase that families make. Because of the overall credit crunch, most families cannot get credit on reasonable terms to finance the purchase of a vehicle. And because of the general economic uncertainty, many families are simply deferring any major expenditures.

The net result is that all auto companies, not just the Detroit-based automakers, have seen a sharp drop in their sales. This means that the revenues received by the companies have declined drastically. As a result, GM, Ford and Chrysler are burning through their cash reserves at an unprecedented rate. As the recent earnings reports indicate, this scenario is not sustainable. If the government does not act to provide immediate assistance, GM, Ford and Chrysler could be forced to liquidate.

The UAW wants to underscore that this would not be a painless, "prepackaged" bankruptcy reorganization as some columnists have suggested. Consumers will not purchase vehicles from a company that has filed for bankruptcy. And bankrupt auto companies would not be able to obtain "debtor-in-possession" financing to enable them to continue operations. Thus, the stark reality is that these companies would be forced into a Chapter 7 liquidation, with their operations ceasing entirely and their assets sold for pennies on dollar.

Devastating Consequences if the Detroit-Based Auto Companies Collapse

If the Detroit-based auto companies are forced into liquidation, the consequences would be truly devastating, not only for UAW members, but also for millions of other workers and retirees across this nation, and for the entire economy of the United States. In addition to the hundreds of thousands of workers who would directly lose their jobs at the Detroit-based auto companies, according to the Center for Automotive Research a total of almost 3 million workers would see their jobs eliminated. This includes persons who work for auto dealers, suppliers of components and materials, and thousands of other businesses that depend on the auto industry. In addition, because the auto manufacturers depend on many of the same suppliers, a disruption in the supply chain would have serious negative consequences for the remaining auto manufacturers.

The liquidation of the Detroit-based auto companies would also have devastating consequences for millions of retirees. The retirees from these companies and their spouses and dependents – about one million persons – could suffer sharp reductions in their pension benefits. And they would face the loss of their health insurance coverage – an especially devastating blow to the roughly 40 percent who are younger than 65 and thus not yet eligible for Medicare. In addition, if the automakers' pension plans are terminated, the Pension Benefit Guarantee Corporation (PBGC) would be saddled with unprecedented liabilities. To prevent the collapse of the PBGC, which would jeopardize the retirement security of millions of workers and retirees, the federal government would have to provide a huge bailout for the pension guarantee program. Furthermore, under existing law, the federal government would be liable for a 65% tax credit to cover the health care costs of pre-Medicare auto retirees costing about $3 billion per year.

The liquidation of the Detroit-based auto companies would have serious negative repercussions for the entire U.S. economy. Almost 4 percent of our nation's GDP is related to the auto industry, and almost 10 percent of our industrial production by value. The collapse of the auto sector would severely aggravate the current economic downturn, sending production and consumer spending into a deeper tailspin while unemployment spirals higher. Federal, state and local government revenues would shrink even further, forcing harmful cuts in a wide range of social services at precisely the time they are most urgently needed.

The UAW submits that it would be far better for the auto industry and its workers and retirees, and for the nation as a whole, for the federal government to take prompt action now to prevent the imminent collapse of the Detroit-based auto companies. The human toll will be far less. And the ultimate cost to the government will be far cheaper.

MYTHS ABOUT THE AUTO INDUSTRY

A number of objections have been raised by various commentators against this type of government assistance to the Detroit-based auto companies. These objections are largely based on myths about the auto industry that do not stand up on closer scrutiny.

A) The Current Problems Facings the Detroit-based Companies Are Not Due to "Overly Rich Union Contracts"

Some commentators have asserted that "overly rich contracts" negotiated by the UAW are to blame for the companies' current situation, and have suggested that workers and retirees should be required to take deep cuts in their wages and benefits. This totally ignores the recent history in the auto industry and the facts regarding wages and benefits at the Detroit-based auto companies.

The truth is that in 2005 the UAW agreed to reopen the contracts mid-term, and accepted cuts in workers' wages and in health care benefits for retirees. Then, in the general 2007 collective bargaining negotiations, the UAW agreed to what industry analysts have called a "transformational" contract that fundamentally altered labor costs for the Detroit-based auto companies. This contract slashed wages for new hires by 50%. Furthermore, new hires will not be covered under the traditional retiree health care and defined benefit pension plans. In addition, this contract stipulated that beginning January 1, 2010 the liability for health care benefits for existing retirees would be transferred from the companies to an independent fund (a Voluntary Employee Beneficiary Association, or VEBA). This agreement has subsequently been approved by federal courts, which have appointed a majority of the trustees who will be independent of the UAW and responsible for managing the VEBA. Taken together, the changes made by the 2005 and 2007 contracts reduced the companies' retiree health care liabilities by fifty percent.

As a result of all these painful concessions, the gap in labor costs that had previously existed between the Detroit-based auto companies and the foreign transplant operations will be largely or completely eliminated by the end of the contracts. Indeed, one industry analyst has indicated that labor costs for the Detroit-based auto companies will actually be lower than those for Toyota's U.S. operations. Thus, the truth is the UAW and our active and retired members have already stepped up to the plate and made the hard changes that were necessary to make our companies competitive in terms of their labor costs.

It is also important to note that union negotiated work rules cannot be blamed for the current problems facing the Detroit-based companies. According to the Harbour Report, the industry benchmark for productivity, union-represented workers are actually more efficient than their counterparts at non-union auto plants. And union-made vehicles built by the Detroit-based auto companies are winning quality awards from Consumer Reports, J.D. Power, and other industry analysts.

The current plight of GM, Ford and Chrysler is simply not attributable to "overly rich union contracts." Instead, it is the result of the larger credit and economic crises that have engulfed our nation, and the unprecedented drop in auto sales that has affected *all* automakers.

Because the recent contracts negotiated by the UAW are now competitive with the rest of auto industry in the U.S., we do not believe there is any justification for conditioning assistance to the Detroit-based auto companies on further deep cuts in wages and benefits for active and retired workers. We would also note that in the cases where the Treasury Department has acted to rescue financial institutions, it has only imposed restrictions on executive compensation. It has never mandated cuts in wages or benefits for rank-and-file workers and retirees. Thus, there is no basis for singling out the auto industry for different treatment.

B) The Current Crisis Cannot Be Blamed on the Detroit-based Companies Producing Gas Guzzling Vehicles

Some pundits also have asserted that the Detroit-based auto companies are to blame for their current predicament because they insisted on producing gas guzzling vehicles, rather than more fuel efficient vehicles that consumers wanted. According to this point of view, GM, Ford and Chrysler simply were not producing vehicles that consumers wanted to buy.

Unfortunately, this argument ignores the fact that the current credit and economic crises have resulted in a sharp drop in sales by *all* auto manufacturers, including the Japanese companies. The immediate problem is not just that consumers aren't buying the vehicles produced by the Detroit-based auto companies. The problem is they aren't buying vehicles from any company!

It is true that earlier this year the sharp spike in gas prices resulted in a sudden shift in the product mix demanded by consumers, with sales of more fuel efficient vehicles increasing, and sales of pickups, minivans and other larger vehicles dropping. This shift in product mix hit the Detroit-based companies the hardest, because their product mix was more oriented towards these larger vehicles. But it also caught Toyota and Nissan by surprise. Because these companies had been aggressively expanding production of larger vehicles, they also experienced significant dislocations.

The Detroit-based auto companies have been investing massive amounts of money to change their product mix and to provide consumers with a wide range of more fuel efficient vehicles. They are aggressively moving ahead with advanced fuel saving technologies. For example, GM plans to introduce the Volt plug in hybrid in 2010.

The landmark energy legislation that was enacted by Congress in 2007, with the support of the UAW and the auto companies, will require substantial improvements in fuel economy until the entire fleet of autos and light trucks sold in the U.S. by all companies achieves at least 35 mpg by 2020. In addition, the Advanced Technology Vehicles Manufacturing Incentive Program (ATVMIP), which was authorized by this legislation and subsequently funded by Congress in the fall of this year, will provide assistance to all automakers – the Detroit-based companies and the foreign transplants – to retool facilities in this country to produce the advanced, fuel efficient vehicles of the future and their key components. This will help to accelerate the introduction of these more fuel efficient vehicles, while ensuring that they are produced by American workers.

Some commentators have questioned why this advanced vehicle retooling program doesn't provide sufficient assistance for the auto companies. The answer is the ATVMIP is part of a long term energy policy that will provide assistance to the auto companies and parts suppliers over a ten year period, tied specifically to the production of very high mileage vehicles. This program was not designed to address the type of immediate cash flow crisis that the Detroit-based auto companies are now facing as a result of the sudden drop in overall auto sales. Even if the ATVMIP is implemented quickly – which is by no means clear – at most it will only provide modest assistance to the Detroit based auto companies in the coming years.

Other observers have questioned whether the ATVMIP could simply be expanded to allow the Detroit-based auto companies immediate access to the entire $25 billion that was authorized and appropriated for this program. The UAW believes this would not make sense because it would undermine the fuel economy objectives of this program. Furthermore, there simply are not enough retooling projects in the short term – for advanced vehicles or more conventional ones – to make this approach feasible.

Some commentators and groups have suggested that any new assistance to the Detroit-based auto companies should be conditioned on even greater improvements in fuel economy. We recognize that President-elect Obama campaigned on a platform that included increases in fuel economy and the production of plug in hybrids, as well as assistance to the auto industry to ensure that the vehicles of the future are produced in this country. The UAW is looking forward to working with the Obama administration and the next Congress to help achieve these objectives.

But we firmly believe it would be an enormous mistake to rush to include these important new initiatives in the current emergency bridge loan for the Detroit-based auto companies. To begin with, we do not believe there is adequate time to develop thoughtful proposals that are workable and effective. In addition, given the desperate situation facing the Detroit-based auto companies, and the devastating consequences their collapse would have for millions of workers and retirees and the entire U.S. economy, the UAW does not believe it is appropriate to hold emergency assistance hostage to broader fuel economy/environmental initiatives.

The Detroit-based auto companies need an immediate bridge loan from the Treasury Department in order to have sufficient cash to be able to continue their operations. These companies will not be able to continue on the path to producing the greener vehicles of the future if they are forced to liquidate in the coming months.

CONCLUSION

The UAW appreciates the opportunity to testify before this Committee on the subject of stabilizing the financial condition of the American automobile industry. We strongly urge Congress to act this week to approve legislation that will provide immediate assistance to GM, Ford and Chrysler to enable them to continue in business, and to avoid the devastating consequences that a collapse of these companies would have for millions of workers and retirees across our country. Thank you.

In: The U.S. Auto Industry and the Role of Federal Assistance   ISBN: 978-1-60741-322-6
Editor: James R. Elliot   © 2010 Nova Science Publishers, Inc.

Chapter 10

TESTIMONY OF MATTHEW J. SLAUGHTER FOR FULL COMMITTEE HEARING, "STABILIZING THE FINANCIAL CONDITION OF THE AMERICAN AUTOMOBILE INDUSTRY"

Committee Chairman Frank, Ranking Member Bachus, and fellow members, thank you very much for inviting me to testify on these important and timely issues regarding the American automobile industry. The Big Three automobile companies have very dedicated and hard-working executives and other workers, and they have many collective strengths and talents.

My name is Matt Slaughter, and I am currently Associate Dean and Professor of International Economics at the Tuck School of Business at Dartmouth, Research Associate at the National Bureau of Economic Research, and Senior Fellow at the Council on Foreign Relations. From 2005 to 2007 I also served as a Member on the Council of Economic Advisers, where my international portfolio included the competitiveness of the American economy and related topics.

I base my testimony to you today on my many years of scholarship and public service on the broad issues of how American companies and the country overall can succeed in an increasingly global economy. And I also base my testimony on two deeply held convictions. One is that although the dynamic and related forces of international trade, investment, and technological change have generated—and have the potential to continue generating—very large gains for the United States overall, these gains do not flow to every single worker, company, and community. The other, given the first, is that one of the paramount policy challenges facing America today is how to both continue realizing the aggregate gains of globalization yet also share these gains more broadly.

Despite these convictions—or rather, as I will explain in my testimony, largely because of them—I do not believe that automobile companies merit any new "bailout" assistance from the federal government.

Any such "bailout" assistance would incur large costs to American workers, companies, taxpayers, and the overall economy. Let me list three such costs.

1. First and, in the long run perhaps most importantly, would be the economy-wide cost of substituting product-market competition with resource allocation set by political rather than economic forces. One of the great U.S. policy successes since World War II has been the bipartisan effort to eliminate laws and regulations that stifle competition and innovation in product markets. With this system, productive U.S. companies expand and force their competitors to adapt. In addition, leading companies from around the world sell in the U.S. market and invest in U.S. factories and offices, ensuring that the U.S. economy is exposed to and strives to meet global best practices. All this dynamism has yielded higher productivity growth, higher average incomes, and greater choices for consumers.

   A bailout of certain U.S. automobile companies could set a precedent to be followed for many years by many companies in many other industries. Given the limited pool of savings available in the U.S. economy, these bailouts would displace productive investments from firms elsewhere in the economy and would thereby impede long-run economic growth and rising standards of living. This cost would admittedly be incurred over the longer term. But that does not make it any less important. If anything, this cost would be all the more important because of the long-term challenges facing our country such as the slow-down in educational attainment and the unsustainable growth in entitlement spending.

2. A second important cost of any bailout would be damage to America's engagement with the global economy. One dimension of this "global cost" would fall on foreign direct investment into the United States. In 2006 foreign-headquartered multinationals engaged in making and wholesaling motor vehicles and parts employed 402,800 Americans—at an average annual compensation of $63,538. Across all industries, insourcing companies in 2006 registered $2.8 trillion in U.S. sales while employing 5.3 million Americans and paying them $364 billion in compensation. But as the world has grown smaller, today the United States faces stiffer competition to attract and retain these companies. Indeed, the U.S. share of global FDI inflows has already fallen from 31.5 percent in 1988-1990 to just 16.0 percent 2003-2005. Will the desire of insourcing companies to operate in America be enhanced by federal government subsidies for their domestic competitors? On the contrary: too many such bailouts would cost America in terms of a smaller, less-dynamic presence of insourcing companies.

   Another dimension of this global cost would fall on U.S.-headquartered multinationals, key U.S. companies which employ over 22 million Americans and account for a remarkable 78.9% of all private-sector R&D. Their success depends critically on their ability to access foreign customers. They do this via exports from their U.S. parents. But even more important is via local sales of their foreign affiliates created via FDI abroad. In 2005, U.S. parents exported $456.0 billion to foreign markets. That same year their majority-owned affiliates tallied nearly $3.7 trillion in total affiliate sales--$8.10 for every dollar in parent exports.

   The policy environment abroad, however, has been growing more protectionist towards the trade and FDI so important to U.S. multinationals. Multilateral efforts to liberalize trade in the Doha Development Round died in July with no prospects for restarting. Even more worrisome are rising FDI barriers. In 2005 and 2006, the United Nations tracked record numbers of new FDI restrictions around the world—

even in major recipient countries such as China, Germany, and Japan. Will U.S.-government bailouts of its "national champions" go ignored by policy makers abroad? No. Instead, U.S. bailouts will likely entrench and expand their protectionist practices. This would erode the foreign sales and competitiveness of U.S. multinationals—and would thereby reduce their U.S. employment, R&D, and related activities as well.

3. A third and more direct cost would be the likelihood that any new taxpayer assistance would go largely or entirely unpaid. Public filings by GM, Ford, and Chrysler make clear that in the past two years they have collectively lost scores of billions of dollars. For Ford, operating losses were $2.8 billion in 2007 and $8.7 billion in first nine months of 2008. The operating losses for General Motors have been even larger: $43.3 billion in 2007 and $21.3 billion in first nine months of 2008. And this total in Ford and GM's operating losses over 21 months of $76.1 billion was incurred almost entirely before the sharp downturn in economic activity and heightened capital-market turmoil since mid-September.

    All this suggests that today the Big Three firms are losing money at a rate in excess of $4 billion a month. Because this underlying dynamic has been at play for quite some time, without fundamental structural changes in these companies an infusion of capital from any source—public or private—runs a high risk of not being repaid. As I address below, a relevant question for taxpayers thus becomes how to structure a different deployment of public funds to support the workers and communities affected by a struggling Big Three.

These three important costs of any new bailout assistance do not imply that the federal government should do nothing at all about the very serious challenges facing the Big Three. Indeed, the federal government can help minimize the economy-wide costs of these challenges. Exactly how will depend on what the future holds for these companies. In struggling industries, one common outcome is for firms to merge. Alternatively or in addition, there is reason to expect that bankruptcy awaits some number of American automobile companies. On this issue, it is important to emphasize two points.

1. Bankruptcy and, more generally, plant closures and job restructurings related to both bankruptcy and mergers, are not uncommon occurrences in the overall U.S. economy. Rather, they are essential for overall economic growth because they are a principal channel through which capital, people, and ideas get reallocated to the most profitable business opportunities.

    Amidst all this dynamism, every single job separation can be difficult for the worker and family involved. This is important to emphasize, and I shall return to it below. But often-heard numbers regarding job reductions must be put in context to be properly understood. Suppose that a bankruptcy filing by one of the Big Three were to lead to 50,000 layoffs. Last week our U.S. Bureau of Labor Statistics reported that in September, the total number of gross job separations was 4.053 million. At an average of about four 40-hour work weeks per month, this means that on average a remarkable 25,000 jobs are destroyed in the U.S. economy every hour that America is open for business. Indeed, my hypothetical 50,000 layoffs from a bankruptcy filing happens every day in the aggregate U.S. economy in less time than this hearing will take.

2. A bankruptcy filing for an automobile company would very likely mean restructuring, not liquidation, in which case many of the company's operations would continue. Much of today's discussions presume that upon filing bankruptcy all jobs at a company—and all those at any suppliers—disappear immediately and forever, with all affected workers rendered unemployed immediately as well. This presumption is simply not an accurate reflection of most bankruptcy proceedings initiated under Chapter 11 rather than Chapter 7 of U.S. federal bankruptcy code. In most bankruptcy cases, many day-to-day operations continue as the company is restructured on many dimensions to restore long-term business viability. And even under Chapter 7 filings, asset sales as part of liquidation often result in continued operation rather than shut-down by the acquirer.

    This is not to say that bankruptcy restructuring is simple or painless. It is not, a point to which I return below. But it is to say that the proper perspective for analysis is not one of immediate and permanent redundancy of the entire company.

So if the future of the American automobile industry may involve some combination of additional downsizing, new mergers, and perhaps even bankruptcy, what role should the federal government play? As stated earlier in my testimony, I regard the proper federal-government focus not to be on impeding market forces but rather on addressing the distributional pressures of these market forces. This focus suggests three areas for federal-government assistance. Let me list these in increasing order of breadth.

1. First, the federal government could help expedite any bankruptcy proceedings. Because of the weak overall U.S. economy minimizing delays in any filing would be of paramount importance. This assistance would help maintain economically sensible activity not just at the Big Three themselves but also at their suppliers as well.

    The exact nature of government assistance in bankruptcy would need to be determined. One possible example might be insuring warranties on new and/or existing cars. The concern has been raised that a bankrupt car company would experience a sharp drop in demand because prospective customers would worry about the quantity and quality of warranted after-sales service. Until such concerns were allayed by actual performance in and beyond bankruptcy, the government could insure such provision.

2. Second, the federal government could extend targeted and temporary aid to workers and communities deemed to be adversely affected by a bankruptcy filing or other industrial restructurings.

    The Big Three are geographically concentrated in certain Midwest communities and states. Many of these areas already face hardship from the national economic slowdown in general and from falling home prices in particular. Plans could be laid now for extending supplemental benefits, beyond standard unemployment-insurance amounts, to whatever workers in whatever communities are deemed worthy of such support.

    The political process would need to determine the appropriate amount and kinds of supports. For now, let me simply state that in light of the size of bailout funds currently being proposed, the potential per-worker supports are extremely large. Today the Big Three employ about 200,000 workers in the United States. If the government reallocated the previous $25 billion in loans allocated to the Big Three and the under-discussion additional amount of at least $25 billion more and planned instead to somehow distribute these taxpayer dollars to workers, this would translate into $250,000 for every single Big Three worker. This could be allocated across several years of unemployment income benefits, of wage-loss insurance upon re-employment, of retraining and relocation expenses: whatever combination of social-safety-net policies we as a country might deem appropriate for these (and perhaps other) workers.

3. Third and perhaps most importantly, the federal government could use this auto-industry crisis as an impetus for meaningfully expanding the economy-wide social contract I mentioned at the outset of my testimony, to better distribute the gains of our dynamic economy.

In recent times, I have researched and written several studies on how public policy could better support American workers and communities while still expanding the global engagement and technological change so critical for raising U.S. living standards.[1] We as a country could do this in many ways: by linking future trade and investment liberalization to a more-progressive tax code; by a fundamental overhaul of our Unemployment Insurance and Trade Adjustment Assistance programs; and by new insurance mechanisms that would allow communities to smooth out their tax revenues. Policies like these would help America grow more equitably in the long run. As the old saw goes, there is no time like the present to start deliberating and implementing such policies.

Let me close by thanking you again for your time and interest in my testimony. I look forward to answering any questions you may have.

End Notes

[1] "A New Deal for Globalization," Kenneth F. Scheve and Matthew J. Slaughter, *Foreign Affairs*, July/August 2007, pp. 34-47. *Succeeding in the Global Economy: A New Policy Agenda for the American Worker*, Grant D. Aldonas, Robert Z. Lawrence, and Matthew J. Slaughter, The Financial Services Forum policy research report, June 2007. *Global FDI Policy: Correcting A Protectionist Drift*, David M. Marchick and Matthew J. Slaughter, Council Special Report, Washington, D.C.: Council on Foreign Relations, June 2008. *An Adjustment Assistance Program for American Workers*, Grant D. Aldonas, Robert Z. Lawrence, and Matthew J. Slaughter, The Financial Services Forum policy research report, July 2008.

In: The U.S. Auto Industry and the Role of Federal Assistance   ISBN: 978-1-60741-322-6
Editor: James R. Elliot   © 2010 Nova Science Publishers, Inc.

Chapter 11

TESTIMONY OF FELIX G. ROHATYN TO THE HOUSE FINANCIAL SERVICES COMMITTEE

Mr. Chairman and members of the Committee:

I am pleased to accept your invitation to review the present situation of the auto industry with you. General Motors, Ford and Chrysler are all in serious jeopardy. The situation is fraught with danger and each of your options carries its own risks. The situation is in some ways similar to the near bankruptcy of New York City in 1975, as well as that of Chrysler in 1980.

After years of operating losses as well as a heavy burden of accumulated legacy costs, GM together with Ford and Chrysler – like New York City thirty years ago – are facing bankruptcy unless the US government is willing to provide them with multi-billion dollar loans. The loans would not guarantee the success of a restructuring but the companies have each submitted a different plan which is intended to bring them to profitability. Absent the loans, however, the companies are likely to fail in time, with serious consequences to our fragile economy.

Government loans, of this type are emergency instruments but have been used in some critical cases with success. Sustained profitability has to be the objective. In May, 1975, New York City was also headed for bankruptcy. Years of operating deficits, failure to make capital investments, high taxes and high costs were driving businesses and residents out of the city. The banks, which normally financed the city, refused to renew their loans absent major reform and Governor Carey and Mayor Beame requested an emergency loan of $1 billion from Washington to tide the city over its next loan maturity. When President Ford refused the request, the city was faced with grim alternatives: either declare bankruptcy or submit New York City to a combination of steep tax increases and brutal budget cuts, which would leave the city in a desperate economic position and with social problems of unknown dimensions. Governor Carey, Mayor Beame and their advisors therefore decided to elaborate our own plan. Time was running out, however. The city needed $1 billion within three weeks, followed by $1 billion per month for the following six months.

We turned to our only potential sources of funds, i.e., the New York City banks and the pension funds of the municipal unions. To provide greater security for bondholders we created a new state agency, the Municipal Assistance Corporation, which had the backing of the state. We were able to raise $1 billion by selling bonds to the public but we still were left with $8 billion to go and still the markets would not reopen to us without government participation. We struggled, for six months, to raise the money from union pension funds, reductions in the work force (60,000 people), loans from the state and restructuring from the banks. But President Ford and his advisors continued to refuse any assistance, seemingly blind to the risks to the markets of such a bankruptcy and eager to make an example of the so-called profligacy of the city.

By the end of November 1975, we had concluded that we could not meet the conditions of President Ford without a crippled city as a result, and New York City was about to file for bankruptcy when we found new allies: the first Western Economic Summit was taking place near Paris, presided by President Giscard d'Estaing of France and Chancellor Helmut Schmidt of Germany. President Ford attended, with other Western leaders and the Chair of the Federal Reserve Bank, Arthur Burns, was a member of our delegation. The French President and German Chancellor warned Dr. Burns of the heavy risks being taken by the Ford Administration's position on New York City. The foreign exchange and the securities markets reacted very negatively and so did the municipal bond markets, making it more and more difficult for even a small municipality to finance.

Giscard d'Estaing and Schmidt warned Ford of a possible global crisis for the dollar and "*the appearance of a bankruptcy by the United States.*" At that point, President Ford and his advisors stepped back from the brink. Upon his return to Washington, Ford agreed to a three-year Federal seasonal loan program which saved our city, but at a heavy price. Deep service cuts, reductions in personnel in the tens of thousands, cancellation of capital programs, as well as the imposition on the city of a state financial control board, the Municipal Assistance Corporation. However, within four years the New York City budget was balanced and the city, with the exception of 9/11, enjoyed thirty years of prosperity. However, it would have been impossible without government participation, which unlocked the participation of the private financial actors (the banks, the insurance companies and the pension funds). In addition, the city elected a new Mayor, Ed Koch, who successfully led the city's restructuring, together with Governor Hugh Carey.

The automotive industry is now in a similar position to New York City in 1975. It has submitted a multi-year operating plan with the management committed to profitability at the end of the period. It would be overseen by a financial control board similar to New York City's. It should produce vehicles consistent with the evolution of fuel and environmental standards. Further savings could be produced through asset sales, downsizing, debt-to-equity swaps and, in the case of Chrysler, savings from synergies in the case of a Chrysler merger, which had been discussed some time ago. The issue in the auto industry is partly about the severe recession as well as about costs that exceed revenues and unexciting product design. Any assistance package has to recognize the need to realign costs with revenues and to deal with realistic assumptions.

There was precedent for these actions: in particular, New York City in 1975 and Chrysler in 1980 both received federal assistance after difficult congressional debate.

In 1979, Chrysler teetered on the edge of bankruptcy and the company struggled to get support for a $1.5 billion loan guarantee which ultimately helped to save the company and 250,000 jobs. The company was able to secure the loan guarantee because labor, management and other stakeholders made significant concessions. The company also benefited from the salesmanship of its new chairman, Lee Iacocca, and the support of Detroit mayor Coleman

Young, as well as state and local governments connected to plants and with tighter government oversight. The company also had to provide a financial and operating plan as well as short and long term cash flow projections. The strategy included sacrifices from everybody with an interest in saving the company. Congress approved the loan guarantee program after a strong debate and Chrysler survived.

The auto industry can only be saved if it takes the lead in environmental and fuel efficiency standards which would benefit the whole country; . It cannot wait much longer and a bankruptcy of one of the lead companies would carry the same risks that caused the President of France and the Chancellor of West Germany to issue their warnings thirty years ago. It is an open-ended risk, which would impact all the stakeholders, and ultimately all of our economy. It is worth remembering an old saying: never take a risk you are not prepared to lose.

I have learned several lessons from this kind of situation:

(1) Be realistic in your assumptions and leave yourself some margin
(2) Act early and do not wait for all the data to be in
(3) Be truthful with all the stakeholders

These have served me well and I believe them to be appropriate in this case.

In: The U.S. Auto Industry and the Role of Federal Assistance   ISBN: 978-1-60741-322-6
Editor: James R. Elliot   © 2010 Nova Science Publishers, Inc.

Chapter 12

TESTIMONY OF ANNETTE SKYORA, NATIONAL AUTOMOBILE DEALERS ASSOCIATION, BEFORE THE HOUSE FINANCIAL SERVICES COMMITTEE, HEARING ON "STABILIZING THE FINANCIAL CONDITION OF THE AMERICAN AUTOMOBILE INDUSTRY"

Good morning, Mr. Chairman and Members of the Committee. My name is Annette Sykora and I am a third-generation car dealer and owner of Smith Ford Mercury in Slaton, Texas, and Smith South Plains Ford, Lincoln- Mercury, Dodge, Chrysler and Jeep in Levelland, Texas. This year, I am also privileged to be the Chairman of the National Automobile Dealers Association (NADA), on whose behalf I am testifying today.

NADA's membership includes nearly 20,000 new car and truck dealers in the United States, both domestic and international nameplates, whose members employ over 1.1 million "Main Street" Americans. Many, many more Americans are employed in businesses that supply goods and services to dealerships. These are good, well-paying jobs that cannot be outsourced. Statistics that document the national economic impact of automobile dealerships in the U.S. are attached to my testimony. Information on specific economic impacts by state can be found on our website at http://www.nada.org.

Mr. Chairman, the economic health and well-being of our nation depends on a robust automotive industry. Nearly 1 in 10 Americans rely on the automotive industry for their livelihood and financial security.

For decades, the nation's auto dealers have been the bellwether for the state of this country's economy. Auto sales constitute 20 percent of all retail spending in the United States and generate up to 20% of the sales tax revenue for state and local governments, many of which are themselves currently facing budgetary shortfalls.

As most of you know, the automobile retail industry is highly credit- dependent and, as such, has been hit especially hard by the recent financial crisis and flagging consumer confidence. Although it is a great time to buy a car with great deals, great incentives, and great vehicles available, the public is not out there shopping.

In fact, for 2008, only an estimated 13.5 million new vehicles are likely to be sold, down from 16.1 million vehicles in 2007---and a 15-year low.

Mr. Chairman, as you evaluate the economic stabilization package before you today, I urge you to take into account one indisputable economic fact: *A resurgence of automotive retailing is necessary for a resurgence in the overall U.S. economy.* A well-capitalized financially sound dealer network is essential to the success of every automobile manufacturer, especially a manufacturer facing economic challenges.

The complex interaction between an auto manufacturer and a franchised new car or truck dealer is unlike any other business relationship in America. While the manufacturer assumes the economic risk attendant to designing and producing vehicles, the dealer assumes the economic risk of retailing those big-ticket items. Franchised dealerships are independently owned businesses, not the "company owned" stores used by many other industries to distribute their products.

As such, it is the dealer – and not the manufacturer – that invests in the land, buildings, facility upgrades, personnel, and equipment necessary to sell and service vehicles. Because of these sizable multi-million dollar dealer investments, manufacturers receive a national retail distribution network at no capital expense and are able to externalize most of the costs associated with the establishment and maintenance of a national retail distribution network for their products. Similarly, customers enjoy a competitive market in which to purchase and service vehicles and convenient locations to respond to safety recalls.

Section 405 of the discussion draft dated November 17, 2008 which is the subject of this hearing today would impose a reporting requirement on the automakers receiving Federal assistance. Among other things, this submission would require a borrower to describe its efforts to "rationalize costs and capitalization with respect to [its] manufacturing workforce, suppliers and dealerships."

Industry trends evidence an orderly, market-based consolidation of the dealer network:

- For more than 50 years, the number of dealerships in the U.S. has been shrinking at a consistent pace, dictated by market conditions. In 1949 there were almost 50,000 dealerships and by 1970 that number was 30,800. During that timeframe virtually all of these held domestic franchises. In 1987, there were 25,150 new-car dealerships; by the end of this year, we expect that number to have dropped to 19,700. Furthermore, of the remaining dealerships only about 14,200 are domestic only.
- What's more, this reduction in dealerships does not reflect a contraction of the overall auto industry. For example, the number of vehicles in operation rose from approximately 125 million in 1976 to almost 250 million in 2007.

While market forces have operated – and will continue to operate – to reduce the number of dealerships, it is important to recognize that dealership reduction is not necessarily the equivalent of dealership rationalization or dealership optimization. There are important counterbalancing factors to consider. The foremost of these are the convenience and competition that consumers receive from an extensive dealer network. Intra-brand competition is very important to consumers. Indeed, the most intense competitor for, say, an individual Ford dealer is the nearest Ford dealer. Therefore, any precipitous decline in the size of the dealer network of any manufacturer could dramatically reduce competition for the sale and service of vehicles.

Mr. Chairman, the franchise system has just celebrated its 100th anniversary. Through those years, it has provided a strong auto retail network for consumers, dealers and vehicle manufacturers alike.

In addition to making long-term capital investments, dealers, unlike other retailers, must pay significant "floor planning" expenses – the wholesale costs associated with acquiring and holding an inventory of new and used vehicles. For an average dealership with a single location, this line of credit averages $3 million.

Despite the fact that both wholesale and retail automotive loans – even when securitized – have continued to perform well, dealers are facing sharp increases in floor plan interest and a decline in the number of lenders willing to finance dealer inventories and fewer lenders willing to finance their inventories. In short, the access to wholesale financing is decreasing and the cost is increasing.

This trend, along with a drastic decrease in consumer confidence, has created severe cash flow problems that are eroding the ability of many dealers to remain viable. By the end of 2008, NADA estimates that at least 700 dealerships and at least fifty-thousand dealership jobs will be lost.

According to the National Association of Minority Automobile Dealers today, there are 2,100 ethnic minority automobile dealers in the U.S. and with the economic turmoil, up to 75 percent of the entire minority dealer body could run out of cash and close their doors by year end. Federal financial assistance is needed immediately to allow these dealers to survive.

If these trends are not halted and reversed, there will be widespread destructive consequences for the dealers, for their employees and for almost every community across the country.

Mr. Chairman, on a related matter, very soon, perhaps even today, the fuel economy increases ordered by Congress last year will be released by the U.S. Department of Transportation. The new CAFE rules are expected to be the largest jump ever in fuel economy standards, and are on track to exceed even what Congress has mandated. In this time of economic uncertainty, the auto industry needs at a minimum regulatory stability and certainty to once again prosper. A single national fuel economy standard provides that certainty and stability, and gives manufacturers a road map to produce the fuel efficient cars of tomorrow. Double regulating fuel economy by some states, under a patchwork of competing rules, would exacerbate the economic challenges facing the industry and actually impair our efforts to achieve energy independence and enhance the environment.

ECONOMIC IMPACT WITHOUT ADDITIONAL FINANCING

Mr. Chairman, simply put, the current state of our national economy cannot withstand the failure of a major automobile manufacturer--it's not a viable option. The repercussions of such would be widespread and immediately felt not just in Detroit but economy wide on every automobile manufacturer -- both foreign and domestic -- on every Main Street nationwide.

Some commentators have suggested parallels between the airline and automobile industries with regard to bankruptcy. However, the automobile industry is fundamentally different.

Should an automaker enter bankruptcy, vehicle sales are likely to plummet. Unlike the purchase of an airline ticket which typically only involves a few hundred dollars and only a few hours in the air, automobile purchases average nearly $30,000 and involve a long-term customer to protect the consumer's investment in areas such as service, parts and warranty. Moreover, the number of available choices for any particular destination in the airline arena is much lower that the number of comparably priced, competitive products in the automobile market.

A Chapter 11 bankruptcy also likely would result in even further constraints on dealership inventories, financing -- raising costs for everyone -- dealers and consumers.

Finally, the sheer complexity and the multiple levels of relationships in our industry -- manufacturers, suppliers, dealers and lending institutions -- means that bankruptcy will have a very broad effect on various sectors of the economy. Simply put, a Chapter 11 bankruptcy would create more problems than it would solve.

POLICY RECOMMENDATIONS

On behalf of NADA, I call upon Congress to move quickly to provide the assistance needed to allow the automotive sector to once again lead our country back to economic health.

In particular, we ask for action in three areas:

1. *Pass the economic stabilization package for the auto industry*
   Mr. Chairman, economic stability will restore consumer confidence in the auto industry. Congress can help to provide stability through a bridge financing program for automobile manufacturers.

2. *Enact a broad economic stimulus for automotive retailing this year*
   Congress should attempt to provide temporary financial assistance to families who are looking to make a new car or truck purchase. This can be done by:

   a. Allowing a temporary deduction of interest on consumer new auto loans and of sales or excise taxes on new vehicle purchases. This will restore consumer confidence, generate showroom traffic and stabilize the auto industry. We commend Senators Barbara Mikulski of Maryland and Kit Bond of Missouri for introducing S. 3684 in the Senate and Congressman Bill Pascrell for agreeing to introduce a companion bill in the House and urge its immediate passage;
   b. Providing for a temporary, refundable consumer tax credit for car and truck buyers;
   c. Funding for state fleet modernization (also known as "cash for clunkers") programs like those in place in Texas and California that encourage consumers to upgrade their older vehicles to newer, more environmentally-friendly models;
   d. Providing for a temporary increase in the expensing/depreciation of business vehicle purchases.

3. ***Target a small business dealer loan guaranty program immediately***

As I've mentioned, many dealers are currently facing working capital challenges, which have already led to the loss of tens of thousands of dealership jobs this year. NADA is working with the Small Business Administration (SBA) to implement a targeted automobile dealer loan guaranty initiative. A similar initiative, implemented in 1980 when the nation's dealers were facing similar financial challenges, successfully helped the industry get back on its feet. Such an initiative requires no new federal programs or federal monies. We urge Congress to support this effort by encouraging the SBA to proceed with our requested initiative as soon as possible and help to ensure that as many dealers as possible are able to participate.

As you can see, we seek support of an economic stabilization package that is focused on the vehicle buying public and on preserving millions of jobs in virtually every community across the country.

In conclusion, NADA and our dealers nationwide stand ready to work with you and the Congress to identify and develop the specific elements that should be adopted to restore consumer confidence, maintain dealer viability, stabilize and strengthen automobile manufacturers and accelerate economic recovery.

Mr. Chairman, the federal government is already helping Wall Street. Now it's time to help Main Street.

Thank you for this opportunity to testify. I am happy to answer any questions.

Attachments:
NADA DATA National Economic Summary

In: The U.S. Auto Industry and the Role of Federal Assistance   ISBN: 978-1-60741-322-6
Editor: James R. Elliot   © 2010 Nova Science Publishers, Inc.

Chapter 13

Testimony by Rick Wagoner, General Motors Corporation to the United States House of Representatives, Financial Services Committee, Washington, D.C.

- **Good morning, Mr. Chairman.**

  - I'm Rick Wagoner, Chairman and Chief Executive Officer of General Motors. Thank you for the opportunity to speak today about the future of America's domestic auto industry.

- **As recent news coverage has made abundantly clear, many people have a picture of GM that has not kept pace with our progress.**

  - Since 2005, we've reduced our annual structural costs in North America by 23 percent, or $9 billion... and expect to reduce them by about 35 percent, or $14-$15 billion, by 2011.
  - We negotiated a landmark labor agreement with the UAW last year that will enable us to virtually erase our competitive gap.
  - And we've addressed pension and retiree health care costs in the U.S., on which we spent $103 billion over the last 15 years.
  - As a result of these and other actions, we are now matching — or besting — foreign automakers in terms of productivity, quality, and fuel economy. By 2010, we'll match them on labor costs, as well.

- On the product side, we're building vehicles that consumers want to buy... like Cadillac CTS, *Motor Trend* magazine's 2008 Car of the Year... and Chevy Malibu, the 2008 North American Car of the Year.
  - We've also made huge progress developing advanced propulsion technologies... like 20 models in the U.S. next year that get at least 30 miles per gallon highway... six hybrids on the road, and three more next year... more than three

million flex-fuel vehicles... the world's largest hydrogen fuel-cell test fleet... and the upcoming Chevy Volt extended range electric vehicle.

- **In short, we've moved aggressively in recent years to position GM for long-term success... and we were well on the road to turning our North American business around.**

  - Last October, following the negotiation of a new labor agreement with the UAW, our stock price climbed to $42.64 per-share... based on analysts' views that we had finally overcome the cost-competitiveness gap with foreign automakers.
  - Since then, our industry has been hit hard by the global financial markets crisis... and the recent plunge in vehicle sales threatens not only GM's ongoing turnaround, but our very survival.

- **In response, we have moved quickly to keep our company on track. Since June, we've:**

  - reduced our North American manufacturing capacity;
  - put parts of the company up for sale;
  - suspend dividend payments;
  - reduced headcount;
  - and eliminated raises, bonuses, and 401(k) matches, and health-care coverages... all designed to improve GM's liquidity by $20 billion by the end of 2009.
  - These actions affect every employee, retiree, dealer, supplier, and investor in our company.

- **Mr. Chairman, I do not agree with those who say we are not doing enough to position GM for success.**

  - What exposes us to failure now is not our product lineup, or our business plan, or our long-term strategy.
  - What exposes us to failure now is the global financial crisis, which has severely restricted credit availability, and reduced industry sales to the lowest per-capita level since World War II.
  - Our industry needs a bridge to span the financial chasm that has opened before us.
  - We'll use this bridge to pay for essential operations... new vehicles and powertrains... parts from our suppliers... wages and benefits for our workers and retirees... and taxes for state and local governments.

- **But if the domestic industry were allowed to fail... the societal costs would be catastrophic:**

  - three million jobs lost within the first year;

- U.S. personal income reduced by $150 billion;
- and a government tax loss of more than $156 billion over three years...
- not to mention the broader blow to consumer and business confidence.
- Such a level of economic devastation would far exceed the government support that our industry needs to weather the current crisis.

- **In short, helping the auto industry bridge the current financial crisis will not only prevent massive economic dislocation now... it will also produce enormous benefits for our country later.**

- And in return, we will repay the taxpayer's faith and support many times over, for many years to come.
- Thank you, and I look forward to your questions.

CHAPTER SOURCES

The following chapters have been previously published:

Chapter 1 – This is an edited, excerpted and augmented edition of a United States Congressional Research Service publication, Report Order Code R40003, dated January 30, 2009.

Chapter 2 – This is an edited, excerpted and augmented edition of a United States Congressional Research Service publication, Report Order Code RL34743, dated November 13, 2008.

Chapter 3 – This is an edited, excerpted and augmented edition of a United States Congressional Research Service publication, Report Order Code RL34297, dated December 27, 2007.

Chapter 4 – This is an edited, excerpted and augmented edition of a United States Congressional Research Service publication, Report Order Code R400058, dated December 8, 2008.

Chapter 5 – These remarks were delivered as Statement of Gene L. Dodaro, Acting Comptroller General of the United States, before the Committee on Financial Services, U.S. House of Representatives, dated December 5, 2008.

Chapter 6 – These remarks were delivered as Statement of James McElya, Executive Chairman, Cooper Standard Automotive, before the Committee on Financial Services, U.S. House of Representatives, dated November 19, 2008.

Chapter 7 – These remarks were delivered as Statement of Alan R. Mulally, President and Chief Executive Officer, Ford Motor Company, before the Committee on Financial Services, U.S. House of Representatives, dated November 19, 2008.

Chapter 8 – These remarks were delivered as Written Statement of Robert Nardelli, Chairman & CEO, Chrysler LLC, before the Committee on Financial Services, U.S. House of Representatives, dated November 19, 2008.

Chapter 9 – These remarks were delivered as Statement of Ron Gettelfinger, President, International Union, United Automobile, Aerospace & Agricultural Implement Workers of America (UAW), before the Committee on Financial Services, U.S. House of Representatives, dated November 19, 2008.

Chapter 10 – These remarks were delivered as Statement of Matthew J. Slaughter, Associate Dean and Professor of International Economics, Tuck School of Business,

Dartmouth, before the Committee on Financial Services, U.S. House of Representatives, dated November 18, 2008.

Chapter 11 – These remarks were delivered as Statement of Felix G. Rohatyn, before the Committee on Financial Services, U.S. House of Representatives, dated December 5, 2008.

Chapter 12 – These remarks were delivered as Statement of Annette Sykora, Chairman, National Automobile Dealers Association, before the Committee on Financial Services, U.S. House of Representatives, dated November 19, 2008.

Chapter 13 – These remarks were delivered as Statement of Rick Wagoner, Chairman and Chief Executive Officer, General Motors Corporation, before the Committee on Financial Services, U.S. House of Representatives, dated November 19, 2008.

INDEX

D

E

F

G